Mastering FORTH,

Revised and Expanded

Martin Tracy

Anita Anderson

Advanced MicroMotion, Inc.

BRADY
New York

B R A D Y

Simon and Schuster, Inc.
Gulf + Western Building
One Gulf + Western Plaza
New York, NY 10023

DISTRIBUTED BY PRENTICE HALL TRADE

Manufactured in the United States of America

1 2 3 4 5 6 7 8 9 10

Library of Congress Cataloging-in-Publication Data

Tracy, Martin, 1946-
Mastering FORTH.

Previous ed. Anderson's name appeared first on t.p.
Includes index.
1. FORTH (Computer program language) I. Anderson, Anita. II. Title.
QA76.73.F24T73 1988 005.13'3 88-8148

ISBN 0-13-559957-1

Contents

Acknowledgments

We have many people to thank for their help on this project. Steve Tabor wrote the preliminary version of chapter 9, and Jennifer Brosious was responsible for all the illustrations and much of the design of the book. Coordination of public relations and marketing was handled by Linda Kahn. Mardi Rollow worked on paste-up and provided much appreciated moral support. Lyndell Martin assisted with the printing and patiently answered the phone. Some of the information we used was provided by the Forth Interest Group (408 277-0668). We especially want to thank Henry Laxen, Michael Perry, and Kim Harris for their help with a language implementation model.

We owe a special thanks to Wil Baden, whose expert rewriting and miniature flowtrees greatly improved chapters 7 and 8 in the second edition of this book. And finally, we would like to thank Charles H. Moore, the father of FORTH, whose foresight we celebrate in this book.

Limits of Liability and Disclaimer of Warranty

Mastering FORTH,

Revised and Expanded

1 Introduction

FORTH is a high-level, stack-oriented language invented by Charles Moore in the early 1970s. Dr. Moore was looking for a simpler and more natural way to communicate with his *third generation* computer—hence the name FORTH (short for *fourth-generation* language). One of FORTH's first applications was to control the giant telescope at the Kitt Peak National Observatory and to analyze the data it collected. Since that time, FORTH has been used in a great many varied and complex projects such as:

- a robot that uses tactile feedback to shear sheep
- an automotive ignition analyzer
- a peach sorter for a California cannery
- an *expert system* for diagnosis of faults in diesel locomotives
- a portable language translator
- numerous word processors, spreadsheets, and data base managers
- controlling a laser fusion laboratory
- programming a *massively parallel processor*

From the beginning FORTH has defied categorization; to begin with, it is designed for both systems programming and applications, and it is interpreted from the keyboard but compiled from mass storage screens. Programming consists of adding new commands to the small but powerful set of commands provided by the language; these commands constitute both the program and actual additions to the language itself.

What Makes FORTH So Special?

- *FORTH is extensible.* Because you can add to the language, you can tailor it to your own needs. And since almost everything in FORTH is written in FORTH—the text editor, assembler, etc.—you can access and alter any of it.
- *FORTH is structured.* Programming with FORTH encourages you to write logically complete, self-sufficient commands, built on existing commands, which are themselves used as the basis of more complex commands. This helps structure program design and simplifies and speeds debugging.
- *FORTH is fast.* FORTH runs much faster than many other high-level languages. Because the interpretation scheme is so elegant, interpreter overhead is minimal. Furthermore, FORTH includes a built-in assembler for speed-critical routines. As a result, FORTH can run almost as fast as machine code itself.
- *FORTH is interactive.* Each new word can be tested as it is defined, and changes can be made and checked on the spot.
- *FORTH is powerful.* It spans a power range from machine code to state-of-the-art structured and extensible languages. FORTH gives you direct access to the resources of your computer while providing you with sophisticated programming and data structures. It encourages you to write high-level programs by making it easy to optimize key sections of your code when you are done.
- *FORTH is transportable.* Only a small nucleus of code needs to be rewritten to move the entire language to a new computer. FORTH has been implemented on almost every computer developed to date.
- *FORTH is compact.* Its simplicity makes for an extremely compact language whose applications actually require less memory than equivalent machine-code programs.

- *FORTH is not restrictive.* You can extend it and experiment with it interactively. The time it takes you to master FORTH will be well spent when you find that your programs run faster, take up less space, do exactly what you want them to, take less time to debug, and provide the basis for more complex programs.

The FORTH-83 Standard

FORTH's extensibility encourages you to form your own personal dialect of the language. At times, however, you may wish to write programs that run unchanged from computer to computer. To facilitate such transportability, the FORTH Standards Team was formed in the mid 1970s to select and recommend a common dialect of FORTH. Their work resulted in the FORTH-83 Standard, which was passed in August 1983.

In this book, we will introduce you to each of the commands required by the FORTH-83 Standard. In addition, we will be using many commands which, while not included in the standard dialect, can be written in the Standard and are therefore transportable. From time to time, we will also present extensions to FORTH which are not addressed by the Standard, such as strings and floating-point arithmetic. When we do, we will remind you that these extensions may differ from one standard system to another.

Most modern commercial FORTHs meet the FORTH-83 Standard partially or completely. We will be taking a close look at several popular FORTH dialects:

- **UR/FORTH** 1.0 by Laboratory Microsystems, Inc.
- **PolyFORTH** ISD-4 1.0 by Forth, Inc.
- **F83** 2.1.0, a popular public-domain dialect by Henry Laxen and Michael Perry. We will refer to this as **L&P F83**.
- **MacFORTH** Plus 3.53 by Creative Solutions, Inc.
- **MasterFORTH** 1.2.4 by Micromotion Products, Inc.
- **ZEN** 1.0, a simple subset of **MasterFORTH.**

You will learn FORTH most effectively if you learn it while seated at your computer, because FORTH is designed to give you immediate feedback on your programs. *Be sure to take the time to install FORTH on your computer before reading any further.* We recommend that you try each example as you come to it and that you answer all of the exercises at the end of each chapter before going on to the next. You will find answers to all the exercises at the back of the book. And please feel free to alter and improve on any of the definitions we present. We hope that you find learning FORTH to be as enjoyable as it is rewarding.

2 Definitions

FORTH is an interactive language. It encourages you to try things out and responds immediately to your commands. To see how this works, start by pressing the <RETURN> key.

<RETURN> **OK**

FORTH says "OK."* You didn't ask it to do anything, but FORTH responded anyway to tell you that it was listening. Regardless of your command, if it can be completed successfully you will see the "OK" when it's done—watch for it.

Commands are called *words* in FORTH. One of the simplest and most useful words is the one which prints a message on the screen. Watch (don't type yet) as we define the word ALICE.

```
: ALICE   ." CURIOUSER AND CURIOUSER!" ;
```

Certain components always appear in the definition of a word.

* In the examples in this book, we will always underline FORTH's response.

Word	Action
:	The colon alerts FORTH that a definition is coming.
ALICE	Every word must have a name. Choose the name to reflect the word's purpose, as you will be asking for it later. Names can be as long as 31 characters.* Use dashes instead of blanks to break up a long name, for example, **A-LONG-NAME**.†
definition	In this case, the *definition* of **ALICE** is the message that you want to be printed, bounded by the *message markers* that tell FORTH where the beginning and end of the message are—**."** (called "dot-quote") and " ("quote"). The **."** must be separated from the message by a blank.
;	The semicolon tells FORTH that the definition is complete.

* **PolyFORTH** words with the same three characters and the same length are indistinguishable. Later we will show you how to change this.

† **PolyFORTH** philosophy discourages the use of hyphenated names.

In painting, the empty space is just as important as the painted area—and in FORTH, the spaces are just as important as the words. All words must be separated by at least one space; otherwise, FORTH wouldn't know where one word ended and another began. For clarity, always add two extra spaces between the name of the definition and the definition itself.

Now, type in the definition for **ALICE** (the shaded boxes are blanks). Don't forget to press <RETURN>.

```
: ALICE  ." CURIOUSER AND CURIOUSER!" ; OK
```

Try out this new definition; type ALICE—and voila!

```
ALICE <RETURN> CURIOUSER AND CURIOUSER! OK
```

Of course the message that a word prints could be anything. To define a word that will print an asterisk, for example, follow the example of **ALICE**.

```
: STAR   ." *" ; <RETURN> OK
```

Check to see that all the elements of a definition are in place: colon plus word name, definition, semicolon. Then try out the new word:

```
STAR <RETURN> * OK
```

Another word that is particularly useful is **CR** (called "carriage return.") Its function is simply to start a new line whenever it appears in your definition. Try defining a word (call it **COLUMN**) that will use **STAR** and **CR** to draw a vertical column of four asterisks.

```
: COLUMN <RETURN>
  CR STAR CR STAR  <RETURN>
  CR STAR CR STAR ; <RETURN> OK
```

When you enter a long definition, you can break it into as many lines as you wish by pressing <RETURN> at the end of each line. FORTH won't answer "OK" until it sees the semicolon at the end of the definition.

Check the display your new word creates.

```
COLUMN <RETURN>
*
*
*
* OK
```

The Dictionary

All words—the ones already present in FORTH (like : and ;), the ones you just defined, the ones you will define later—are stored in its *dictionary*. Here is a summary of the words you have just used plus **STAR** and **COLUMN**, the words you just created. New words appear at the end of the dictionary.

Word	Action
:	Enters a new definition into the dictionary. Used in the form: : <name> definition ;
;	Terminates a definition.
."	Puts a message into a definition. When the definition is later executed, the message is printed. Used in the form: ." message"
CR	Moves display *carriage* to the next line.
STAR	Prints an asterisk.
COLUMN	Prints a column of asterisks.

Much of the magic of FORTH is the ease with which it remembers (*compiles*) and carries out (*executes*) the definitions in the dictionary. When you type a new line and press `<RETURN>`, control is passed to a word called the *text interpreter*. This interpreter reads the line word by word, from left to right, separating each word from its neighbors by the spaces between them.

:	STAR	." *"	;
word 1	word 2	word 3	word 4

As each word is found in the dictionary, its definition is executed. When all words have been executed, the text interpreter prints "OK" and waits for the next line.

If the word executed is `:`, a new definition is created in the dictionary; its name is given by the first word following the `:` —in this case, "STAR." Subsequent words are then compiled into the definition until the word `;` is encountered. It is important to realize that no asterisk is printed when **STAR** is compiled.

Learning to distinguish between when a word is created and when it is executed is one of the keys to understanding FORTH.

Modularity

Once you defined **STAR**, you were then able to immediately use it to create the more complex word **COLUMN. STAR** and **COLUMN** could then serve as *modules* in the construction of even more complex words. FORTH encourages modular programming by making it easy to create and name new definitions. Each new word can be immediately tested simply by typing its name. You can enhance both efficiency and style with the following principle:

Words should do as little as possible. By keeping words simple, you can use them in more situations within many other definitions.

Let's design some simple modules which, when combined with **STAR**, **CR**, and **COLUMN**, let you print giant letters made of asterisks. One way to group asterisks is to include them within the message markers. Define a word, for instance, that will start a new line and print five asterisks in a horizontal row—call it **ROW**.

```
: ROW   CR ." *****" ; <RETURN> OK
```

Does it behave the way you expected?

```
ROW <RETURN> ***** OK
```

Now try a more complicated project: a word that will print a giant capital L. Do you see already how such a word can be defined using words you already have?

```
: L   COLUMN ROW ; <RETURN> OK
```

At this time you may see a warning like

```
L Isn't Unique
```

This is not an error; FORTH is simply telling you that the word **L** has already been defined. When this happens, FORTH will use the most recent definition—your definition— which is what you want it to do anyway.

Check to see if **L** works correctly.

```
L <RETURN>
*
*
*
*
***** OK
```

What if you wanted to draw a capital "T"? There are several ways to do it. One way would involve first defining a word that would space over two blanks from the margin so that you could center the stem of the "T."* Call this new word INSET.

```
: INSET   ."   " ; <RETURN> OK
```

When you combine **INSET** with **STAR** and **CR**, you can create **STEM:**

```
: STEM <RETURN>
   CR INSET STAR CR INSET STAR <RETURN>
   CR INSET STAR CR INSET STAR <RETURN>; OK
```

Check to see that **STEM** works.

```
STEM <RETURN>
  *
  *
  *
  * OK
```

---

* Remember, whatever is inside the message markers is displayed on the screen as is—whether it's intelligible words, characters, or just blank spaces.

Now the "T" is easy—just combine **ROW** and **STEM.**

```
: T    ROW STEM ; <RETURN> OK
```

Check the result:

```
T <RETURN>
*****
    *
    *
    *
    * OK
```

In Summary

The programs you will want to write will involve more complicated functions with more useful applications than drawing letters, but the principles remain the same. Think modular. By using FORTH words that are already available or that you have defined, you will be able to accomplish complex tasks in less time. It will also be easier to find your mistakes, since each word is labeled for easy reference and can be tested independently. Modular programming looks like a well-built pyramid, starting at the bottom level with words like **STAR** and **CR** and using them to build higher levels.

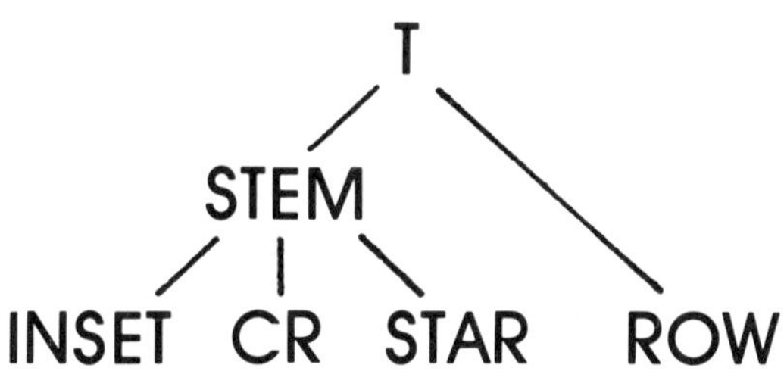

The word is the program. There's no distinction between words and programs; **STAR** is a program, and so is **T**. All your FORTH programs will be combinations of previously defined words. That's why it's so important to understand definitions right at the beginning.

EXERCISES

Here are some simple exercises for you to try. You'll find the answers in the back of the book. Just remember, every `:` has a `;` , and every `."` has a `"`.

1. Combine the actions of **`CR`**, **`INSET`**, and **`STAR`** into the new word **`BLIP`**, which will return, indent two spaces, and print one asterisk. Redefine **T** to use **`BLIP`** instead of **`STEM`**. Using only **`STAR`**, **`ROW`**, **`BLIP`**, and **`CR`**, make the new words **`I`** **`C`** and **`E`**. Each letter should be no higher and no wider than five characters.
2. Define a word **`BOOP`** which, combined with **`ROW`**, lets you create the words **`H`** and **`U`**, which (guess what!) print the block-letters "H" and "U."
3. You have been asked to print a giant homecoming banner for Somewhere Technical High School. Using only words you have already written, create the word **`BANNER`** which, when executed, prints "HI-TECH" vertically on your terminal in large block letters.

3 The Stack

It would be quite impossible to build a dictionary large enough to hold a separate definition for every number. In fact, numbers are never found in the dictionary. What happens if you type 459 ? (We assume at this point you know to press <RETURN>, so we are not going to show it any more.)

```
459 Ok
```

The text interpreter scans the input stream and finds the string of characters "459". It next searches the dictionary for a definition with the name "459". When the search fails, the text interpreter passes the string to an internal procedure which attempts to convert it into a number. In this case, the conversion succeeds, and the number 459 results (to be continued below.)

If the word you type is neither the name of a definition nor a number, the conversion fails, and the text interpreter assumes you've made an error. Execution stops, and the name is returned to you with a question mark. Try typing the nonsense word **GORF**.

```
GORF
GORF ?
```

If the conversion to a number succeeds, where does FORTH leave the number? On the stack.

One way to imagine the FORTH stack is to think of a giant spring-loaded rack with numbers on it. Whenever a number is found in the input stream, FORTH puts or *pushes* that number onto the stack. Try typing some numbers, separating them by spaces (and don't forget the <RETURN>).

```
1 2 3 Ok
```

As each number is read and interpreted, it is pushed onto the stack, on top of any numbers already there.

When you take the numbers off again (*popping* them from the stack), their order is reversed. You cannot pop number 1 until you first pop numbers 3 and 2. This kind of a stack is sometimes called a *Last In, First Out* or *LIFO* stack.

You can use the word . ("dot") to pop a number from the stack and display it on your screen—try it.

```
. 3 Ok
```

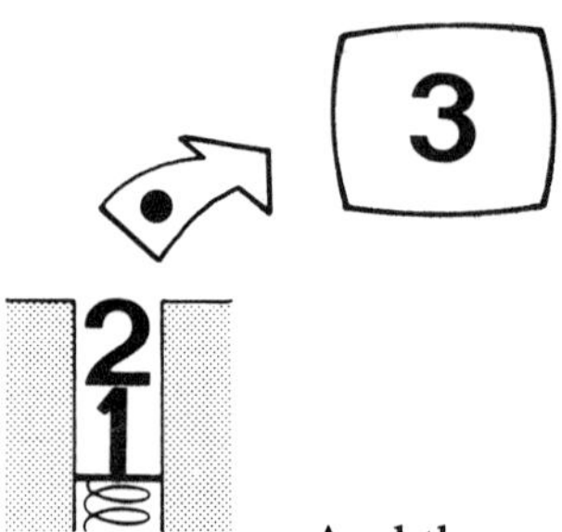

And then print the rest out too.

```
. . 2 1 Ok
```

The order in which these numbers are stacked is crucial to understanding FORTH. It is your responsibility to know the condition of the stack and the order of the numbers on it for accurate programming.

What happens if you type a `.` now?

```
. 0 ? Stack?*
```

The stack is empty and FORTH gives you an error message. (This condition is known as *stack underflow.*)

To see the what's on the stack, type `.S`.

1 2 3 Ok
.S
1 2 3 <-Top†

The numbers are still there.

.S
1 2 3 <-Top

The easiest way to clear the stack of all numbers is to lightly slap the keyboard and then press <RETURN>.

```
hncq3 hncq3 ?
```

This generates a nonsense word which FORTH is unable to execute. This kind of error empties the stack.

```
.S
<-Top**
```

The number of items on the stack is given by **DEPTH,** which, like most FORTH words, leaves its result on the stack.

---

* Or Empty! or some such message.

MacForth menus include a debug switch. When it is on, the stack contents are printed after each line is executed.

† Or Stack: 3 2 1 or some such message.

** As you may have guessed, each FORTH has a unique but recognizable set of informative messages.

```
10 9 8 Ok
DEPTH .S
10 9 8 3 <-Top Ok
DEPTH . 4 Ok
aeblgm,; aeblgm,; ?
DEPTH . 0 Ok
```

Addition

One of the unusual features of FORTH is the order in which numbers are entered for arithmetic operations. Instead of

```
3 + 4
```

as you might expect, FORTH uses

```
3 4 +
```

This idea, known as postfix notation or RPN (Reverse Polish Notation), makes sense when you think about FORTH's stack. It also makes complicated algebraic expressions easier to enter, as we will see later.

The word **+** ("plus") removes the top two numbers (or *arguments*) from the stack, adds them together, and leaves the result on top of the stack.

Use **.** to see the result:

```
3 4 + . 7 Ok
```

Now you can see why we need postfix notation; both numbers must be already on the stack before **+** can operate. To add a series of numbers, you can enter them this way:

```
5 13 + 1 + 14 + 25 + . 58 Ok
```

or this way:

```
5 13 1 14 25 + + + + . 58 Ok
```

Either way, **+** must find (at least) two numbers on the stack when it operates.

When a number appears inside a word definition, the compiler records the number for future use. The number won't be pushed onto the stack until the word is later executed.

```
: DOZEN 12 ;
DEPTH . 0
DOZEN . 12
```

We will no longer show the **Ok** at the end of each line, but you will see it on your screen.

Subtraction

Postfix notation is used by all arithmetic operators, including subtraction.

```
7 3 - . 4
```

The operator **-** ("minus") needs blanks on both sides, just like any other word. Don't confuse this with the *minus-sign* which must immediately precede negative numbers.

```
-7 3 + . -4
```

Speaking of negative numbers, **NEGATE** changes the sign of the top number on the stack.

```
3 NEGATE . -3
DEPTH . 0
```

Consider how you might define **-** using **NEGATE**:

```
: -   NEGATE + ;
```

The complementary word **ABS** will give you the absolute value of any number.

```
-3 ABS . 3
3 ABS . 3
```

Multiplication and Division

The word ***** ("star") pops the top two stack numbers, multiplies them together, and pushes the result back onto the stack.

```
3 -4 * . -12
```

Division is more complicated because it produces both a quotient and a remainder. The word **/** ("slash") gives you the quotient alone.

```
15 6 / . 2
```

The word **MOD** gives you the remainder alone.

```
15 6 MOD . 3
```

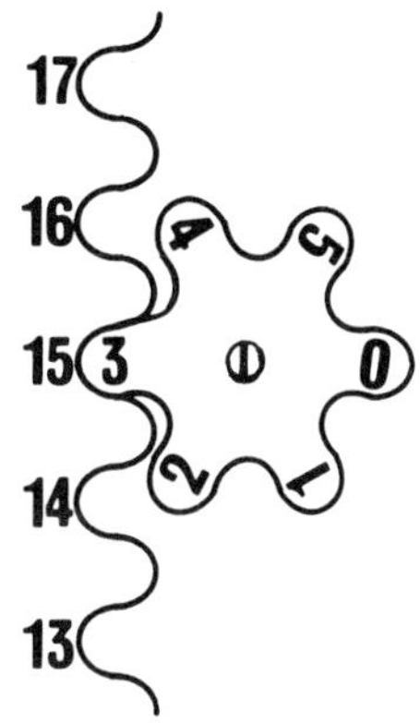

Note that 6 **MOD** will always return a number from zero to five. We will make use of this later in writing a random number generator.

The word **/MOD** ("slash-mod") combines these functions, leaving the quotient on top of the stack and the remainder underneath.

```
15 6 /MOD . . 2 3
```

Division is "floored," meaning that if the result is negative and has a remainder, the quotient nearest to minus infinity (rather than nearest to zero) is returned.

```
-16 3 / . -6*
```

The remainder returned by **MOD** always has this property:

```
Numerator = (Quotient * Denominator) + Remainder
```

Check it out.

```
-16 3 MOD . 2
 -6 3 * 2 + . -16
```

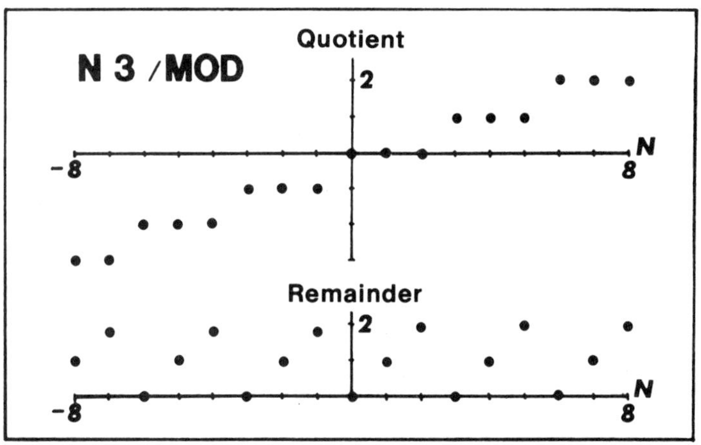

Division by zero is meaningless and the result is unpredictable.

---

* **polyFORTH** specifies that MOD and /MOD use *unsigned* arguments. -16 is treated as 65520 to give a quotient of 21840 and a remainder of 0.

MacForth division *rounds towards zero* rather than *floors towards minus infinity*. -16 3 / yields a quotient of -5 and a remainder of -1.

MAX and MIN

The pair of words **MAX** and **MIN** are useful in limiting numbers to lie within a given range. As you may have guessed, **MIN** will give you the smaller of two numbers

```
17 53 MIN . 17
78 -22 MIN . -22
```

while **MAX** gives you the larger of the two.

```
4 3000 MAX . 3000
-8 -10 MAX . -8
```

For example, you may wish to limit a thermostat control to the range between 62 to 75 degrees Fahrenheit. The expression

```
62 MAX 75 MIN
```

will do this for you.

```
: COMFORT   62 MAX 75 MIN ;
55  COMFORT . 62
65  COMFORT . 65
90  COMFORT . 75
```

Arithmetic Expressions

One advantage of postfix notation is apparent when you try to work with complicated algebraic equations that have parentheses. With postfix notation, no parentheses are required. The following problem:

$$\frac{4(3+2)}{(1+7)}$$

can be written in postfix notation like this:

```
3 2 + 4 * 1 7 + / . 2
```

Let's walk through this example step by step, noting the stack contents at each point:

Word	Action	Stack
3	Pushes 3 onto stack.	3
2	Pushes 2 onto stack.	3 2
+	Adds top two numbers.	5
4	Pushes 4 onto stack.	5 4
*	Multiplies top two numbers.	20
1	Pushes 1 onto stack.	20 1
7	Pushes 7 onto stack.	20 1 7
+	Adds top two numbers.	20 8
/	Divides top two numbers.	2

Outer Limits

Ultimately, all numbers in a computer are represented by conveniently grouped *bits* of zeroes and ones. Most FORTHs have stacks that are either 16 or 32-bits wide. The arithmetic operators expect and produce *single-precision* signed numbers as wide as the stack. An integer is a *whole number* with no fractional parts. That's why 21 divided by 5 gives 4 instead of 4.2 or *four and one-fifth.*

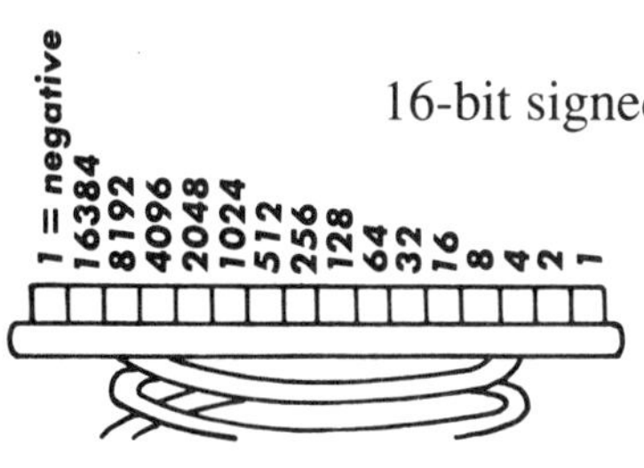

16-bit signed numbers are somewhat limited in size.*

* **MacForth** uses 32-bit single precision numbers, which can be as large as 2,147,483,647. Most vendors supply 32-bit implementations for selected processors.

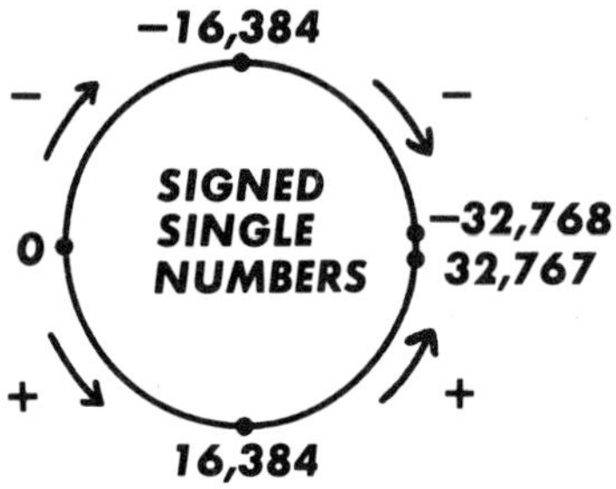

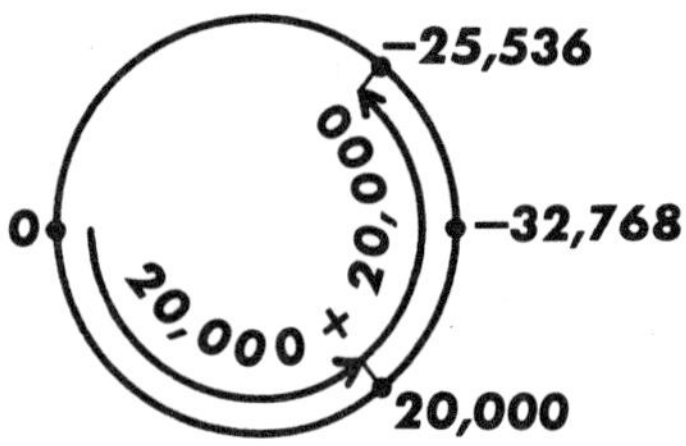

0000000000000000 is 0
0111111111111111 is +32,767

1111111111111111 is -1
1000000000000000 is -32,768

Adding 1 to the largest positive number gives you the largest negative number:

```
32767 1 + . -32768
```

Other calculations can yield equally surprising results:

```
20000 20000 + .   -25536
20000       2 * . -25536
```

Fortunately, FORTH has ways of dealing both with extra-large *double* numbers and with fractions, as we will see in later chapters.

Stack Notation

The arguments required by each FORTH word and the result left on the stack after execution are so important that we use a special notation to keep track of them. The arguments required on the stack *before* execution are shown to the left of a single dash and the results *after* execution are shown to the right.

```
before - after
```

Numbers on the stack appear in order of entry, so the number furthest to the right will be the top number of the stack. If no numbers are needed or produced, no stack diagram is necessary.

Here are the definitions of the words we have used so far in this chapter:

Word	Stack	Action
.	n	Prints number on top of stack.
+	n n2 - n3	Adds two numbers, giving n3.
-	n n2 - n3	Subtracts n2 from n, giving n3.
*	n n2 - n3	Multiplies two numbers, giving n3.
/	n n2 - n3	Divides n by n2, giving quotient n3.
MOD	n n2 - n3	Divides n by n2, giving remainder n3.
/MOD	n n2 - n3 n4	Divides n by n2. n3 is the remainder and n4 is the quotient.
MIN	n n2 - n3	Returns the smaller of n and n2.
MAX	n n2 - n3	Returns the larger of n and n2.
NEGATE	n - n2	Changes the sign of n.
ABS	n - n2	Gives the absolute value of n.
DEPTH	- n	Returns the number of items now on the stack.
.S		Prints the items on the stack without disturbing them.

Shortcuts

Certain common calculations have shortcuts in FORTH. These are words which are both faster and shorter than their alternative sequences; they should be substituted whenever possible. One such word is **1+** , which works like a 1 followed by a +.

```
13 1+ . 14
```

The words **1-** , **2-** , **2*** , and **2/** are analogous. **2*** is available in most FORTHs, but is not required by the FORTH-83 Standard

Word	Stack	Action
1+	n - n2	Adds 1 to n.
2+	n - n2	Adds 2 to n.
1-	n - n2	Subtracts 1 from n.
2-	n - n2	Subtracts 2 from n.
2*	n - n2	Multiplies n by 2.
2/	n - n2	Divides n by 2.

MacForth adds **3+ 3- 4+ 4- 4* 4/ 5+ 5- 6+ 6- 7+ 7- 8+ 8- 8* 8/ 10+ 10- 10* 16+ 16- 16* 16/** and **0MAX.**

Putting It All Together

Now that you know how to define FORTH words and use basic arithmetic operators, you can begin thinking of ways to accomplish specific tasks. Here's a set of words, for example, that function together as a "change optimizer" program. They will take a random assortment of change and tell you how to present this amount with the smallest number of coins.

The first part of the program converts all the coins to their penny values so that they can be totaled.

```
: CHANGE      0 ;
: QUARTERS    25 * + ;
: DIMES       10 * + ;
: NICKELS     5  * + ;
: PENNIES          + ;
```

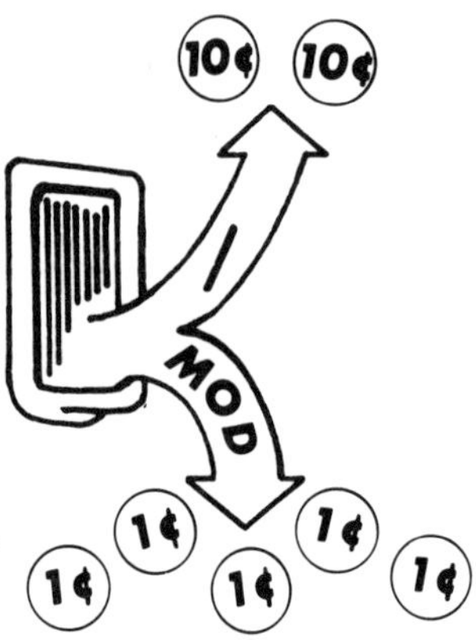

The first word, **CHANGE,** merely sets up the running total by putting a 0 on the stack. The word **QUARTERS** takes a number you provide, multiplies it by 25, adds it to the number on the stack (0), and leaves the result on the stack. **DIMES** and **NICKELS** multiply their respective numbers by 10 and 5 and add this to the total already on the stack.

PENNIES simply adds the number of loose pennies to the number on the stack. If the definitions of **PENNIES** is simply **+** , why have a word at all? Why not just use **+** in the program? Simply for readability.

Now your input can be expressed in this form:

```
CHANGE 3 QUARTERS 6 DIMES 10 NICKELS 112 PENNIES
```

What's on the stack at this point? The sum of 3 * 25, 6 * 10, 10 * 5, and 112.

```
. 297
```

The second part of the program redistributes the total starting with the largest denomination, quarters—so as to produce the smallest number of total coins. This is done with the word **INTO**.

```
: INTO
   25 /MOD CR . ." QUARTERS"
   10 /MOD CR . ." DIMES"
   5  /MOD CR . ." NICKELS"
           CR . ." PENNIES" ;
```

INTO divides the number on the stack first by 25; the quotient is printed on a new line followed by the message **QUARTERS**. The remainder stays on the stack to be divided by 10, and so forth. The final remainder represents the number of pennies left over; it is printed as is, followed by the message **PENNIES**.

When you use the program, the result looks like this:

```
CHANGE 3 QUARTERS 6 DIMES 10 NICKELS 112 PENNIES INTO
11 QUARTERS
2 DIMES
0 NICKELS
2 PENNIES
```

EXERCISES

1. The area of a triangle is given by the formula $\frac{b*h}{2}$

   where b is the base of the triangle and h is its height (which is always perpendicular to the base).

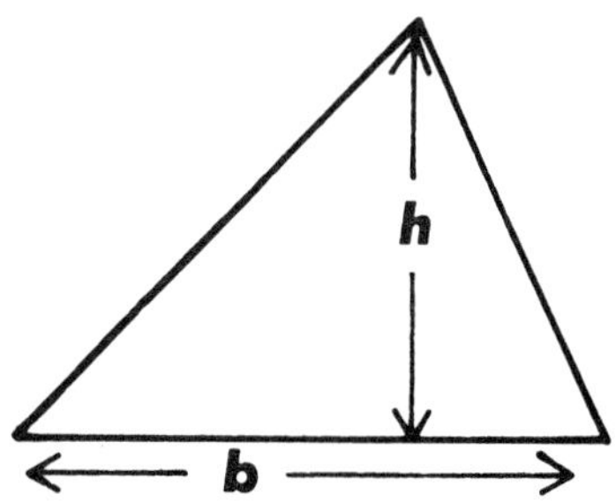

Define a word **TRIANGLE** which, given the base and height as arguments on the stack, computes and prints the area of the triangle. Since it's always a good idea to label your results, **TRIANGLE** should produce a result that looks something like this:

```
10 14 TRIANGLE
THE AREA IS 70
```

2. Write a phrase which limits the number on top of the stack to be a positive integer, but no more than 100. Test it against several numbers. Hint: first make it into a definition.

3. After a busy day waiting tables, you notice that your tips include several strange coins. Modify the change machine to handle these coins. Their values, in pennies, are

FRANCS	worth 27 cents.
KRONOR	worth 13 cents.
MARKS	worth 40 cents.
TOKENS	worth 75 cents.

The output of the change machine should look exactly like the one in this chapter. Write extra words to handle your new income and produce a result like the following:

```
CHANGE 4 QUARTERS 3 FRANCS 6 NICKELS 2 TOKENS INTO

14 QUARTERS
1 DIMES
0 NICKELS
1 PENNIES
```

4. Evaluate the following expressions:

a. `5 + 4 + 3 + 2 + 1`

b. `(1 * 3) + (2 - 4)`

c. 5^4

d. `((76 * 20) / (45 / 3))`

e. $3^2 + 2(3 * 5) + 5^2$

4 Stack Manipulation

You will often need to alter the contents of the stack. You might want to make copies of certain numbers, delete others, move them around, or a combination of these. To make changes such as these, you can use FORTH's stack manipulation commands.

DUP

DUP ("dupe" as in *dup*licate) takes the top number off the stack, makes a copy of it, and puts both numbers back on the stack.

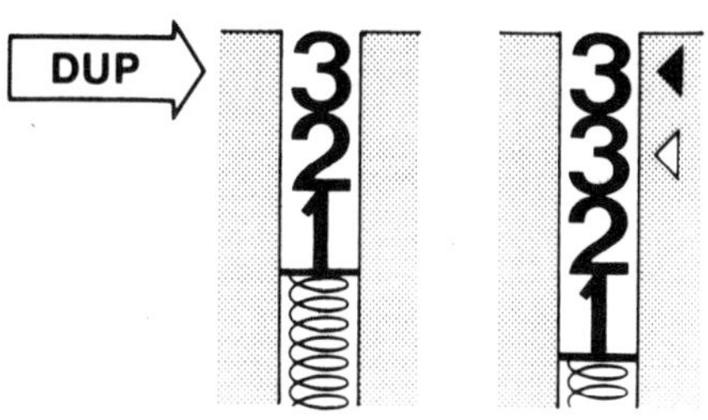


```
1 2 3 DUP .S
1 2 3 3 <-Top
```

Write the word **DOUBLE,** which multiplies a number by two and prints the results. You need **DUP** to write the word **DOUBLE** because you want to print the number being multiplied as well as multiply it, which takes two copies.

```
: DOUBLE  ." TWICE " DUP . ." IS " 2* . ;
4 DOUBLE TWICE 4 IS 8
```

DROP

DROP is the opposite of **DUP**; it takes the top number on the stack and discards it.

```
7 9 11
DROP . 9
DROP
```

Here's a likely definition of **MOD** that would use **DROP** to get rid of the quotient and leave the remainder.

```
: MOD   /MOD DROP ;
```

SWAP

SWAP simply exchanges the top two items on the stack.

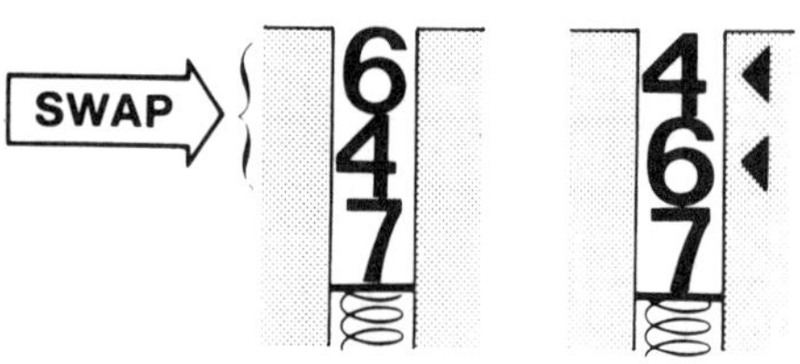


```
7 4 6
DUP . 6
SWAP . 4
.S
7 6 <-Top
DROP DROP
```

SWAP is especially useful whenever you have to deal with two numbers at once. In the following example, you need to keep track of how many events are completed and how many are still to be performed. Each computation must be performed at the top of the stack, so you need to **SWAP** the two numbers each time.

```
: EVENTS   0 ;
: TICK   1+ DUP . ." COMPLETED, "
   SWAP  1- DUP . ." TO GO "  SWAP ;
: FINISH   . ." COMPLETED. " DROP ;
10 EVENTS
TICK 1 COMPLETED, 9 TO GO
TICK 2 COMPLETED, 8 TO GO
TICK 3 COMPLETED, 7 TO GO
FINISH 3 COMPLETED
```

The word **FINISH DROP**s the number of incomplete events, since there is no point in printing this number and since it's a good idea to clear the stack before the next program.

OVER

DUP copies the top item on the stack; **OVER** copies the item beneath it, leaving the copy on top of the stack. For example, suppose you want a copy of the top two items on the stack. Let's call the word that does this **2DUP** ("two-dupe"). A good definition of **2DUP** would be

```
: 2DUP   OVER OVER ;
```

Why doesn't **DUP DUP** work the same way as **2DUP**? Let's try some numbers and see.

```
1 2 3 DUP DUP .S
1 2 3 3 3 <-Top
azddk azddk ?
1 2 3 2DUP .S
1 2 3 2 3 <-Top
qoiav qoiav ?
```

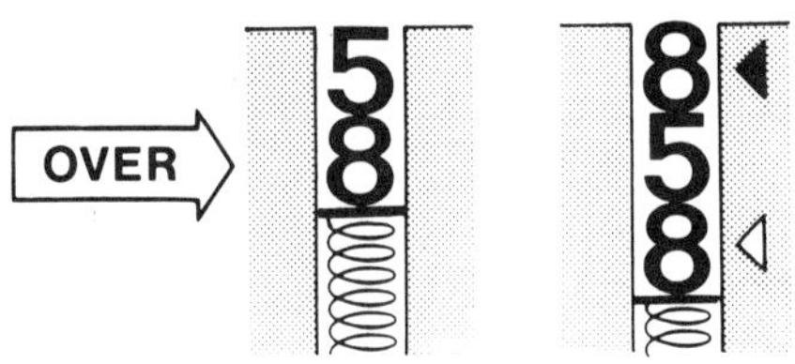

All **DUP** can do is make a copy of the number on top of the stack; you need **OVER** to get at numbers further down and make copies of them.

PICK

You can select or *pick* any item on the stack with **PICK***. As with **OVER**, the selected item is copied and the copy moved to the top of the stack. However, you must first push the "index" or number of the item you want on the stack. The top item has an index of zero, the second item has an index of one, and so on.

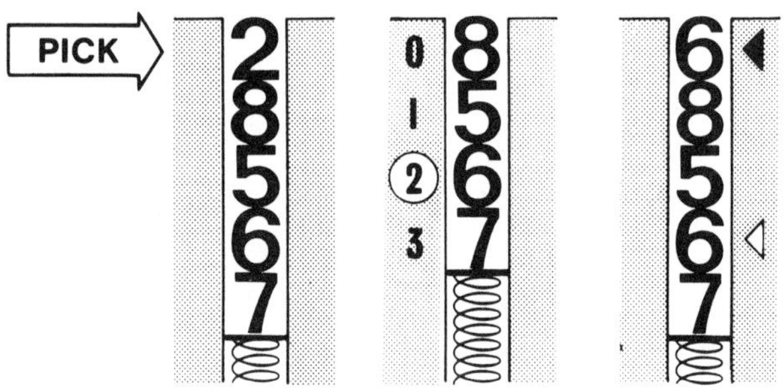

Suppose you would like to calculate the volume of a box. To do this, you need to multiply three items: the length, the width, and the height. You would like to print these measurements with appropriate labels before printing the volume. The word **VOLUME** uses **PICK** to accomplish this for you:

```
: VOLUME
   CR ." LENGTH: " 2 PICK .
   CR ." WIDTH : " 1 PICK .
   CR ." HEIGHT: " 0 PICK .
   CR ." VOLUME: " * * .  ;
```

* **polyFORTH** defines **PICK** in the FORTH-83 compatibility blocks.

```
5 8 9 VOLUME
LENGTH: 5
WIDTH : 8
HEIGHT: 9
VOLUME: 360
```

PICK is the most general stack copy command. We can define the other copy commands **DUP** and **OVER** by using **PICK** with the proper index:

```
: DUP    0 PICK ;
: OVER   1 PICK ;
```

But both **DUP** and **OVER** are usually much faster and produce less code than a corresponding **PICK** plus its argument does.

ROT

The commands **DUP, DROP, SWAP**, and **OVER** let you move or copy the top two items on the stack in any way you choose. Likewise, the command **ROT** ("rote" as in *rot*ate) lets you reach the third item on the stack. **ROT** moves the third item to the top of the stack. As with **SWAP**, the number is moved rather than copied. The second and top items are renumbered to become the new third and second items.

```
9 5 6 .S
9 5 6 <-Top
ROT .S
5 6 9 <-Top
ROT .S
6 9 5 <-Top
ROT .S
9 5 6 <-Top
```

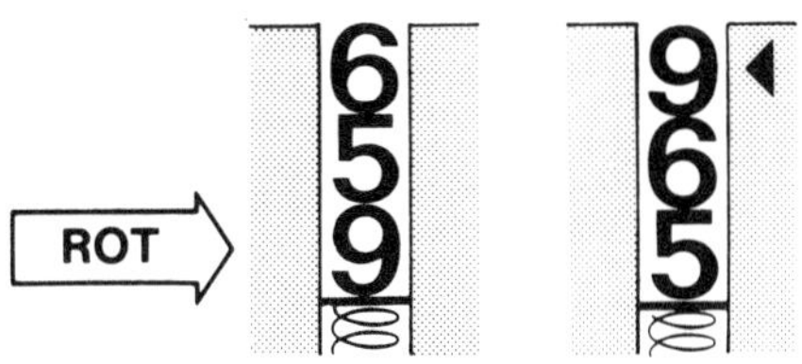

The phrase **ROT ROT** is the reverse of **ROT.** It moves the top item on the stack to the third position.* Keeping the same numbers as in the last example, this is how **ROT ROT** would rearrange them:

```
9 5 6 ROT ROT .S
6 9 5 <-Top
ROT .S
9 5 6 <-Top
```

Suppose that three numbers on the stack represent three quantities and that you need to increment the third quantity by one. You could do this by alternating **ROT** and **ROT ROT** (that is, bringing the third number up to the top of the stack, incrementing it, and putting it back again).

```
9 5 6  ROT 1+ ROT ROT .S
10 5 6 <-Top
```

ROLL

ROLL takes **ROT** a step further†. Instead of moving just the third number on the stack to the top, **ROLL** will move any number you specify to the top, no matter how far down on the stack it is. Knowing what's on the stack, you simply indicate the index of the number you want moved to the top. **ROLL** takes the same kind of index argument as **PICK**; that is, the top item is numbered zero, the second item is numbered one, and so on.

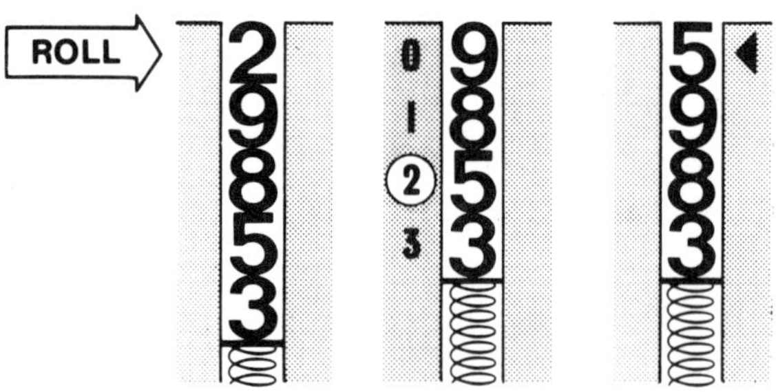


```
3 5 8 9 2  ROLL .S
3 8 9 5
3 ROLL .S
8 9 5 3
```

* **L&P F83** and **URFORTH** have the word **-ROT** ("not-rote" or "dash-rote") which is equivalent to **ROT ROT** but is much faster.

† **polyFORTH** defines **ROLL** in the FORTH-83 compatibility blocks.

ROLL is the most general stack manipulation command. We can define the more specific commands **SWAP** and **ROT** by using **ROLL** with the proper index.

```
: SWAP   1 ROLL ;
: ROT    2 ROLL ;
```

The command **0 ROLL** does nothing. **ROLL** is quite a slow primitive. It is hardly ever used in actual practice.

Here is a list of all the simple stack manipulation commands we've learned so far:

Word	Stack	Action
DUP	n - n n	Duplicates the top stack item.
DROP	n	Discards the top stack item.
SWAP	n n2 - n2 n	Swaps the top two stack items.
OVER	n n2 - n n2 n	Copies the second item on the stack to the top of the stack.
PICK	... i - n	Copies the index-numbered item to the top of the stack. The top item has an index of zero, the second item an index of one, and so on.
ROT	n n2 n3 - n2 n3 n	Moves the third item on the stack to the top of the stack.
ROLL	... i - n	Moves the index-numbered item to the top of the stack. The top item has an index of zero, the second item an index of one, and so on.

The *i* in the stack diagrams for **PICK** and **ROLL** means a single number used as an *index*.

Double Stack Operators

Most of the simple stack operators you have learned have an equivalent which operates on a pair of items at a time. We have already seen how **2DUP** lets you duplicate a pair of items. Here is a list of the double operators, their arguments, and their results:

Word	Stack	Action
2DUP	n n2 - n n2 n n2	Duplicates the top pair of items.
2DROP	n n2 -	Drops the top pair of items.
2SWAP	n n2 n3 n4 - n3 n4 n n2	Swaps the top two pairs of items.
2OVER	n n2 n3 n4 - n n2 n3 n4 n n2	Copies the second pair of items and moves them to the top of the stack.
2ROT	n n2 n3 n4 n5 n6 - n3 n4 n5 n6 n n2	Moves the third pair of items to the top of the stack.

The double stack operators are especially useful when dealing with paired quantities such as fractions (which have a denominator and a numerator), graphics (which have x and y coordinates), and complex numbers (which have a real part and an imaginary part). You may have noticed that **2PICK** and **2ROLL** are missing from our list. That's because the stack seldom contains more than six items (or three pairs).

Putting It All Together

The height of a falling object above the ground can be determined at any time (**t**) if its initial height (h_0) and its initial downward velocity (v_0) are both known. The height of the object is given by the formula

$$height = h_0 - (v_0 * t) - 16t^2$$

where height is in feet and velocity is in feet per second. We can write a **FORTH** word which takes an initial height, initial velocity, and a time t (entered in that order) from the stack and leaves the final height of the object after t seconds.

```
: HEIGHT
   SWAP OVER *
   SWAP DUP * 16 * + - ;
```

Let's take some numbers—say, an initial height of 1000 feet, an initial velocity of 100 feet per second, and a time of 3 seconds—and follow the computation.

Word	Stack	Action
	1000 100 3	
SWAP	1000 3 100	**SWAP**s time and velocity.
OVER	1000 3 100 3	Copies and moves time.
*	1000 3 300	Multiplies velocity by time.
SWAP	1000 300 3	**SWAP**s product and time.
DUP	1000 300 3 3	**DUP**s time.
*	1000 300 9	Squares time.
16	1000 300 9 16	Adds 16 to the stack.
*	1000 300 144	Multiplies 16 by time squared.
+	1000 444	Adds product to velocity times time.
-	556	Subtracts sum from initial height.

Don't take our word for it, though—try out **HEIGHT** for yourself.

```
1000 100 3 HEIGHT 556
```

We can do more with this problem, particularly to make the entry of the values clearer. In a case like this, it helps to *echo* the inputs by printing them on the screen properly labeled. The addition of a word that "surrounds" the original problem-solving word takes care of this need. It also can take care of exceptions—say, if the initial height was so low (or the velocity so high or the time too long) that the final height was less than 0, which wouldn't make sense. The **0 MAX** in the following word, **HEIGHT?**, makes sure that no values less than 0 will be displayed. polyFORTH normally retains only the first three characters of a name and its length. To prevent inadvertent redefinitions, this word would be renamed **?HEIGHT.**

```
: HEIGHT?
   CR ." INITIAL HEIGHT   : " 2 PICK .
   CR ." INITIAL VELOCITY: " OVER .
   CR ." HEIGHT AFTER " DUP .
   ." SECONDS: "   HEIGHT 0 MAX . ;
```

Now try the same values to see how much easier the result is to read.

```
1000 100 3 HEIGHT?
INITIAL HEIGHT : 1000
INITIAL VELOCITY: 100
HEIGHT AFTER 3 SECONDS: 556
```

And increase the time to 6 seconds to see that the **0 MAX** is doing its job.

```
1000 100 6 HEIGHT?
INITIAL HEIGHT : 1000
INITIAL VELOCITY: 100
HEIGHT AFTER 6 SECONDS: 0
```

Exercises

1. Assuming x y and z are single-precision numbers, find FORTH phrases which match these stack diagrams:

   a. x y - x y x
   b. x y - x x y
   c. x y z - x z
   d. x y z - y z
   e. x y z - z y x
   f. x y z - y x z
   g. x y z - x x y z
   h. x y z - x y y z

2. **L&P F83** supports several additional stack operators. Using only **`DUP`** **`DROP`** **`SWAP`** **`OVER`** **`ROT`** and **`PICK`**, see if you can define them.

`3DUP`	n n2 n3 - n n2 n3 n n2 n3	Duplicates the top three stack items.
`NIP`	n n2 - n2	Deletes the second stack item.
`TUCK`	n n2 — n2 n n2	Duplicates and *tucks* the top stack item under the second item.

Can your definition for **`3DUP`** be improved by using **`2DUP,`** **`2DROP,`** **`2SWAP,`** **`2OVER,`** or **`2ROT`**?

3. Given two single-precision numbers x and y on the stack, with y on top, find FORTH phrases which evaluates these expressions:

a. $x + y^2$ b. $x^2 + y^2$
c. $3xy$ d. $x^2 + 2xy + y^2$

Given x y and z, with z on top, find phrases for these expressions:

e. $(x + y)/z$ f. $(x + y)/(x - z)$
g. $xy + xz$ h. $xz^2 + xy^2 - yz^2$

4. The area of a rectangle can be determined from the coordinates of either pair of opposite corners. Coordinates are usually given as a pair of numbers, with the horizontal coordinate given first. If we call the coordinates of one corner **`X1`*** and **`Y1`** and the coordinates of the other corner **`X2`** and **`Y2`**, the area is calculated by the formula

```
(X2 - X1) * (Y2 - Y1)
```

Define a word which expects all four coordinates on the stack and which returns and appropriately labeled result.

`RECTANGLE` x1 y1 x2 y2 computes and prints the area of a rectangle, given the coordinates of two opposite corners.

`RECTANGLE` works like this:

```
41 44 58 80 RECTANGLE
THE AREA IS 612
```

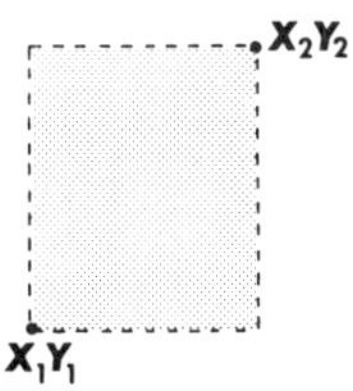

* **polyFORTH** and **MasterFORTH** line editors use the command **X** to delete a line. For safety, **X** should not be used as the name of a definition.

5. Polynomials such as

   $y = x^4 - 3x^3 + 17x^2 - 4x + 5$

   can be rapidly evaluated using Horner's method. The polynomial is factored and the innermost phrase is computed first.

   $y = (((x - 3)x + 17)x - 4)x + 5$

   Write the word **POLY** which takes its argument x from the stack and leaves its results y there.

   ```
   7 POLY . 2182
   ```

5 The Editor

Programming with FORTH is never a one-shot operation. Inevitably you will want to add or change something later as you think about your work a second time or devise a new purpose for your program. FORTH includes a separate program called the editor which makes it easy to both retain and improve upon existing words.

Words, Words, Words

All the words provided in FORTH as well as all the definitions you may add are compiled in the dictionary. You can use the command **WORDS** to examine the contents of the dictionary.* First, type in the following definitions:

```
: MARKER ;
: DANCE ." CHARLESTON" ;
: MUSIC ." SWING" ;
```

When you type **WORDS**, the name of each word in your dictionary will be listed on the screen, starting with the latest definition. To interrupt the listing, hit any key, or follow the instructions printed by **WORDS**. To continue the listing, hit a key again; otherwise, hit <RETURN> to abort the listing.

* Older FORTHs use **VLIST** instead. **PolyFORTH WORDS** can be loaded as an option.

```
WORDS
MUSIC DANCE MARKER... <Hit any key> <RETURN>
```

As we have seen, you can redefine words if you think of a newer or better definition, and FORTH will automatically use the latest version.

```
: DANCE ." HUSTLE" ;
: MUSIC ." ROCK" ;

DANCE HUSTLE
```

The new definitions are added to the dictionary, but the previous definitions are still there.

```
WORDS
MUSIC DANCE MUSIC DANCE MARKER ...
```

To remove definitions from the dictionary, type **FORGET**, followed by the name of the word.

```
FORGET DANCE

MUSIC SWING
```

FORGET not only removes a definition (the latest **DANCE**), but also all the definitions which follow it (the latest **MUSIC** too.) Your dictionary now looks like this:

```
WORDS
MUSIC DANCE MARKER ...
```

Try it again.

```
FORGET DANCE

WORDS
MARKER ...
```

There is a limit to what you can **FORGET.**

```
FORGET DUP FORGET ? Protected
```

This is FORTH's way of saying that words below a certain critical point in the dictionary cannot be forgotten.

If you want to restore a forgotten word, you can type it in again and recompile it. But a long definition would mean a lot of retyping. When you create a FORTH word from the keyboard, the carefully typed lines that go into its definition are gone forever. There is no easy way to reconstruct the lines you typed (called the *source code*) from the word that is now part of the dictionary (called the compiled or *object code*). You need some way of saving what you type so that the words you create can be recreated as needed.

Files and Screens

Fortunately, there is a way to save lines of source code—by typing them into computer *memory*. We have already seen one kind of memory—the FORTH stack. The stack holds the arguments and *remembers* the results of the words you use. Another kind of memory holds the dictionary and remembers new definitions. These two types of memory are usually called *main* memory because they are immediately accessible to the computer.

Another kind of memory is called *mass storage*, which is often cheaper and larger than main memory. Cassettes, floppy disks, and hard disks are examples of mass storage. It is the job of a program called the *operating system* to move information from mass storage to main memory and back again.

FORTH provides many of the functions of an operating system. It lets you type lines of source code to be saved in mass storage. You can then direct the text interpreter to read from mass storage rather than from the keyboard. The text interpreter reads the lines it finds there exactly as if you had typed them in again.

Mass storage is typically divided into a number of files. A file simply holds an ordered collection of information, much like a file folder in a file cabinet. A catalog gives the name of each file and its location in mass storage.

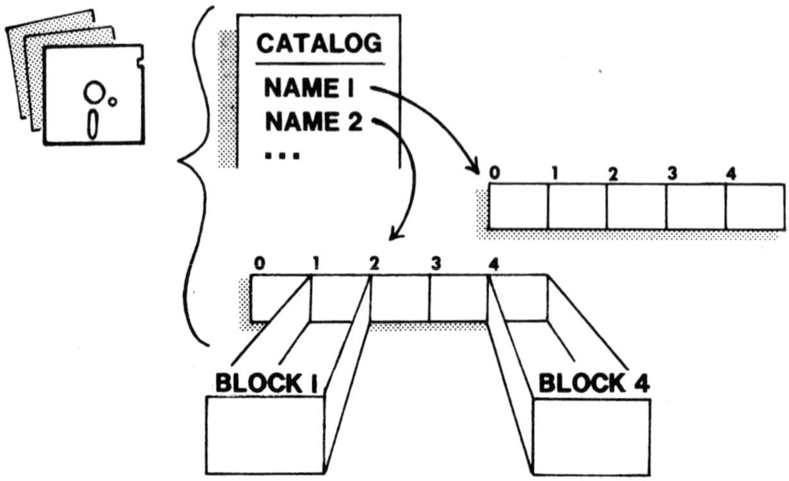

Many FORTHs further divide each file into conveniently sized *blocks*, which are moved in and out of main memory on request. Some polyFORTH systems do not use files.The mass storage device is simply divided into blocks. MacForth uses the normal Macintosh files, which appear to be a continuous text file, rather than a series of blocks. UR/FORTH supports both text and block files. The blocks are numbered sequentially, starting with zero. A block which is used to hold source text is sometimes called a *screen*. Screens are divided into 16 lines of 64 characters each. These are enough lines for several definitions.

Selecting a File

The program which enables you to type source text into a screen is called the *editor*. A well-designed editor lets you move, insert, and delete lines of source text. You can insert words within a line, search screens for a match with a given word, or replace one word with another. In short, the editor gives you control over the source text and encourages you to improve it.

Editors differ remarkably— some FORTH systems even give you a choice of editors. We will describe two general-purpose editors: *screen-oriented* editors that let you type text directly into a 16 line area on your console screen, and *line-oriented* editors where all the editing is done in a command line at the bottom of the screen. We will further assume that you are using a floppy diskette or hard disk for mass storage and that you are somewhat familiar with the operating system of your computer.

Before using the editor, you must create or select a file to be edited. The files available to you are listed in a catalog and can be displayed with a command like **DIR** or with the same command that you would normally use with your operating system.

MacFORTH

Creative Solutions has taken great pains to follow the standard Macintosh file interface. When you first boot MacForth Plus, you will be in a new *untitled* text file. Any commands you type go into this file. The mouse, the clipboard, and all other editing tools will work in a familiar manner. To execute or compile the last line you typed, press <ENTER> instead of <RETURN>. To execute or compile several lines, select them and press <ENTER>. Any output is inserted in the file, where it may be cut and pasted or otherwise edited. To execute or compile an entire source file, pull down the **File** menu and select **Include.**

To save a source file, click the close box and you will be asked to name it (if it's new). To select a different source file, pull down the **File** menu and select **Open**. That's all there is to it. MacForth users may wish to skip to the exercises at the end of this chapter.

UR/FORTH

When you first boot **UR/FORTH** , it selects the file **FORTH.SCR** if it is present in the same subdirectory. You can use **DIR** to list the other available files— source files end in **.SCR.** To select another file, type **USING** followed by the name of the file.

```
USING COMPUSR
```

If the suffix is omitted, **.SCR** is assumed. To make a new file, type **MAKE** followed by the name of the file, then select it with **USING.**

```
MAKE SAMPLE
USING SAMPLE
```

The file is created empty but is automatically extended as you edit it. To invoke the editor, type **EDIT**. UR/FORTH uses a screen editor. To enter the display, press the space bar or <ENTER>. To leave the display, press <ESC>. Press it again to return to Forth.

It is possible to select files from the editor simply by typing the number of the file as it appears in the upper left of the display. If the file you want isn't there, type "U" and then name the file. Press <F1> for help.

L&P F83

Use **DIR** to list the available files— source files end in .BLK. To select a file, type **OPEN** followed by the name of the file.

```
OPEN KERNEL86.BLK
```

To make a new file, type **CREATE-FILE** followed by the name of the file. **CREATE-FILE** needs to know how many blocks to make the file. To make a 32 block file called **SAMPLE.BLK**, you would type

```
32 CREATE-FILE SAMPLE.BLK
```

This also selects the file. To extend this file by, say, 10 blocks, type **10 MORE**.

Laxen and Perry's F83 uses a line-oriented editor. To invoke the editor, type **ED**. The first time you type **ED** you will be asked for your *id*. Just type in your initials for now. To edit screen 5, type

```
5 EDIT
```

When you are through editing, type **DONE**. Be sure to close all files with **FLUSH** before returning to the operating system with **BYE**.

PolyFORTH

The polyFORTH main source file FORTH.SRC is opened when you first boot. The remaining source files are generally opened when you type **HI**. You will often find a list of files to be opened on block 8 or block 11 of FORTH.SRC.

To see which files are available, type **DIR**. PolyFORTH source files end in .SRC. To see which files have been opened, type **.MAP**. To the left of each file name you will see its unit number. To select a file, type its unit number and the command **UNIT**.

```
2 UNIT ( generally selects FORTH2.SRC)
0 UNIT ( generally selects FORTH.SRC)
```

To add a file to the units map, use **CHART**, followed by the name of the file.

```
CHART MYFILE
```

If the suffix is omitted, **.SRC** is assumed. There is no simple word like **CHART** for making a new file. We recommend that you carefully type in the following definition:

```
: MAKE
   >R  AUNIT DUP BL WORD COUNT MAP
   OVER VOLUME * RELATIVE  R> NEWBLOCKS ;
```

To make a 32 block file called **SAMPLE.SRC**, you would enter

```
32 MAKE SAMPLE.SRC
```

Then type **.MAP** and select the appropriate unit.

PolyFORTH uses a line-oriented editor. To invoke the editor, type **L**. This lists the most recently edited block, initially 0, and enables the editor. When you are through editing, type **FLUSH**. All files are automatically closed when you return to the operating system with **BYE**.

MasterFORTH and ZEN

MasterFORTH and its subset ZEN use *gerunds* to manipulate files. Type **DIR** to see a list of available files. Source files end in **.SCR.** To select a file, type **USING** followed by the name of the file.

```
USING SAMPLE
```

If the suffix is omitted, **.SCR** is assumed. To make *and select* a new file, type **MAKING** followed by the name of the file.

```
MAKING MYFILE
```

The new file **MYFILE.SCR** will be four screens long. To extend it by 10 screens, type

```
10 MORE
```

Both MasterFORTH and ZEN are shipped with the file **SAMPLE.SCR** for you to practice on.

```
USING SAMPLE
```

MasterFORTH uses a screen-oriented editor. To invoke it, type the number of the screen to edit, followed by the command **EDIT**.

```
3 EDIT
```

To leave the editor, press <ESC> once for ZEN, and twice for MasterFORTH. ZEN provides both a screen-oriented editor *and* a line-oriented editor. To use the line editor, type **L**. This lists the most recently edited block, initially 0, and invokes the editor. In either case, all files are automatically closed when you return to the operating system with **BYE**.

LIST, LOAD, and THRU

Before continuing further, make or select a file for editing practice. If you want to examine a screen in this file, you can list its contents by typing the screen number, followed by the word **LIST**. See if there's anything on screen 1 of your file.

```
1 LIST
```

Assume for now that you see the following definition typed into your screen.

```
: SIMPLE
   CR ." This is easy!" ;
```

The word **SIMPLE** is not yet part of the dictionary:

```
SIMPLE SIMPLE ?
```

To redirect the text interpreter to read a screen instead of the keyboard (that is, to compile the screen), you would simply type the screen number followed by the word **LOAD**.

```
1 LOAD
```

Has **SIMPLE** been compiled?

```
SIMPLE This is easy!
```

Comments

Now imagine that screen 2 of your file holds the definitions of some trickier words.

```
2 LIST

  SCR# 2
   0 \ Somewhat trickier words.
   1 : TRICKY ( start# - end#)
   2 \ Starting equals ending number.
   3     3 +   ( add 3)
   4     2*    ( multiply by two)
   5     2-    ( subtract 2)
   6     2/    ( divide by two)
   7     2-    ( subtract two again) ;
   8
   9 : TRICK2 ( start# — end#)
  10 \ The answer is always 3.
  11     DUP  3 * 7 +
  12     OVER + 5 + 4 /
  13     SWAP -  ;
  14
  15*
```

* Line-oriented editors usually display the line numbers to the left of the screen. These numbers are not really part of the screen, and screen-oriented editors may omit them entirely.

This screen shows how to use comments and indentation to make a definition easier to understand. Line 0 describes the contents of the screen in general terms. The *backslash* \ , which begins the line, is a FORTH word that causes the text interpreter to ignore all text to the right of the backslash for the rest of the line.\ works for text files, too.

PolyFORTH users can add \ this way:

```
: \ >IN @ 64 + -64 AND >IN ! ; IMMEDIATE
```

This would be a good definition to practice editing and **LOAD**ing.

Therefore, the text "Somewhat trickier words" is not compiled into the dictionary.

By convention, line 0 of each screen in a file describes the words on that screen. This makes it possible to quickly determine the contents of a file by reading line 0 of each screen. UR/FORTH uses **QX** to list line 0 of the first 50 screens. In polyFORTH and ZEN, **QX** takes as an argument the starting screen number, for example, **10 QX**.

Several FORTHs provide **INDEX** , which takes two arguments, the starting and ending screen numbers:

```
10 40 INDEX.
```

The line 0 comment often contains other useful information, such as the initials of the programmer who created the screen and the date the screen was last modified.

Line 1 reads

```
1 : TRICKY ( start# - end#)
```

The left parenthesis (called "paren") is also used to add comments to source text. All text up to and including the next right parenthesis is treated as a comment. The first line of source text for a definition should include a *paren* comment giving the stack notation for the definition (its arguments and results). Paren comments are also useful to explain the less obvious words within a definition. Comments should be used carefully, however, for these reasons:

- Too many comments can make the definition difficult to read.
- Comments about what a definition is supposed to be doing tend to be believed, even if the code is incorrect!

The word **TRICKY** is a good example of using too many comments. The comment "subtract 2," for example, doesn't really need to follow **2-**.

Well-chosen names, indentation, and comments are the keys to writing easily readable definitions.

You can compile a range of screens with the command **THRU**. **THRU** needs the starting and ending screen numbers to compile.

```
FORGET SIMPLE
2 3 THRU
```

Screens 2 and 3 will be compiled just as if you had typed **2 LOAD** followed by **3 LOAD**.

One last remark about comments: screen 0 of a file cannot be read by the text interpreter— neither **LOAD** nor **THRU** can be used to compile it. Therefore, you can use screen 0 as a full screen of commentary on the words defined in the file and their use. You don't need any backslashes or parentheses either, because the screen is never compiled.

Screen-Oriented Editors

Use **LIST** to find a blank screen for editing practice, or else make yourself a new file. You will shortly be writing source text on this screen and editing it. Because you will be typing directly into the screen, you will need a set of non-printing keys to invoke the editing functions. On some computers you do this by pressing both the <CONTROL> key and a normal key at the same time. *WordStar-style* editors work this way. On other computers, you may have special editing or function keys marked with arrows, logos, or other symbols. We will assume that your terminal has at least the four cursor arrow keys.

To edit screen 3, type:

```
3 EDIT*
```

---

* **UR/FORTH**: type **EDIT**, then **E**, then the screen number.

You'll see the empty screen with the cursor in the upper lefthand corner (called the "home" position).

Just for practice, type in these three lines, hitting <RETURN> at the end of each line:

```
This is line one.
This is line two.
And this is line three.

_
```

The *underscore* shows the position of the cursor. Press the up-arrow twice to move the cursor up two positions to the beginning of line 2. Notice that the cursor travels right through the "A" in line 3 without changing it. You can move the cursor to the right without disturbing line two by pressing the right-arrow key. Move to the second word (with five right-arrows).

```
This is line one.
This is line two.
And this is line three.
```

A more efficient way to move right is to use <TAB>, which puts the cursor at the beginning of the next word. Try two <TAB>s.

```
This is line two.

This is line two.
```

If <TAB> doesn't work, try pressing <CONTROL> and the right arrow at the same time.

<Shift-TAB> takes you to the beginning of the previous word, or try pressing <CONTROL> and the left arrow at the same time.

```
This is line two.
```

Use the <TAB> and the arrow keys until the cursor is positioned over the period in line 2.

```
This is line two.
```

Now type over the period with a comma.

```
This is line two,_
```

Move the cursor down to the beginning of line 3. Type over the capital "A" with a small "a" and you will see:

```
This is line one.
This is line two,
and this is line three.
```

Try advancing to the next screen* and typing in the following definition:

```
\ Famous Quotes
: LAVOISIER
\ 18th century chemist.
   CR ." To call forth a concept"
   CR ." a word is needed."
   CR ." —Lavoisier" ;
```

Let's add some new natural— for example, Lavoisier's first name (Antoine). First, position the cursor over the L of his last name.

```
   CR ." —Lavoisier" ;
```

Press the <INSERT> key. If you have no such key, try the WordStar Command <CONTROL-V>. A message should appear somewhere near your screen to remind you that "insert mode" is active. Now type in "Antoine" (and a space).

```
   CR ." —Antoine Lavoisier" ;
```

Notice how the characters to the right of the cursor are pushed over automatically to make room for your new material. If you insert too many characters, the end of the line may be pushed off the righthand edge of the

---

* On IBM PCs, try pressing the <PgDn> to move forward one screen and <PgUp> to move back. If that fails, try <CONTROL-N> for the *next* screen and <CONTROL-B> to move *back* one screen. If that fails, too, this would be a good time to read the editor chapter in your system documentation.

screen. Some editors will prevent you from inserting more characters; others will warn you with an audible *beep*. To leave *insert mode*, press the <INSERT> key again— it toggles you in and out of insert mode.

Now take out what you've just put in. You can do this several ways. You can use the backspace key to delete the character to the left of the cursor, for example. Make sure the cursor is still over the "L" in "Lavoisier," then press backspace three times.

```
CR ." —Antoi_   Lavoisier" ;
```

Although the cursor has moved three positions to the left, erasing as it goes, the remainder of the line didn't move at all. This leaves you with three blanks between names. You can delete one of the extra blanks, or any other character under the cursor, by using the <DELETE> key, or try the WordStar command <CONTROL-G>. Press it three times.

```
CR ." —AntoiLavoisier" ;
```

The actions of erasing and moving the remainder of the line to the left can be combined by using backspace while in the insert mode. Try typing <INSERT>, followed by five backspaces.

```
CR ." —Lavoisier" ;
```

The five letters to the left of the cursor have been deleted and the remainder of the line has moved left five positions. Choose the method of character deletion which seems the most comfortable to you.

If you have inadvertently changed a screen, there is usually a special key that will restore it to its original condition.* When you have finished editing, press <ESC>. FORTH screen editors usually have a rich repertoire of additional commands for deleting lines, moving lines or screens within or between files, and other courtesies.* It is often useful to be able to search the file for a string and replace it with another string, and most FORTH screen

---

* **UR/FORTH** uses <F10> or <CONTROL-Z>. **ZEN** uses <CONTROL-U>. **MasterFORTH** uses the command line— press <Escape> then type **FRESH**. Return to the editor with <RETURN>.

editors provide this capability.† Searching always takes place from the current cursor position on the current screen forward to the end of the file. To search the entire file, first move to screen 0. Consult your system documentation for further information.

The Line Editor

Use **LIST** to find a blank screen for editing practice, or else make yourself a new file. You will shortly be writing source text on this screen and editing it. To invoke the line editor, type **L**. This lists the most recently edited block, initially 0, and enables the editor. To see the next screen, type **N** (try it!).** To move back a screen, type **B**. Line 0 is displayed at the bottom of your screen, or in highlight or inverse video to show you that it is the *active* line, and that the line editor is available for editing it. You can change the active line with the command

```
n T
```

Line **n** becomes the active line. To replace it, type

```
P <text>
```

The **P** command puts the following text into the active line, replacing what was there. The variation **U** <text> puts the text under the active line. Try entering a line of your choice. The remaining lines move down to accommodate the new active line.

---

* **UR/FORTH**, **MasterFORTH**, and **ZEN** even support a line stack for pushing lines in one screen and popping them in another.

† **UR/FORTH** uses <F7> for search and <F8> for search and replace. You will be prompted for the arguments. <CONTROL-L> repeats the previous search and replace operation.

ZEN uses the line editor for search and replace. **MasterFORTH** also uses a line editor syntax which is executed from its command line. Press <ESC> to move to the command line and <RETURN> to return to the editor.

** **L&P F83**: use **N L** to move forwards and **B L** to move backwards in the file.

To delete the active line entirely, type:

```
X
```

The remaining lines move up to fill the gap. The deleted line is saved in a special *insert buffer*. Typing **P** or **U** followed immediately by <RETURN> puts the text in the insert buffer into or under the active line. For example, the following sequence will move line 6 to line 9:

```
6 T X<RETURN>
8 T U<RETURN>
```

At this point, find an empty screen and experiment with these line editing commands.

Editing an entire line to add or change a word is a clumsy operation, at best. You can also edit characters within a line at the current cursor position. The command

```
I <text>
```

inserts text at the cursor. The remaining characters on the line move to the right to accommodate the insertion. Characters on the extreme right may be pushed off the line and lost. The command

```
F <text>
```

finds the next occurrence of the given text and repositions the cursor there. The search is made from the current cursor position to the end of the screen. To search the entire screen, first reposition the cursor with **0 T.** The command

```
E
```

erases the last text found. The command

```
D <text>
```

finds and deletes the given text. It is exactly equivalent to an **F** command followed by an **E** command. The command

```
R <text>
```

replaces the text last found with the text following the command.

For example, to replace the first **0=** on the screen with **NOT**, use the sequence

```
0 T F 0=
R NOT
```

Line editor commands can be combined on a single line by separating them with a caret ("^").

```
0 T F 0=^R NOT
```

The text following an **F** or **D** command is copied into a special *find buffer*. Subsequent **F** or **D** commands followed immediately by <RETURN> find or delete the text in the find buffer. If you execute the example above, typing **F**<RETURN> will take you to the next occurrence of "0=". If the search fails, you will see a message like "Not found."

The **S** <text> command works like the **F** command except that it scans for the text from the current screen to the end of the file. In PolyFORTH and L&P F83 the **S** command takes an argument equal to the last block number to search. ZEN always searches to the end of the file. To search the entire file, first move to screen 0. When you have finished editing, save your changes to disk by typing **FLUSH**.

Many FORTHs which support the line editor also support *shadow screens*. A shadow screen is a documentation screen associated with a source screen. Select a source screen from one of your system files and note which words are defined on it. Now select the shadow screen. PolyFORTH uses type **Q.** The shadow blocks are kept in a separate file, ending with the prefix .DOC. This file is usually mapped out one **UNIT** higher than the source file.

L&P F83: type `A`. The shadow blocks are kept in the last half of the source file.

ZEN does not support shadow screens.

You should be looking at the documentation associated with the words on the source screen.

Finishing Up

When you edit a screen, you are actually editing a copy of the screen which was moved from mass storage to main memory by the operating system. How and when the operating system rewrites the edited screens to mass storage varies from system to system. The FORTH-83 Standard command **SAVE-BUFFERS** is guaranteed to write all altered screens to disk. In addition, many FORTHs support the command **EMPTY-BUFFERS**, which re-initializes the disk buffers. Any changes not written to disk are lost. This may be exactly what you want, if you have written bad information to a screen but have not yet saved it to disk.

Exercises

Retype the definitions you used in Chapter 2 into an empty screen in your file—use as many screens as you wish. Be sure to use comments and indentation to make the definitions easy to understand. Use **`LOAD`** or **`THRU`** to compile these screens. Do the definitions work correctly? If not, **`FORGET`** them, correct the source screens, and try compiling them again.

6 Variables, Constants and Arrays

Computer memory comes in many types. One type of memory we have seen is the FORTH *LIFO* stack. It keeps a few top items handy but requires extra manipulation to reach items buried more deeply.

Another type of memory is called *random-access memory* (or just RAM). Each item in RAM is equally accessible and can be obtained in any order. This is possible because each location in RAM has its own fixed numerical address. Each location has an *address*—a number assigned to it by the computer according to its own internal system. You can think of RAM as a long series of slots on a very large table.

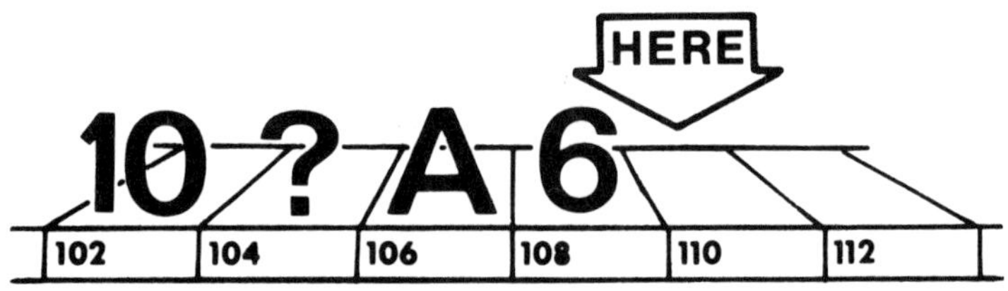

Each slot contains a *value*. The value could be any number of things—the square root of 2, your checkbook balance, even the address of another location.

Be sure you understand that there is a difference between the address of a location and the value stored at that location.

Since all addresses tend to look alike, FORTH lets you give some of them names for easy reference and readability.

Variables

Some values change quite frequently—the number of inches of rain so far this season, for example, or the number of boxes of detergent in a supermarket's stock. When you want to use these values in your program without the hassle of manipulating them on the stack—and with the added convenience of referring to them by name—you should use a variable. Let's set up a variable that will have the name **RAIN**.

```
VARIABLE RAIN
```

What exactly have you done?

The interpreter creates a new dictionary word with the name **RAIN**. It then finds the address of the first available or *free* RAM location. This is given by the word **HERE**.

```
HERE . 110
```

The interpreter then assigns the name **RAIN** to this location, and updates **HERE** to point to the next free location. **RAIN** will now leave the address of this location on the stack.

```
RAIN . 110
HERE . 112
```

A *byte* in computer jargon means the smallest unit of memory that has its own address. On many computers, a byte contains 8 *bits* (zeroes or ones), and so has 1 of 256 different values (0 to 255). This is large enough to hold a printable character, but is too small for general use. For this reason, bytes are usually grouped into *cells*.

A FORTH-83 cell is 16-bits wide. The FORTH-83 stack is also 16 bits, or one cell, wide. However, some modern computers, like the Novix NC4016 or the TMS320C25, are *cell-addressed*. The smallest addressable unit is a cell and so a cell is the same as a byte. In contrast, 32-bit FORTH implementations usually group *four* bytes into a 32-bit cell.

To hide the differences between these implementations, we introduce three new words: **CELL CELLS** and **CELL+**. Their FORTH-83 definitions are:

```
2 CONSTANT CELL*                  ( number of bytes per cell)

: CELLS ( n - n2)   2* ;          ( number of bytes per n cells)
: CELL+ ( a - a2)   2+ ;          ( advance to the next cell address)
```

We will use *a* to refer to an address in a stack diagram. The equivalent definitions for cell-addressed FORTHs are:

```
1 CONSTANT CELL

: CELLS ( n - n2)   1  ;
: CELL+ ( a - a2)   1+ ;
```

For 32-bit implementations you would use:

```
4 CONSTANT CELL

: CELLS ( n - n2)   4 * ;
: CELL+ ( a - a2)   4 + ;**
```

Find an empty source screen or file and enter the appropriate definitions for your implementation. This will be your *prelude*, which you should **LOAD** or **INCLUDE** each time you start FORTH.

In the example above, **HERE** has been advanced by one cell to point to the next empty cell. This cell that is skipped belongs to the variable **RAIN**. **RAIN**, however, occupies more than one cell of memory. When we add the variable **RAIN**, we add the four characters of its name and another 4 or 5 bytes of overhead.

At this point the cell **RAIN** contains an unknown value. Let's *initialize* **RAIN** with a useful number. Assume that there have been 12 inches of rain so far this season.

---

* The word **CONSTANT** will be introduced later in this chapter.

** **MacForth** would use

```
4 CONSTANT CELL

: CELLS   4* ;
: CELL+   4+ ;
```

```
12 RAIN !
```

The value 12 is placed on the stack and the address of the variable **RAIN** (110 in this example) is pushed on top of it. The operator `!` ("store") then moves the 12 to the RAM location **RAIN**, replacing the unknown value that was previously there.

See if the value of **RAIN** is now really 12.

```
RAIN . 110
```

Whoops! The value isn't on the stack; the address is. (Your **RAIN** is probably at a different address anyway; we chose the number 110 just for convenience.) You need the new word `@` ("fetch") to get to the value of **RAIN**.

```
RAIN @ . 12
```

The word `@` takes an address from the stack (left there by **RAIN**) and copies the value it finds there onto the stack. In other words, `@` replaces an address with its value.

Note that you could get exactly the same result by using the address of **RAIN**, if you knew it. Ordinarily, however, you will never have to worry about the specific address of a variable; the name is all you need.

The process of bringing a value to the stack and printing it can be shortened with the word **?** ("question"), which combines **@** and **.** . FORTH-83 doesn't require **?** but most FORTHs supply it anyway. If yours doesn't, add it to the prelude this way:

```
: ?   @ . ;
```

```
RAIN ? 12
```

Changing the value of a variable is as simple as initializing it. Suppose it rained an inch yesterday, bringing the season's total to 13; you can store the new total just like you did the old one.

```
13 RAIN !
```

You'll find that the old total has now been replaced.

```
RAIN ? 13
```

An easier way to keep running totals is to let FORTH do the computation for you. Suppose yet another inch of rain falls; you could store this information as follows:

```
RAIN @ 1+ RAIN !
```

Review the elements of this program to be sure that you understand them:

Word	Stack	Action
RAIN	a	Pushes the address of **RAIN** on the stack.
@	13	Pops the address off the stack, gets the value at that address, and pushes it on the stack.
1+	14	Adds 1 to the number.
RAIN	14 a	Pushes the address of **RAIN** on the stack again.
!		Stores 14 at the address, removing both numbers.

Check to be sure that the total is correct.

```
RAIN ? 14
```

Since adding to running totals is such a common operation, a special word, **+!** ("plus-store") will add the second number on the stack to the value stored at the address on top of the stack, saving you some steps. Try adding another 1 to **RAIN** this way.

```
1 RAIN +!
RAIN ? 15
```

It is also possible to add the value of one variable to that of another variable. You could set up a variable called **TODAYSRAIN** that keeps track of daily rainfall, for example, and then add that total to the running total stored in **RAIN.** If rainfall today was 2 inches, here's what you would do:

```
VARIABLE TODAYSRAIN

2 TODAYSRAIN !
TODAYSRAIN @ RAIN +!
RAIN ? 17
```

You can also include variables in definitions. Instead of adding a 1 to **TODAYSRAIN** every time an inch of rain falls, you can define a word that will take care of this for you—call it **DRIP**.

```
: DRIP   1 TODAYSRAIN +! ;
```

TODAYSRAIN currently has a value of 2. Suppose it rains 3 inches today.

```
DRIP DRIP DRIP
TODAYSRAIN ? 5
```

A Random Example

Variables are useful whenever a named quantity has changing values. For example, one kind of random number generator generates a new random number by applying a formula to a previous random number.

new number = ([old number * b] + 1) mod m

This new random number in turn becomes the previous random number (the *seed*) the next time around. We can use a variable called **SEED** to keep track of this number. Here is a simple random number generator **RAND** that uses **SEED**.

```
VARIABLE SEED
1234 SEED !

: RAND ( - n)
   SEED @ 5421 * 1+  DUP SEED ! ;
```

Check **RAND** against the formula. **SEED @** gives us the previous random number, which we initialized to 1234. This is multiplied by 5421 (our **b**) and is added to 1. The multiplication operator ***** limits the product to a one-cell result, which is equivalent to performing a **MOD** of 65536 (our **m**) on the result (equivalent to 2147483648 **MOD** on 32-bit implementations). Here is **RAND** in action:

```
RAND RAND RAND . . . 7793 1072 -10837
```

We might also need to produce a more limited range of random numbers. We might want to pick a random card (only 52 choices) or throw dice (only 6 choices per die). We can limit the size of any number to a useful range with the **MOD** function. For example, any number **MOD** 52 gives a result from 0 to 51. We could include **MOD** within a new **RANDOM**, which is based on **RAND**:

```
: RANDOM ( n - n2)
   RAND SWAP MOD ;*
```

* **MacForth** division of a negative number by a positive number gives a negative remainder. To keep the dice positive, use this definition:

```
: RANDOM   RAND ABS  SWAP MOD ;
```

RANDOM will return a number from 0 to n-1. By adding 1 to whatever **RANDOM** returns, we get a number from 1 to n. If n is 6, we will get a number from 1 to 6, which is exactly what we need to model the throw of a die.

```
: DICE ( - n n2)
   6 RANDOM 1+ 6 RANDOM 1+ ;

DICE . . 2 5
DICE . . 4 1
```

Using **MOD** to limit the range of random numbers greatly reduces their randomness. This is because the digits on the right of a number produced by **RAND** are less random than the digits on the left. We will give you a better definition of **RANDOM** in a later chapter. If you wish to know more about random numbers and their generation, you might read *Algorithms* by Robert Sedgewick (Addison-Wesley, 1983).

Constants

Some values just never change—the number of days in a week, grams in a kilogram, etc. You can assign a name to any constant value with the word **CONSTANT**. Because you know the value of a constant when you first set it up, creating the constant and initializing it can be done in one step. Let's set up a constant to hold the number of days in a week.

```
7 CONSTANT DAYS/WEEK
```

And when you want to see the value or work with it, this is all you need to do:

```
DAYS/WEEK . 7
```

Note that no `@` is necessary. A constant puts its value on the stack, ready for you to use.

Constants are more than convenient and readable; they are also fast. If you define a constant to be the number 12, like this:

```
12 CONSTANT DOZEN
DOZEN . 12
```

using **DOZEN** is likely to be faster than putting a 12 on the stack.

A Closer Look

Before going on, it's worthwhile to examine in more detail how variables are really set up. When you type

```
VARIABLE <name>
```

two separate actions take place:

1. A new definition is created in the dictionary with the name <name> and instructions to push the address of the first free RAM cell (which usually follows the definition) on the stack. This much is done internally with the word **CREATE**.
2. The first free cell of RAM is reserved for the variable <name>. The word **HERE** is updated to point to the next free cell, which normally follows the cell just reserved. This much is done internally with the word **ALLOT**, which needs to know the number of free *bytes* to be reserved.

Since a variable occupies one free cell, here is a possible definition of **VARIABLE**:

```
: VARIABLE   CREATE  CELL ALLOT ;
```

Any word which uses **CREATE** to make a new dictionary entry is called a *defining word*. The defining words we have met so far are **:** **VARIABLE** and **CONSTANT**.

Arrays

A logical grouping of identically sized variables is called an array. What are arrays good for? Mainly, convenience and saving space. The convenience comes in when you can refer to the whole group by one name, enhancing readability. Arrays save space, too, by eliminating much of the computer housekeeping necessary to name each individual cell in an array.

What sorts of things would you want to group in an array? You might want to keep track of the calories you take in daily and add them up weekly, for instance. Instead of setting up seven variables, one for each day of the week and all in different memory locations, you can group the seven variables in an array and simplify the process of entering the values and keeping track of the totals.

The word **VARIABLE** is not what we want to set up arrays; as we've just seen, it **ALLOT**s only one cell of memory. But by splitting the action of **VARIABLE** into **CREATE** and **ALLOT**, you can **ALLOT** as many bytes as you need to hold all the elements in your array.

For example, to create the calorie array **CALS**, first you need to make a new definition with the name **CALS**, and then you need to allot enough cells for 7 days' worth of calories, one cell per day:

```
CREATE CALS  7 CELLS ALLOT
```

You now have a whole row of consecutive cells in memory, with the first cell named **CALS**.

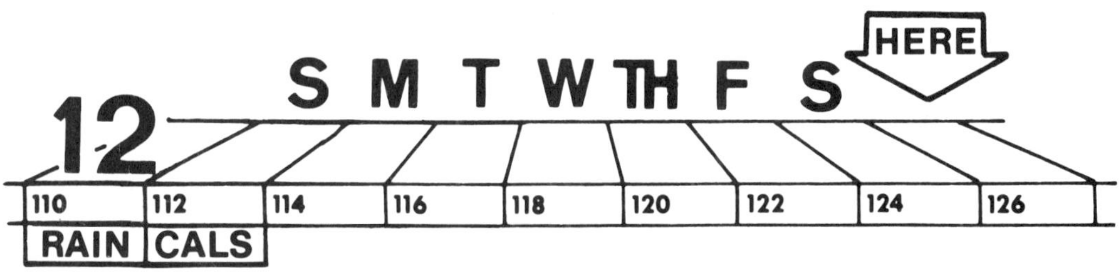

The action of **CALS**, like any new word defined by **CREATE**, is to leave the address of the first reserved cell which follows it on the stack. If you can find the address of the first cell, you can find the address of any cell by adding the appropriate offset, or distance between them. Since an offset is a difference between two memory addresses, it is given in bytes. Here's how it works:

Suppose your caloric intake on Sunday (the first day of the week) was 1200. Simply store that number at the beginning of **CALS**:

```
1200 CALS !
```

On Monday you took in 2000 calories. All you need to do is increase the address of **CALS** by one cell to store the 2000 in the right place:

```
2000 CALS CELL+ !
```

Rather than trying to remember the offset for each day—which could get very difficult if you had a large number of offsets. Use constants to name each offset and make it easier on yourself.

```
0 CELLS CONSTANT SUNDAY
1 CELLS CONSTANT MONDAY
2 CELLS CONSTANT TUESDAY
3 CELLS CONSTANT WEDNESDAY
4 CELLS CONSTANT THURSDAY
5 CELLS CONSTANT FRIDAY
6 CELLS CONSTANT SATURDAY
```

Now when you want to store 1800 calories for Tuesday, this is all you need to do:

```
1800 CALS TUESDAY + !
```

You can also set FORTH to the task of adding up each day's caloric intake so that all you have to do is enter each meal. Your Wednesday, say, starts with a 450-calorie breakfast.

```
450 CALS WEDNESDAY + !
```

Later you eat a 600-calorie lunch.

```
600 CALS WEDNESDAY + +!
```

The **+** adds the offset, and the **+!** adds the calories.

```
CALS WEDNESDAY + ? 1050
```

This is tedious, isn't it—typing in **WEDNESDAY +** every time you want to enter another meal or check the total? By factoring out repetitive material such as **WEDNESDAY +** , you can simplify your input considerably. Several steps are necessary to do this, but they need to be entered only once—and you may be using your **CALS** array for a long time, long enough to appreciate the extra convenience.

First, set up a variable to hold the offset for the current day.

```
VARIABLE TODAY
```

Second, a word to enhance readability. **IS-TODAY*** will take the offset you give it and store it in **TODAY**.

```
: IS-TODAY ( n )   TODAY ! ;
```

Third, a word to set the value of **TODAY**'s offset to 0, in case it still has the value from last week in it.

```
: WAKE-UP   0 CALS TODAY @ + ! ;
```

Fourth, a word to store calories at the proper offset.

```
: MEAL   CALS TODAY @+! ;
```

And fifth, a word to put the total on the stack so that you can display it.

```
: TOTAL   CALS TODAY @ + @ ;
```

Now you can use the words in this sequence, plugging in caloric values such as these:

```
THURSDAY IS-TODAY
WAKE-UP
800 MEAL
450 MEAL
1000 MEAL

TOTAL . 2250
```

* **polyFORTH** philosophy discourages hyphenated names. You might use **DAYTIME** instead.

You may have noticed the repetition of **CALS TODAY @ +** in the preceding examples. Could this be factored out as well?

Tables

Arrays provide a good way to store tables and to access the information in them for computation or display. Entering each value in the table separately can be a chore if you have to take two steps to allot space and initialize the value. Fortunately, the word `,` ("comma") combines these two operations. It reserves the next free cell and initializes it to whatever value is on top of the stack.

Let's make up a table to hold postal fees; then you can design a program that will take the number of ounces a package weighs, look up the proper fee in the table, and tell how much postage to put on your package. In our mythical postal system, the first 3 ounces cost 40 cents; 20 cents per ounce is added for the next 4 ounces; and 10 cents per ounce additional charge is made for the next 9 ounces, which brings the postage for one pound to $2.10. The table has one entry for each ounce:

```
CREATE POSTAGE-TABLE
0   , 40  , 40  , 40  , 60  , 80  , 100 , 120 , 130 , 140 ,
150 , 160 , 170 , 180 , 190 , 200 , 210 ,
```

Now you need a word to *look up* values in the table. Call it **OUNCES**.

```
: OUNCES ( n )
   CELLS POSTAGE-TABLE + @ CR . ."  CENTS" ;
```

When you type a number followed by **OUNCES**, FORTH knows to multiply the number by **CELL** (to get the offset), **@** the value at that offset, return the carriage, and print the value followed by the message "CENTS." See how it works:

```
5 OUNCES 80 CENTS
6 OUNCES 100 CENTS
```

Byte Arrays

If the values to be stored in an array are small (from 0 to 255), you can save memory by storing them in an array of bytes rather than an array of cells. The operators `!`, `@`, and `,` have the byte-sized equivalents **C!** ("C-store"), **C@** ("C-fetch"), and **C,** ("C-comma"). The "C" stands for "character" because a single printable character can be neatly stored in one byte of memory.

When you move a value from the stack to RAM memory with **C!**, the high-order byte is discarded. When you copy a byte value from RAM to the stack with **C@** , the high-order byte is made zero. The order of bytes within a variable is undefined, so don't **C@** from a variable unless you first **C!** into it.

We can rewrite the postage example to use an array of bytes. The table is built with **C,**

```
CREATE POSTAGE-TABLE
0   C, 40  C, 40  C, 40  C, 60  C, 80  C,
100 C, 120 C, 130 C, 140 C, 150 C, 160 C,
170 C, 180 C, 190 C, 200 C, 210 C,
```

and the new definition for **OUNCES** is

```
: OUNCES ( n )
   POSTAGE-TABLE + C@ CR . ." CENTS" ;
```

Check to see that it produces the same results.

```
5 OUNCES 80 CENTS
```

Word	Stack	Action
!	n a	Stores the value n at the given address.
@	a - n	Reads the value n at the given address and pushes it on the stack.
?	a	Prints the value stored at the given address.
+!	n a	Adds n to the value stored at the given address.
VARIABLE	<name>	Creates a one-cell variable named <name>. When <name> is executed, it will push the address of this cell on the stack.
CONSTANT	<name>	Creates a constant named <name> with a value of n. When <name> is executed, the value n will be pushed on the stack.
CREATE	<name>	Creates a dictionary entry named <name>. When executed, <name> will push the address of the first memory cell which follows the word <name> onto the stack. No memory is actually reserved by **CREATE**.
ALLOT	n	Reserves n bytes of RAM memory. **ALLOT** usually follows a defining word.
,	n	Reserves one cell of memory, initializing it to the value n.
C!	byte a	Stores the byte on the stack at the given address.
C@	a - byte	Reads the byte at the given address and pushes it on the stack.
C,	byte	Reserves one byte of memory, initializing it to the byte value.

Double Variables and Constants

Paired quantities, such as spatial coordinates or complex numbers, can be stored in and retrieved from special double-sized variables and constants. Use **2VARIABLE** and **2CONSTANT** to build the named 2-cell quantities.* Use **2@** and **2!** to move the paired quantities to and from the stack.

* **MacForth** does not supply **2VARIABLE** and **2CONSTANT**. You can add them to your prelude this way:

```
: 2VARIABLE   VARIABLE  CELL ALLOT ;
: 2CONSTANT   CREATE  , ,  DOES>  2@ ;
```

CREATE–DOES> will be introduced in a later chapter.

```
12  20  2CONSTANT BOTH

BOTH .S 2DROP
STACK: 12 20

2VARIABLE HIS-AND-HERS

1 10 HIS-AND-HERS 2!
HIS-AND-HERS 2@ .S 2DROP
STACK: 1 10
```

The high-order item of the pair, that is, the one closest to the top of the stack, is stored in the first 2 bytes of the **2VARIABLE**.

```
HIS-AND-HERS @ . 10
```

Word	Stack	Action
2VARIABLE	<name>	Creates a 2-cell variable named <name>. When <name> is executed, it will push the address of the first cell on the stack.
2CONSTANT	<name>	Creates a double constant named <name> with the value pair n and n2. When <name> is executed, this pair will be pushed on the stack.
2!	n n2 a	Stores the pair n and n2 at the given address.
2@	a - n n2	Reads the pair n and n2 from the given address and pushes them on the stack.

Exercises

1. Write a word **EXCHANGE** which exchanges the values of two variables. **EXCHANGE** is used like this:

```
VARIABLE X  2 X !
VARIABLE Y  5 Y !

X Y EXCHANGE
X ? 5
```

2. The Forth Interest Group (FIG) FORTH supports a form of **VARIABLE** which takes its initial value from the stack. Write a defining word **FIG-VARIABLE** which creates this kind of variable.

```
10 FIG-VARIABLE WHAT
```

```
WHAT ? 10
```

3. You will often find that an extra stack is just what you need to solve a problem. Try creating your own stack with an array called **STACK** and the words **PUSH** and **POP**. **PUSH** and **POP** should work like this:

```
3 PUSH
4 PUSH
POP . 4
POP . 3
```

You'll need an additional variable to keep track of the next available stack position. **PUSH** should do something reasonable even if your **STACK** is full. (Hint: use **MAX** and **MIN.**) What might **POP** do with an empty stack?

4. Add these stack manipulation words to the pseudo stack created in the example above:

>P	(n ; P: - n)	Pushes n on the pseudo stack.
P>	(- n ; P: n)	Pops n from the pseudo stack.
PDUP	(P: n - n n)	**DUP**s n on the pseudo stack.
PDROP	(P: n)	**DROP**s n from the pseudo stack.
PSWAP	(P: n n2 - n2 n)	**SWAP**s n and n2 on the pseudo stack.

7 Flow of Control

Often you will come to a point in your program where a decision needs to be made—that is, if the temperature of a room is over 85 degrees, turn the air conditioner on. Or suppose you are programming a dice game like *craps*. The first time you roll the dice, you need to see if their total equals 12 or 2; if it does, you lose, and if it doesn't, you can continue playing.

The decision-making process can always be divided into two parts: first, information about a circumstance or *condition* on which the decision depends (in the case of craps, whether the total equals 12 or 2); and second, what the possible responses will be (to end the game, to reroll, etc).

Every time FORTH checks for a condition, it expects to find a number on the stack with one of two values—true or false—called a *boolean flag*. True is represented by -1, false by 0. These flags are left on the stack by words called *logical operators*, and are used to decide between alternative courses of action. For example, the following words compare two numbers to each other and leave a true/false condition on the stack, depending on what they find:

Word	Stack	Action
=	n n2 - f	*Equal* returns *true* (-1) if n equals n2.
>	n n2 - f	*Greater-than* returns *true* if n is greater than n2.
<	n n2 - f	*Less-than* returns *true* if n is less than n2.

Here are the comparison operators in action:

```
11 12 =  .  0
12 12 =  . -1
6  5  >  . -1
11 6  <  .  0
-6 6  <  . -1
```

Though at this point it is necessary to print the flags to see how the logical operators work, remember that you will usually leave them on the stack to be passed on to the next part of the program.

Another group of logical operators compares a single number on the stack to zero.

Word	Stack	Action
0=	n - f	*Zero-equals* returns *true* if n equals 0.
0>	n - f	*Zero-greater*-than returns *true* if n is greater than 0.
0<	n - f	*Zero-less-than* returns *true* if n is negative.

```
5  0= .  0
0  0= . -1
5  0> . -1
-5 0< . -1
5  0> .  0
```

The operator **0=** can be used to reverse the value of a flag.

```
0  0= . -1
-1 0= .  0
```

AND, OR, and NOT

The logical operators **AND OR** and **NOT** allow you to make more sophisticated decisions based on conditions returned by the other logical operators. **AND** returns true only if the top and second flags on the stack are true. **OR** returns true if either the top or second flag (or both) is true.

```
0 5 < 5 8 < AND . -1
0 9 < 9 8 < AND .  0
3 3 = 3 4 = OR  . -1
3 5 = 3 6 = OR  .  0
```

NOT , like **0=**, reverses the top *boolean* flag on the stack.

```
5 5 = NOT . 0
5 6 > NOT . -1
```

We will show you later how to use **AND OR** and **NOT** to manipulate non-boolean values. Meanwhile, be sure that when you form a logical expression (combination of conditions) that at least one of the arguments to **AND OR** and **NOT** is a boolean flag.

Let's suppose your computer has a built-in clock which you've used to store the current month (a number from 0 to 11) and current year (a 4-digit number like 1984) into the variables **MONTH** and **YEAR**. Now suppose you would like to write a word called **DAYS** which returns the number of days in the current month. One approach you could take would be to create a table of twelve entries, one entry for each month. But if the month is February (that is, its value is 2) and if the year is a leap-year (that is, it is evenly divisible by 4), then you will need to add 1 to the number of days (28). The logical expression which, if *true*, means to add one the number of days, looks like this:

```
MONTH @ 2 = YEAR @ 4 MOD 0= AND
```

Word	Stack	Action
AND	f f2 - f3	Returns *true* if flags f and f2 are both *true*.
OR	f f2 - f3	Returns *true* if either flag f or f2 (or both) is *true*.
NOT	f - f2	Returns *true* if flag f is false and false if it's *true*.

Conditional Structures

Logical operators record information about circumstances or conditions in the form of *true/false* boolean flags, which they leave on the stack. We can then use these flags to select among alternative choices of action. Let's write a word that will examine a flag and do different things depending on what it finds. If the flag is true, it will print "true"; if it is false, it will print "false." Here's how you set it up:

```
: TRUTH   IF ." TRUE  " ELSE ." FALSE " THEN ;
```

The word **IF** removes and examines the flag on top of the stack. If it is true, **IF** continues executing the words which follow until it reaches **ELSE**; if it is false, **IF** skips ahead to continue execution with the first word which follows **ELSE**. In either case, execution continues with the words following **THEN**, if any. Try out **TRUTH** with some comparisons:

```
10 3 > TRUTH TRUE
10 3 < TRUTH FALSE
```

It is often helpful to diagram these alternate pathways— this is particularly true as the choices grow more complicated. We'll use a variation of traditional flowcharts to display what we've just done.

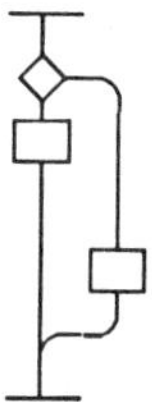

```
: TRUTH ( flag)
        IF ( )
           ." TRUE  "
         ELSE
           ." FALSE "
        THEN ;
```

In this method, the boxes used in the flowchart are too small to have anything put inside them. Instead there is associated text to the right of, and parallel to, the boxes. For flow diagrams there will not be more than one box in a horizontal line. It is easy to see that any flowchart can be pulled and stretched into this form. A box like is used to indicate an action or group of actions. A box like ⊥ ø(or ⊥) is used to show a test or decision. An action or group of actions will often be included with the test. The associated text can be informal description for program design or actual program source. Our use will be mostly actual program source. The direction of flow will always be straight down for actions in sequence or a true condition. For a false condition the flow will be to the side. When we don't go straight down we will always go to the right and down, or to the left and up, that is, *clockwise*. Thus it is not necessary to have arrows showing the direction of flow.

In this and the next chapter, which are both about flow of control, we will include flow diagrams like this with all our examples. These diagrams are not part of FORTH, but are included to help you understand how flow of control is handled in FORTH. The diagrams do not show anything that is not already present in the FORTH code, but they make the intent of the actual code clearer. In other chapters we will sometimes include these diagrams when we think that they will be helpful.

In some decisions, the alternative is to do nothing. In that case, take it out—it's optional. An example of a situation like this is a word that checks the stock of some item (say, boxes of detergent) in a supermarket. If the number of boxes goes below some number, called a "reorder point," then a message prompting the user to reorder is displayed. If there are enough items in stock, no action is taken. Let's make 12 the reorder point for all items. You could start by creating a constant equal to 12.

```
12 CONSTANT REORDER-POINT
```

The word **IN-STOCK** compares the number of boxes in stock with the constant:

```
: IN-STOCK ( n)
   REORDER-POINT <
   IF ." TIME TO REORDER " THEN ;

15 IN-STOCK
10 IN-STOCK
TIME TO REORDER
```

```
: IN-STOCK ( n)
        REORDER-POINT < IF (  )
           ." TIME TO REORDER "
        THEN ;
```

Now let's get back to the craps game and see what these conditional structures can do.

Once you have rolled the dice and added the total, you need to examine the total and make some decisions. One thing you might do is print the message "Craps! You lose" if you roll a total of 2 (snake eyes) or 12 (boxcars) on the first throw.

```
: SNAKE-EYES ( n)
   2 = IF ." CRAPS! YOU LOSE " THEN ;

: BOXCARS ( n)
  12 = IF ." CRAPS! YOU LOSE " THEN ;
```

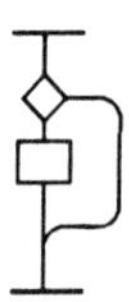

```
: SNAKE-EYES ( n)
        2 = IF (  )
           ." CRAPS! YOU LOSE "
        THEN ;
```

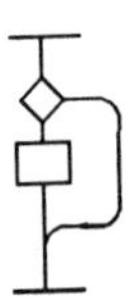

```
: BOXCARS ( n)
        12 = IF (  )
           ." CRAPS! YOU LOSE "
        THEN ;
```

Test these words with a reasonable total (from 2 to 12, just as you would get with two dice) and see if they work.

```
2 SNAKE-EYES CRAPS! YOU LOSE
5 SNAKE-EYES
12 BOXCARS   CRAPS! YOU LOSE
```

Since you need to perform two tests on the same total, you should **DUP** the total first:

```
: CRAPS ( n n2)
   + DUP SNAKE-EYES BOXCARS ;
```

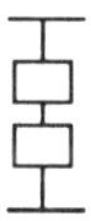

```
: CRAPS ( n n2)
   + ( total) DUP SNAKE-EYES
   BOXCARS ;
```

These words illustrate the importance of modularity: **CRAPS** is made from the two modules **SNAKE-EYES** and **BOXCARS**, each of which has simple, yet clearly defined actions. You could have redefined **SNAKE-EYES** to include the **DUP**, thereby making the definition of **CRAPS** shorter, but this would have limited the usefulness of **SNAKE-EYES** in other situations where a copy of the total was not necessary. Remember, words should do as little as possible.

Other Truths

Conditional structures (such as **IF—THEN** and **IF—ELSE—THEN**) will react to any non-zero value as if it were a *true* (-1) flag:

```
25 TRUTH TRUE
-3 TRUTH TRUE
```

This is especially useful in programming situations where if there is a non-zero quantity you want to do something; otherwise you want to do nothing. This feature also lets us use subtraction to test equality—only equal numbers subtract to be zero.

Look again at the word **INTO** which you defined in chapter 3. It took an assortment of change, converted it into pennies, and redistributed them into the highest coin denominations. But in a real program situation, there might not be any change to redistribute. How would you tell FORTH to execute **INTO** only if it found change left over on the stack? You can write a new word, **?INTO**, to check for this.

```
: ?INTO ( n)
   DUP IF INTO ELSE DROP THEN ;
```

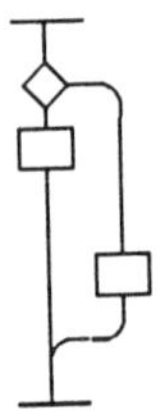

```
: ?INTO ( n)
   DUP IF
      INTO (  )
   ELSE
      DROP (  )
   THEN ;
```

Note that you had to **DUP** the number on the stack before checking it; if you didn't, **IF** would have removed the number, and there wouldn't have been a copy left for **INTO** to work with. If the number representing the amount of change was 0, however, there would still be a copy of it left after **ELSE** was executed, so a **DROP** is necessary to leave the stack clean.

This situation comes up so often in FORTH that a special word, **?DUP** ("question-dup"), has been written to factor out the inevitable **DROP**. It **DUP**s the top number on the stack only if it's true. Just for fun, one possible definition of **?DUP** is:

```
: ?DUP   DUP IF DUP THEN ;
```

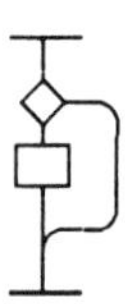

```
: ?DUP ( n - n n, or 0)
   DUP IF
      DUP ( n n)
   THEN (n n, or 0) ;
```

In FORTH, words which expect a flag on the stack are given a name which begins with a question-mark, such as **?INTO** *and* **?DUP**. *Words which print results have names which include a* **.** *(dot) like* **.S** *and* **."**. *There are other naming conventions in FORTH, but these two are used the most often.*

Here is an improved version of **?INTO** using **?DUP**:

```
: ?INTO ( n)
   ?DUP IF INTO THEN ;
```

```
: ?INTO ( n)
   ?DUP IF
      INTO (  )
   THEN ;
```

Look again at **CRAPS**. On the first throw, you would roll the dice and check for a total of 2 or 12. If the total is 2, there's no need to check to see if it's also 12. Since the categories are mutually exclusive, it makes no sense to check for both. This is even more important when you have more things to check for; for example, in some versions of craps, a sum of 3 on the first throw also loses.

What you need in a case like this is a system of *nested* conditional structures. To make the system even more efficient, try to factor out the repetitive elements of the structure before you try nesting. In this case, we can isolate the losing message in a word called **SORRY!**.

```
: SORRY!   ." CRAPS! YOU LOSE! " ;
```

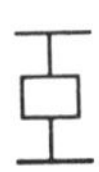

```
: SORRY! ( n - n)
   ." CRAPS! YOU LOSE! " ;
```

Notice how **SORRY!** fits into the following structure:

```
: CRAPS2 ( n n2)
   + DUP 2 =
   IF DROP SORRY!
   ELSE DUP 3 =
     IF DROP SORRY!
     ELSE 12 =
       IF SORRY! THEN
     THEN
   THEN ;
```

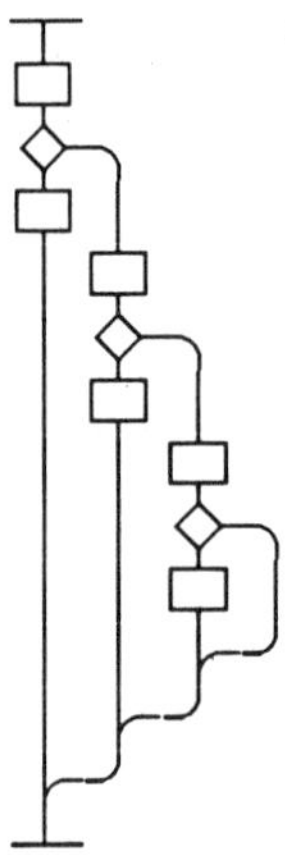

```
: CRAPS2 ( n n2)
   + ( total) DUP 2 =
         IF    DROP (  )
                SORRY!
         ELSE    DUP 3 =
            IF    DROP (  )
                   SORRY!
            ELSE    12 =
               IF (  )
                      SORRY!
               THEN
            THEN
         THEN ;
```

Note the indentations in the program. As in an outline, the conditional structures are contained within each other, like boxes within boxes. Such indentation can become very complicated. In a real game of craps, for example, you have to check for 2 or 12 or 3 (the losing combinations) and 7 and 11 (the winning combinations)— five mutually exclusive possibilities. Notice in the following example how the rearrangement of words makes the program easier to read.

To complete the craps program for the first throw you will need a winning message.

```
: WIN!   ." YOU WIN!" ;
```

You'll also need a variable to hold the total "point" in case the game continues:

```
   VARIABLE POINT
```

Here is the completed program:

```
: FIRST-THROW ( n n2)
   +  ( only the total counts )
   DUP  2 = IF DROP SORRY! ELSE
   DUP 12 = IF DROP SORRY! ELSE
   DUP  3 = IF DROP SORRY! ELSE
   DUP  7 = IF DROP WIN!   ELSE
   DUP 11 = IF DROP WIN!   ELSE
   POINT !     (otherwise)
   THEN THEN THEN THEN THEN ;
```

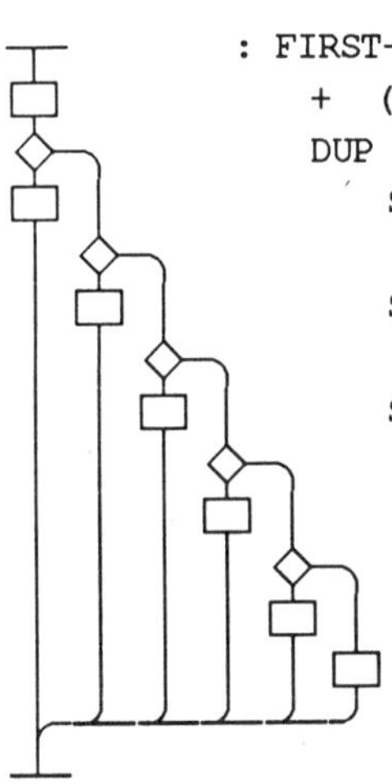

```
: FIRST-THROW ( n n2)
   +  ( Only the total counts.)
   DUP  2 = IF   DROP (  )
      SORRY!
         ELSE   DUP 12 = IF   DROP (  )
      SORRY!
         ELSE   DUP  3 = IF   DROP (  )
      SORRY!
         ELSE   DUP  7 = IF   DROP (  )
           WIN!
         ELSE   DUP 11 = IF   DROP (  )
           WIN!
         ELSE   POINT ! (  ) ( Otherwise)
         THEN THEN THEN THEN THEN ;
```

Try out this *multiple-choice* control structure:

```
2 1 FIRST-THROW CRAPS! YOU LOSE!
6 1 FIRST-THROW YOU WIN!
3 2 FIRST-THROW
POINT ? 5
```

Word	Stack	Action
IF	f	Used in a definition in the form **IF-ELSE-THEN** or simply **IF-THEN**. If flag is true, ...
ELSE		... the words following **IF** are executed (but the words following **ELSE** are skipped); ...
THEN		... if false, the words following **ELSE** are executed (if the **ELSE** part exists).
?DUP	n - 0 or n n	Duplicate n if it is non-zero.

Exercises

1. Now that you have learned the comparison, logical, and flow of control operators, define **MAX** and **MIN**.
2. Given **0<** and **0=**, define **0>**.
3. Define the new logical operator, **NAND**, in terms of the current logical operators **AND**, **OR**, and **NOT**. **NAND** returns false if both of its operands are true; otherwise it returns true.

```
0  0 NAND . -1
-1 0 NAND . -1
0 -1 NAND . -1
-1 -1 NAND . 0
```

4. For advanced students—given **NAND**, define the other logical operators **AND**, **OR**, and **NOT**.
5. Complete the definition of **DAYS** described in this chapter. To test days, store month and year values into the variables **MONTH** and **YEAR** and check your results.

```
4 ( APRIL) MONTH !  1980 YEAR !
DAYS . 30
```

Don't forget to test February on a leap year.

6. Here's a number-guessing game for you to program. The computer starts with a secret number from 1 to 100. You try to guess the number. With each guess, the computer responds "WARMER" if the new guess is closer than the old one, and "COLDER" if it is not. If you guess within 2 of the number, you're "HOT," and if you guess the number exactly, you're told how many guesses you took. The action looks something like this:

```
GAME  ( Sets the secret number.)
10 COLDER
80 WARMER
75 HOT!
73
YOU WON IN 4 GUESSES!
```

Use **RANDOM** (from the last chapter) to set the secret number. What is a reasonable response to the first guess?

8 Loops

An extension of the idea of taking an action if a condition is true, is to repeat an action until a condition is true. In flow-of-control terms, this is called an *indefinite loop*. For example, in a dice game you continue to throw dice until you win or lose.

Indefinite Loops

An interesting conjecture about positive integers is tested in the following program:

```
: WHATSIT ( n )    \ Test a conjecture.
   BEGIN  DUP 1 AND   ( is n odd?)
     IF  3 * 1+  ELSE  2/  THEN
     DUP . DUP 1 =
   UNTIL  DROP ;
```

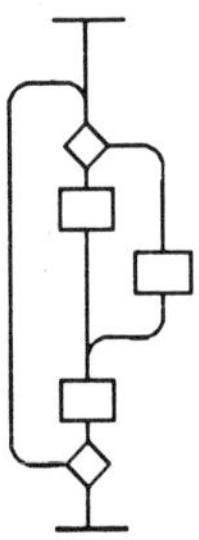

```
: WHATSIT ( n )    \ Test a conjecture.
   BEGIN
      DUP 1 AND ( Is n odd?)
      IF   3 *   1+
      ELSE   2/
      THEN
      DUP .    DUP 1 =
   UNTIL   DROP ;
```

We will be showing you all definitions from this point on with appropriate comments and indentation.

We can summarize the action of **WHATSIT** thus: " Pick a number. If the number is odd, multiply it by three and add one; if it's even, divide by two. Repeat with the result you obtain until the result equals one." The *interesting conjecture* is that, although you are multiplying by three but dividing only by two, the result will eventually equal one. Although we can demonstrate this for all the positive integers that can normally be expressed in a computer, to-date no one has proved that it will hold for all integers whatever.

Here's a breakdown of the elements in **WHATSIT**:

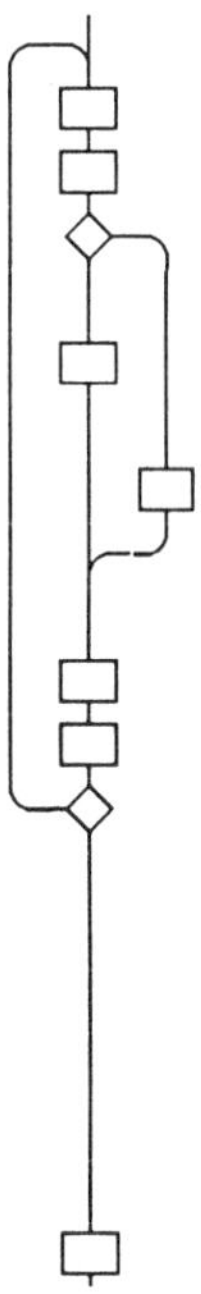

Word	Stack	Action
	n	The starting number.
BEGIN	n	Marks the beginning of an indefinite loop.
DUP	n n	Copies n.
1 AND	n f	Flag is true if n is odd.
IF	n	Executes the following code IF flag is true; otherwise, skips to **ELSE**.
3 * 1+	n2	Multiplies n by 3 and adds 1. Skips to **THEN**.
ELSE	n	Executes the following code (IF flag was false).
2/	n2	Divides n by 2.
THEN	n2	Marks the end of a conditional path. Both **IF** and **ELSE** continue here.
DUP .	n2	Copies n and then prints it.
DUP 1 =	n2 f	Creates a true flag if n2 equals 1.
UNTIL	n2	Marks the end of an indefinite loop. If the flag is false, execution will return to the most recently compiled **BEGIN**; otherwise, execution continues with the following code. In other words, execution repeats at **BEGIN** until the flag is true .
DROP		Cleans the stack by **DROP**ping the 1.

Enter **WHATSIT** from the keyboard (or **LOAD** it from a screen) and try it out.

```
40 WHATSIT 20 10 5 16 8 4 2 1
25 WHATSIT 76 38 19 58 29 88 44 22 11 34
17 52 26 13 40 20 10 5 16 8 4 2 1
```

In the **BEGIN—UNTIL** construct, the test that decides whether the program exits the loop is found at the bottom of the loop. This means that the code sequence within the loop will always be executed at least once:

```
1 WHATSIT 4 2 1
```

An alternate form of the indefinite loop puts the loop test at the beginning. Look at this definition of **CLEAR**:

```
: CLEAR ( ? )
\ empties the stack.
   BEGIN    DEPTH WHILE    DROP    REPEAT ;
```

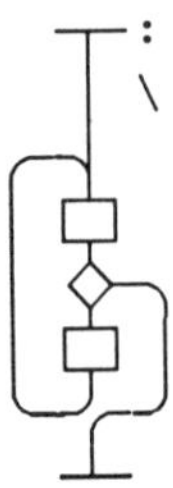

```
: CLEAR ( any — none )
\ empties the stack.
        BEGIN
           DEPTH
        WHILE
           DROP
        REPEAT ;
```

Here is **CLEAR** in more detail:

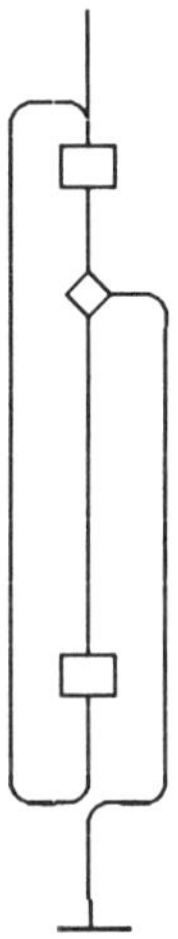

Word	Stack	Action
	?	Anything could be on the stack here.
BEGIN	?	Marks the beginning of an indefinite loop.
DEPTH	? n	Leaves the number n of items on the stack, not including n itself.
WHILE	?	Executes the following if n is true, that is, if there are items on the stack (**DEPTH** > 0). If n is false, execution skips to the word following **REPEAT**. In other words, the program exits the loop when the stack is empty.
DROP	?	**DROP**s an item from the stack. The stack might now be empty.
REPEAT		Continues execution at the most recently compiled **BEGIN**.
;		Ends the definition. **WHILE** skips to here when it exits the loop.

Ending The Game

We now have all the programming elements we need to complete the dice game *craps*. For your convenience, here is a copy of **DICE** and **FIRST-THROW** from the earlier chapter:

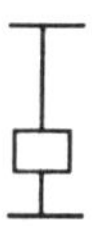

```
: DICE ( - n n2)
\ throws two die.
   6 RANDOM 1+  6 RANDOM 1+ ;

VARIABLE POINT  \ holds the "point" total.
```

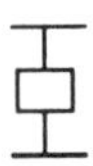

```
: SORRY!
   ." CRAPS! YOU LOSE!" ;
```

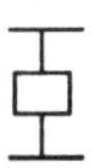

```
: WIN!
   ." YOU WIN!" ;
```

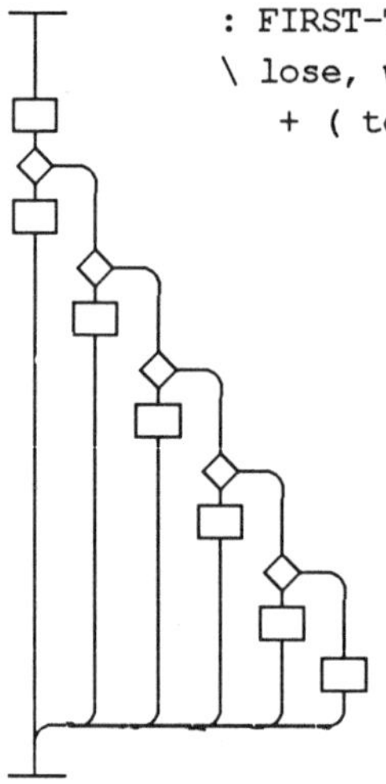

```
: FIRST-THROW ( n n2)
\ lose, win or continue.
   + ( total)\ Only the total counts.
         DUP  2 =
         IF   DROP (  ) SORRY!
                ELSE   DUP 12 =
                IF   DROP (  ) SORRY!
         ELSE   DUP  3 =
         IF   DROP (  ) SORRY!
                ELSE   DUP  7 =
                IF   DROP (  ) WIN!
          ELSE   DUP 11 =
          IF   DROP (  ) WIN!
          ELSE   POINT ! (  )\ Otherwise.
          THEN THEN THEN THEN THEN ;
```

If the game continues beyond the first throw, you must keep throwing dice until the total of a throw is equal to your point (and you win) or else equals seven (and you lose). A **BEGIN—UNTIL** construct which plays the game might look like this:

```
BEGIN
  CR  DICE 2DUP  . .  +
  DUP 7 =   IF  SORRY! TRUE ( game over)  ELSE
  POINT @ = IF    WIN! TRUE ( game over)  ELSE
  FALSE ( otherwise keep playing)
  THEN THEN
UNTIL
```

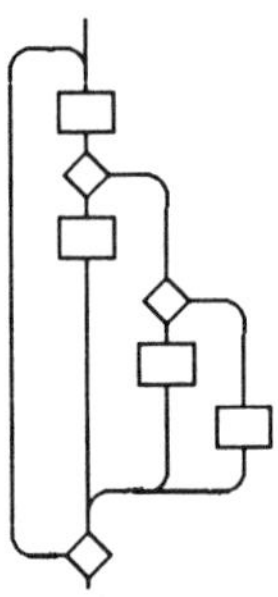

```
BEGIN
   CR   DICE ( n1 n2) 2DUP . .    + ( total)
          DUP 7 =
          IF   DROP (  ) SORRY!   TRUE ( true)\ Game over.
   ELSE   POINT @ =
   IF (  ) WIN!   TRUE ( true)\ Game over.
   ELSE   FALSE ( false)\ Otherwise keep playing.
   THEN THEN
UNTIL
```

BEGIN-UNTIL and **BEGIN-WHILE-REPEAT**, like **IF-ELSE-THEN**, are *compile-only* constructs. This means that, while you can compile them into a definition, you could never type them in directly from the keyboard.

When we give an example like the one above, we do not expect you to try it out until it appears later within a definition. **TRUE** and **FALSE** are constants. If your **FORTH** doesn't include them, their definitions are as follows:

```
 0 CONSTANT FALSE ( boolean false)
-1 CONSTANT TRUE  ( boolean true)
```

The **TRUE** and **FALSE** are necessary to inform **UNTIL** whether to continue playing or not.

The word **EXIT** lets us simplify situations like this, in which we simply want to stop playing when the game is over. **EXIT** exits a definition immediately, no matter how deeply nested it is within **BEGIN-UNTIL**, **BEGIN-WHILE-REPEAT**, or **IF-THEN-ELSE** constructs. We can use **EXIT** to improve our game.

```
BEGIN
  CR  DICE 2DUP . .  +
  DUP 7 =   IF  SORRY! DROP EXIT ( game over) THEN
  POINT @ = IF   WIN!       EXIT ( game over) THEN
  FALSE
UNTIL
```

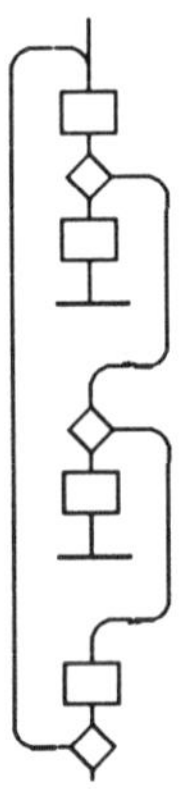

```
BEGIN
   CR   DICE 2DUP . .  +
         DUP 7 =
         IF   DROP (  ) SORRY!
            EXIT ( game over)
         THEN
         POINT @ =
         IF (  ) WIN!
            EXIT ( game over)
         THEN
         FALSE
UNTIL
```

EXIT doesn't affect the stack, so we need **DROP** to remove the total of the dice if we lose. We need **FALSE** to tell **UNTIL** to keep playing. In fact, many FORTHs use the word **AGAIN** to replace **FALSE UNTIL**. **AGAIN** can be used to emphasize that the only valid exits from our dice loop are winning or losing.

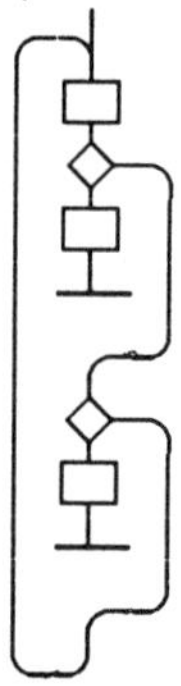

```
BEGIN
   CR  DICE ( n1 n2) 2DUP . .   + ( total)
     DUP 7 =
     IF  SORRY!   DROP
        EXIT \ Game over.
     THEN
     POINT @ =
     IF (  ) WIN!
        EXIT \ Game over.
     THEN
AGAIN
```

And now, here is the completed craps program:

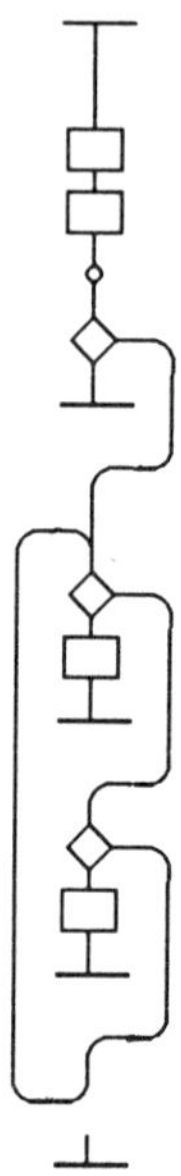

```
: CRAPS
\ the game of craps.
   0 POINT !
   CR   DICE ( n1 n2) 2DUP . .   FIRST-THROW (  )
   ( Game won or lost on first throw?)
       POINT @ 0=
       IF   EXIT   THEN

   BEGIN   CR   DICE ( n1 n2) 2DUP . .   + ( total)
              DUP 7 =
              IF   SORRY!   DROP (  )
                  EXIT ( Game over.)
              THEN ( total)
              POINT @ =
              IF (  ) WIN!
                 EXIT ( Game over.)
              THEN
   AGAIN ;
```

The word **EXIT** cannot be used to improve **FIRST-THROW** because **EXIT** exits only the word it is in. Win, lose, or otherwise, **FIRST-THROW** must return to **CRAPS** when it is done. The variable **POINT** is used to communicate between **FIRST-THROW** and **CRAPS.** **POINT** will be set to the non-zero point total only if the game is to continue.

Finite Loops

Finite loops are loops which are guaranteed to end after a certain number of repetitions. They are often used for counting or for repeating an action a given number of times. Look closely at the following example:

```
: SIX-SHOOTER
\ a simple DO—LOOP.
   6 0 DO    CR    ." BANG!"    LOOP ;
```

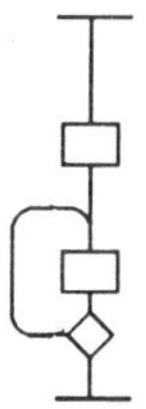

```
: SIX-SHOOTER
\ A simple DO—LOOP.
   6 0
   DO
      CR    ." BANG!"
   LOOP ;
```

```
SIX-SHOOTER
BANG!
BANG!
BANG!
BANG!
BANG!
BANG!
```

DO-LOOPS must follow these rules:

- **DO-LOOP**s are compile-only constructs, and are always used within a definition.
- Every **DO** must have a **LOOP**, just as every **IF** must have a **THEN**.
- The *upper limit* of the loop (6) appears first in the structure.
- The *lower limit* or *index* (0) appears second. This number is incremented each time the loop is repeated.
- The actions to be executed appear between **DO** and **LOOP**.

The Return Stack

Before we continue our discussion of finite loops we need to look at the internal FORTH stack called the *return stack.* FORTH uses this stack to keep track of program execution whenever one word calls another. For example, in the word **CRAPS**, before FORTH executes **FIRST-THROW**, it first pushes an address onto the return stack. This *return address* tells FORTH where in **CRAPS** to continue execution when it returns from **FIRST-THROW**. FORTH pops the return stack and returns to this address whenever it executes either a semicolon or an **EXIT**.

To avoid confusion, we will continue to call the normal FORTH stack the *parameter stack*, or the *data stack*, or simply, *the stack.* When we refer to the return stack, we will call it by its full name, the return stack.

The return stack can come in quite handy as an extra stack. Three words are provided in FORTH to let you use this stack.

Word	Stack	Action
>R	n	("to-R") removes the top item from the parameter stack and pushes it onto the return stack.
R>	n	("R-from") removes the top item from the return stack and pushes it onto the parameter stack.
R@	n	("R-fetch") copies the top item of the return stack to the parameter stack.

If you use the return stack, you must use it carefully:

- **>R**, **R>**, and **R@** should only be used within a definition.
- Items pushed on the return stack before entering a **DO–LOOP** cannot be accessed while in the loop.
- Items pushed on the return stack from within a **DO–LOOP** must be removed before terminating the loop.
- The return stack must be restored to its original state before leaving a definition with a semicolon or **EXIT**.

You can define a word which multiplies three coordinates by a scaling factor like this:

```
: 3DTIMES ( x y z n - nx ny nz)
   DUP >R * ROT
   R@ * ROT
   R> * ROT ;
```

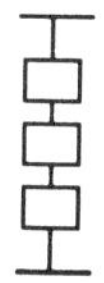

```
: 3DTIMES ( x y z n - nx ny nz)
   DUP >R   * ( x y nz) ROT ( y nz x)
   R@ * ( y nz nx) ROT ( nz nx y)
   R> * ( nz nx ny) ROT ;
```

DO-LOOPS also use the return stack to keep track of the progress of the loop. Study this definition of **SIGMA**, to see how the two stacks work together.

```
: SIGMA ( n - n2)
\ sum the integers from 0 to n-1.
   DUP 0= IF  EXIT  THEN  ( exceptional case)
   0  ( running total) SWAP 0  ( initial index)
   DO  I +  LOOP ;
```

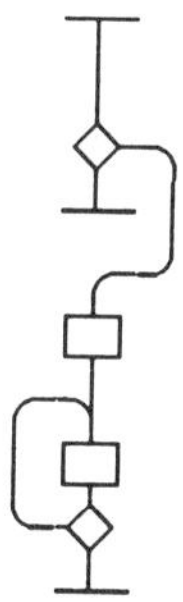

```
: SIGMA ( n - n2)
\ sum the integers from 0 to n-1.
   DUP 0=
   IF  EXIT  THEN ( Exceptional case.)

   0 SWAP ( sum n) 0 ( Initial index.)
   DO ( sum)
      I +
   LOOP ;
```

```
0 SIGMA . 0
1 SIGMA . 0  ( 0)
2 SIGMA . 1  ( 0 + 1)
5 SIGMA . 10 ( 0 + 1 + 2 + 3 + 4)
```

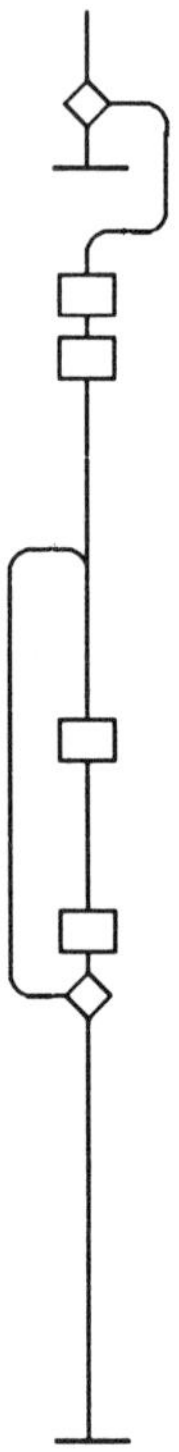

Word	Stack	Action
	n	is the upper limit plus 1.
DUP 0=	n flag	If n is zero, ...
IF EXIT THEN		... do something reasonable.
0	n sum	Initializes the running total.
SWAP 0	sum n 0	The top two items on the stack specify an initial count value (index) of 0, and an upper limit of n-1.
DO	sum	Marks the beginning of the loop. The initial value and upper limit are moved to the return stack.
I	sum **I**	The current index of the loop is copied from the return stack to the parameter stack by the word **I**.
+	sum	Adds **I** to the running total.
LOOP	sum	First, adds 1 to the current index (on the return stack). If the current index then equals the upper limit, the index and limit are removed from the return stack and execution continues with the next word; otherwise, execution returns to the most recently compiled **DO**.
;	sum	Ends the definition and returns to the address popped from the return stack, as usual.

By using the return stack, **DO-LOOP**s don't clutter up the data stack with the index and limit of the loop.

Here are two other ways in which **SIGMA** could be defined.

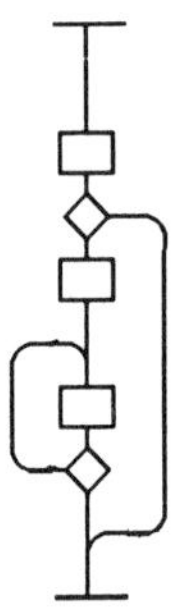

```
: SIGMA ( n — sum)
\ Sum the integers from 0 to n-1.
  DUP
        IF
           0 SWAP ( sum n) 0
           DO ( sum)
              I +
           LOOP
        THEN ;
```

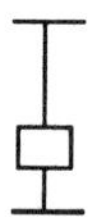

```
: SIGMA ( n — sum)
\ Sum the integers from 0 to n-1.
  DUP 1- *   2/ ;
```

The word **+LOOP** lets you increment the loop index by any integer. **+LOOP** is used like **LOOP**, except that it adds the number it finds on top of the stack to the loop index each time through the loop. For example, to count from 1 to 20 by 3, use the **DO-+LOOP** sequence in **20-BY-3**.

```
: 20-BY-3
   21 1  DO  I .  3 +LOOP ;
```

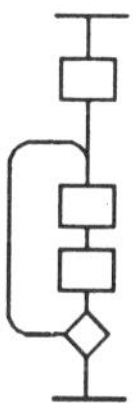

```
: 20-BY-3
   21 1
   DO
      I .
      3
   +LOOP ;
```

```
20-BY-3 1 4 7 10 13 16 19
```

+LOOP exits the loop when the index *crosses the boundary* between the limit minus 1 and the limit—that is, it stops the loop just after it increments the index from 19 to 21, which crosses the boundary between 20 (the limit 21 minus 1) and 21. In fact, the **DO-LOOP** is just a special case of the **DO-+LOOP** in which the increment is always one.

It's easiest to picture the action of **LOOP** and **+LOOP** if you think of the integer numbers arranged in a circle, with the largest possible integer connected to the smallest possible integer. When the loop prints the 19, **+LOOP** tries to move the index up 3 (to 22), but in the process it crosses the border between 20 (limit minus 1) and 21 (limit) and so does not return to the **DO**. Because **LOOP** checks only for boundary crossing, it can count and index memory addresses as easily as it counts integers.

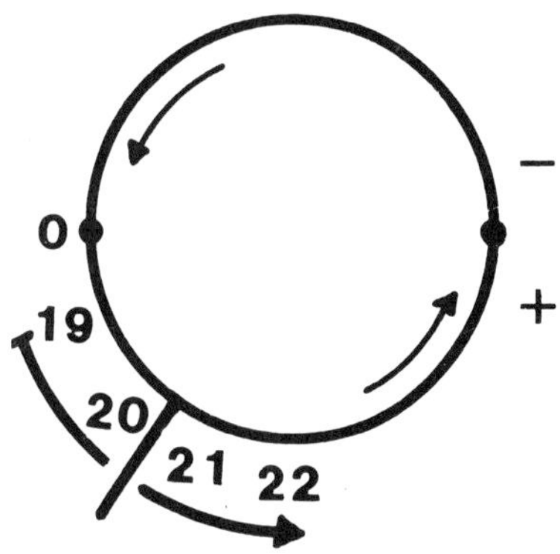

Such an image also helps explain why, when the loop parameters are set, the upper limit should always be a number greater than the index. If you set up loop parameters such as 3 and 3, for example, the loop would begin at 3 and continue around all possible integers until it stopped at 2, which is probably not what you had in mind. MacFORTH **DO** tests for this condition. If the limits are the same, the loop is skipped. PolyFORTH **DO-LOOP**s would execute only once.

Errors such as these can be tricky to spot. An incorrect definition of **CLEAR** using a **DO-LOOP** would be

```
: CLEAR ( ? )
\ empties the stack.
   DEPTH 0 DO  DROP  LOOP ;
```

This version of **CLEAR** correctly empties the stack as long as there are items to be **DROP**ped. But if the stack is empty, the loop index and limit will both be 0, and far too many items will be dropped.

One way to fix this problem would be to insert an **IF-THEN** *clause* that would check the stack for 0 items before giving the go-ahead to run the loop.

```
: CLEAR ( ? )
\ empties the stack.
   DEPTH ?DUP IF 0 DO  DROP  LOOP THEN ;
```

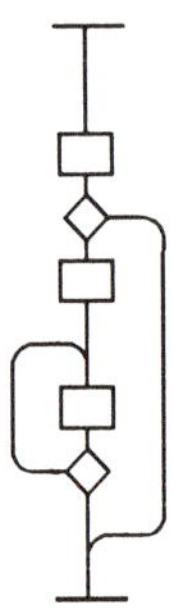

```
: CLEAR ( ? )
\ Empties the stack.
   DEPTH ?DUP
        IF
           0
           DO
              DROP
           LOOP
        THEN ;
```

A shorter and neater way to handle the problem is to use the word **?DO** ("question-do"), which will start a loop only if the upper limit is unequal to the initial index. UR/FORTH, MasterFORTH, and L & P F83 all support the **?DO–LOOP** construct. With **?DO**, **CLEAR** looks like this

```
: CLEAR ( ? )
\ empties the stack.
   DEPTH 0 ?DO  DROP  LOOP ;
```

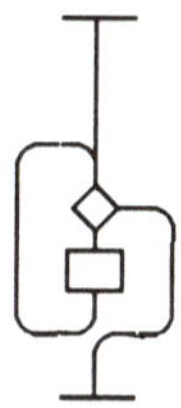

```
: CLEAR ( ? )
\ Empties the stack.
  DEPTH 0
       ?DO
          DROP
       LOOP ;
```

Nested Loops

Loops, like **IF-ELSE-THEN** constructs, can be nested to any level. You could use a nested loop to take a list and compare each item in that list with each item in a second list. To do this, you will need both an inner and an outer loop index. The word **I** always gives you the innermost loop index. while the word **J** gives you the index of the next outermost loop. The word **ODDS** uses nested loops this way to examine probabilities in dice-throwing.

```
: ODDS ( sum - n)
\ there are n ways to make the sum by throwing 2 dice.
   0  ( the initial n)
   7 1
   DO  ( outer loop)
   7 1
     DO  ( inner loop)
       DUP I J + =  ( dice total=sum?)
       IF  SWAP 1+ SWAP  THEN
     LOOP
   LOOP
   DROP CR . ." OUT OF 36 WAYS " ;
```

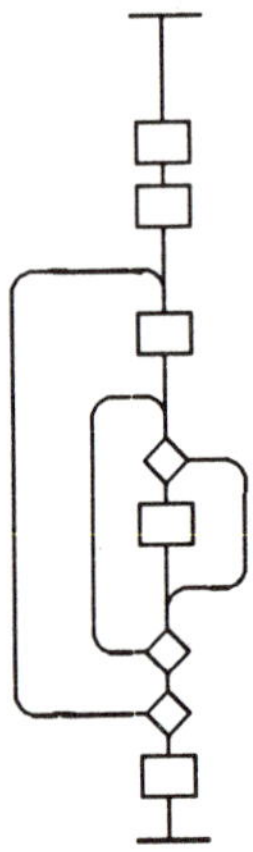

```
: ODDS ( sum - n)
\ Display how many ways to make sum by throwing 2 dice.
   0  ( sum n)
   7 1
   DO
      7 1
      DO
         OVER I J + = ( Sum = dicetotal? )
         IF   1+   THEN

      LOOP
   LOOP
   SWAP DROP ( n) CR   . (  ) ." OUT OF 36 WAYS " ;
```

```
4 ODDS
3 OUT OF 36 WAYS

2 ODDS
1 OUT OF 36 WAYS
```

If you are nesting more than two loops, you will need to use variables or the data stack itself to hold a copy of the additional loop indices.

Leaving Loops

DO-LOOP uses the return stack to hold the index and limit of a loop. This places two important restrictions on what can be done from inside a **DO-LOOP**:

- Any item pushed onto the return stack before entering the loop cannot be reached from inside the loop. The following sequence is meaningless:

  ```
  >R  DO  R@ . LOOP  R>
  ```

- Any item pushed onto the return stack after entering the loop prevents the loop index from being reached. The following sequence is also meaningless:

  ```
  DO  0 >R I . R> DROP  LOOP
  ```

- The word **EXIT** cannot be used from inside a **DO-LOOP**. The return address cannot be reached.

You can, however, terminate execution of a **DO-LOOP** at any time with the word **LEAVE**. Before leaving a **DO-LOOP**, you *must* remove any items you have pushed onto the return stack from within the loop. **LEAVE** leaves the loop immediately, but does not exit the definition itself. You can use it to search an array for a match with a given key as follows:

```
CREATE KEEPERS  100 ALLOT  ( 50 cells)

: MATCH ( key - index true or  0)
\ find key in KEEPERS.
\ Returns index and true if key is found;
\ otherwise returns only false.
   FALSE ( assume no match) 50 0
   DO  DROP  DUP KEEPERS I + @ =  ( match?)
     IF  I SWAP TRUE LEAVE
     THEN FALSE  2 ( two bytes per cell)
  +LOOP
   SWAP DROP  ( drops key) ;
```

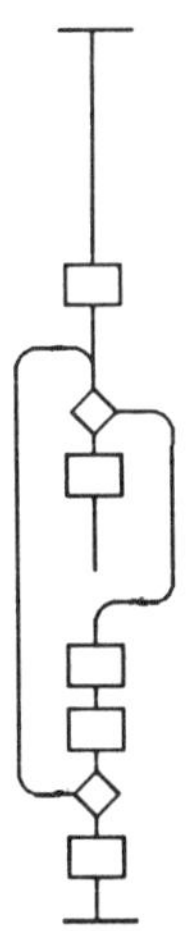

```
CREATE KEEPERS   50 CELLS ALLOT
: MATCH ( key — index true, or false)
\ Find key in KEEPERS.
\ Returns index and true if key is found;
\ otherwise returns only false.
   FALSE ( key false) 50 CELLS 0
   DO
      DROP ( key) DUP KEEPERS I + @ =  ( match?)
      IF   I SWAP ( index key) TRUE ( index key true)
         LEAVE
      THEN ( key)
      FALSE ( key false)
      CELL ( key false cellsize)
   +LOOP ( index key true, or key false)
   SWAP DROP  ( index true, or false) ;
```

If the key is found, execution leaves the loop but remains in **MATCH** to drop the key. In the case of nested loops, **LEAVE** leaves only the loop which contains it.

UNDO

A string search is a classical programming problem. When you search for characters in a string, you generally use a **DO—LOOP**. You leave the loop in one of two circumstances:

1. The search is successful. You leave the loop immediately.
2. The search fails. You leave the loop because it is exhausted.

The problem is that once you have left the loop, how do you know if the search was successful?

One solution is to maintain a flag on the stack.

```
: SEARCH
   ... 0 ( flag) ROT ROT
   DO  DROP ( compare strings here) =
     IF  TRUE LEAVE  THEN  0 ( flag)
   LOOP ;
```

If the search is successful, the flag will be true.

A better solution is to leave the loop *and the word that contains it* as soon as the search is successful.

```
: SEARCH
   DO  ( compare strings here) =
     IF  TRUE  UNDO EXIT  THEN
   LOOP  FALSE ;
```

The command **UNDO** undoes the loop by discarding the index, limit, and any other loop items on the return stack before leaving the word with **EXIT**. Only ZEN includes **UNDO** in its word set. PolyFORTH would define **UNDO** this way:

```
: UNDO   R>  2R> 2DROP  >R ;
```

MacFORTH, UR/FORTH, and L&P F83 would define this way:

```
: UNDO   R>  R> R> R> 2DROP DROP  >R ;
```

UNDO has the additional charm that it can leave a word from a nested loop, as in **UNDO UNDO EXIT**.

Word	Stack	Action
BEGIN		Used in a definition in the form **BEGIN-UNTIL** or
WHILE	flag	**BEGIN-WHILE-REPEAT**. Marks the start of a word sequence for repetition. A **BEGIN–UNTIL** loop executes until flag is true;
REPEAT		a **BEGIN–WHILE–REPEAT** loop executes until the flag is false. When the loop finishes, execution continues with the word following the
UNTIL	flag	**UNTIL** or **REPEAT**.
EXIT		Exits a definition immediately. Can't be used inside a DO-LOOP.
AGAIN		Used with **BEGIN** in the form **BEGIN-AGAIN** to mark a word sequence for indefinite execution.
DO	limit n	Used in the form **DO-LOOP** or **DO-+LOOP** Marks a word sequence for repetition until the loop index, (initially n) crosses the boundary between the loop limit and the limit-1.
LOOP		**LOOP** increments the index by 1 with each repetition.
+LOOP	n	adds the increment on top of the stack to the index with each repetition. When the loop finishes, execution continues with the first word following **LOOP** or **+LOOP**.
I	- i	Copies the loop index of the innermost loop to the stack.
J	- j	Copies the loop index of the next outermost loop to the stack.
?DO	limit n	Used in the form **?DO-LOOP** or **?DO-+LOOP**. **?DO**, unlike **DO**, skips the loop if the initial index n equals the limit.
LEAVE		Leaves the innermost **DO-LOOP** or **DO-+LOOP** immediately, but does not leave the definition.
UNDO		Discard all loop parameters on the return stack in preparation for leaving a word with **EXIT**.

Exercises

1. The ACME Pack-Me company packs products into boxes. If a box of the proper size is not available, the next largest size will do. Boxes range in size from 0 to 9, and the following quantities are on hand (in the initialized array **BOXES**):

```
CREATE BOXES
3 , 2 , 0 , 4 , 0 , 1 , 4 , 2 , 2 , 3 ,
```

   In other words, there are currently 3 boxes of size 0, 2 of size 1, etc. Define a word **BOX?** which, when a box size is requested, returns the actual size to use and decrements **BOXES** accordingly.

```
5 BOX? 5 ( use size 5)
5 BOX? 6 ( no more size 5 so use size 6)
```

   If there are no suitable boxes at all, say so.

2. Write the word **STARS** which prints a given number of asterisks on a line.

```
6 STARS ******
3 STARS ***
```

3. Define the utility word **BOUNDS** which, given a starting address and length in bytes, converts them to a form suitable for examining a range of addresses with a **DO-LOOP**.

```
8050 ( address) 10 ( count) BOUNDS .S
8060 8050 <-Top
```

4. Write the word **HISTOGRAM** to display the elements of an array in histogram form. Histogram expects the starting address and number of cells in the array to be on the stack. For each cell, it prints a line of stars, the number of stars equal to the number in the cell. If you apply **HISTOGRAM** to the **BOXES** array from the first exercise, you would see

```
BOXES 10 HISTOGRAM
***
**

****

*
****
**
**
***
```

Limit the number of stars to a reasonable value.

9 More on Numbers

So far we have been working with integer or *single-precision* arithmetic. Most programming requires only integer arithmetic, even if you might think that the problem would require larger or more accurate numbers.

Numbers like 121.08 and 894 5/8 are called rational numbers; they aren't integers but can be expressed as the ratio of two integers. 121.08 is the same as 12108/100, and 894 5/8 is the same as ([8 * 894] + 5)/8 or 7157/8. In FORTH we can represent this second number in two ways:

```
894 5 8 / +
```

or

```
894 8 * 5 + 8 /
```

Either of these computations gives you 894, because the `/` function drops the fractional part of the quotient. Now try multiplying 894 5/8 by 2, using these two different computations (the exact answer is 1789.25).

```
894 8 * 5 + 8 / 2* . 1788
894 8 * 5 + 2* 8 / . 1789
```

What happened? In the first example, `/` dropped the fraction before the calculation was complete, and the answer came out too low.

It's usually more accurate to divide after multiplying.

Another sort of calculation you may want to do is percentages. What is 37% of 182? To solve this on paper you would multiply 182 by 37 and divide by 100 to get 67.34. Let's write a FORTH word to do percentages.

```
: % ( n n2 - n3) * 100 / ;
182 37 % . 67
```

So far, so good. Now try 37% of 1820 (it should be 673.4).

```
1820 37 % . 18*
```

What happened? The word `%` multiplied 37 by 1820, giving 67340. But this is larger than the largest positive single number, 32767, so a meaningless product was left on the stack.

Double Numbers

What we need is a 32-bit number, or *double* number, to hold the intermediate product until the calculation is complete. Double numbers range from –2,147,483,648 to +2,147,483,647. This range is large enough to hold any possible product of two single numbers.

The FORTH-83 Standard double-number extension provides a rich set of double-number operations. We have already seen the stack manipulators **2DUP**, **2DROP**, **2SWAP**, **2OVER**, and **2ROT**.† We have also seen the memory operators **2!**, **2@**, **2CONSTANT**, and **2VARIABLE**. There are double-number equivalents to many of the other operators we have studied. MacForth 32-bit precision is sufficient for most calculations. For this reason, MacForth does not include any double-number math operators.

---

* **MacForth** 32-bit single-precision integers will correctly calculate 673 as the answer.

† **MacForth** does not include **2ROT**.

Word	Stack	Action
D+	d d2 - d3	d3 equals d plus d2.
D-	d d2 - d3	d3 equals d minus d1.
DMAX	d d2 - d3	d3 is the greater of d and d2.
DMIN	d d2 - d3	d3 is the lesser of d and d2.
DABS	d - d2	d2 is the absolute value of d.
DNEGATE	d1 — d2	changes the sign of d.
D2/	d - d2	Divides d by 2.
D.	d	Prints d.
D<	d d2 - flag	Returns true if d is less than d2.
D=	d d2 - flag	Returns true if d equals d2.
D0=	d - flag	Returns true if d is 0.
Many FORTHs also provide:		
D2*	d1 — d2	Multiplies d by 2.

Given these operators, many others can be defined, for example:

```
: D> ( d d2 - f)   2SWAP D< ;
```

When a double number is pushed on the stack, the most-significant *high-order* cell is pushed on top of the least-significant *low-order* cell. A single number can therefore be extended to a double number by pushing a zero on top of it if it is positive, or a minus one if it is negative. The word **S>D** ("S-to-D") does exactly that. **S>D** assumes that true is represented by -1. Some older FORTHs use 1 instead. If so, the definition of **S>D** changes to

```
: S>D   DUP 0< NEGATE ;
```

You may wish to add the appropriate **S>D** to your prelude.

```
: S>D ( n - d)   DUP 0< ;
```

This is the only way that double numbers can be created under the FORTH-83 Standard. However, in many FORTHs, ending a number with a decimal point automatically converts it to a double number.

```
1 S>D . . 0 1
1 S>D D. 1
1. D. 1
700000. D. 700000
```

When a double number is stored in memory, the high-order cell is stored at the low-order address.

```
2VARIABLE TWOSOME
3 S>D TWOSOME 2!
TWOSOME 2@ D. 3
TWOSOME @ . 0
TWOSOME 2+ @ . 3
```

The word `*/` ("star-slash") combines the multiplication and division we need for fractions or decimals but uses a double-number intermediate product to ensure accurate results.* The divisor must be on top of the stack and the multiplier just underneath. Compare these two calculations:

```
15000 10 * 5 / . 3785 ( wrong   )
15000 10 5  */ . 30000 ( correct )
```

Let's rewrite `%` using `*/`.

```
: PERCENT ( n n2 - n3)   100 */ ;
1820 37 PERCENT . 673
```

We can also use `*/` to calculate the the area of a circle, given its radius. Integer numbers can't represent π as 3.14159... but we can substitute 31416 / 10000. The formula for the area would then be

```
: AREA ( n - n2)
   DUP *  31416 10000 */ ;
```

* **MacForth** uses a 64-bit intermediate product.

Surprisingly, it is possible to get even better precision by using 355/113 for π instead of 31416/10000. Many mathematical constants can be expressed as the ratio of two single numbers.

Constant	Value	Substitution
π	3.141592	355/133
√2	1.414213...	19601/13860
√3	1.732050...	18817/10864
e	2.718281...	28667/10546
√10	3.162277...	22936/7253

Rounding

At times, we need to know how large the remainder of a division is. For example, this remainder might represent pennies left over from a compound interest calculation. Or we might need to examine the size of the remainder to determine whether we should adjust or *round* the quotient before we discard or *truncate* the remainder.

The word ***/MOD** ("star-slash-mod"), like **/MOD**, leaves the remainder on the stack, just underneath the quotient. Unlike ***/**, it uses a double-number intermediate product. We can then use the remainder to round a result to the nearest single number.

```
: ROUND%   100 */MOD SWAP 50 + 100 / + ;
```

Look at how this works with a real problem, say 15% of 3518.

Stack	Action
3518 15	Pushes arguments on the stack.
100 `*/MOD`	Multiplies 3518 by 15, giving an intermediate double number. Divides this product by 100, leaving a quotient (527) and a remainder (70) with the quotient on top. The remainder will be between 0 and 99.
`SWAP`	Swaps the quotient and the remainder so you can test the remainder for size.
50 `+`	Adds 50 to the remainder, leaving a sum between 50 and 149.
100 `/`	Divides the modified remainder by 100, leaving a quotient of either 0 or 1 on the stack.
`+`	Adds the new quotient to the old quotient. If the new quotient is 0 (that is, if the original remainder was less than 50) the old quotient remains unchanged; if the new quotient is 1 (that is, the original remainder was equal to or greater than 50) the old quotient is rounded up.

Check and see what your answer is.

```
3518 15 ROUND% 528
```

Sometimes you must round up. Say you are planning a school for 2450 students. You know that 7% of Americans are left-handed, and you want to plan for an adequate number of left-handed desks.

```
: ROUNDUP% ( n n2 - n3)
  100 */MOD SWAP 99 + 100 / + ;
2452 7 ROUND%   . 35
2452 7 ROUNDUP% . 36
```

Adding 99 to the remainder instead of 50 ensures that if there is any remainder at all, the program will round up the number.

Unsigned Numbers

Signed integers are 16-bit numbers ranging from -32768 to 32767. The left-most bit, called the *sign bit*, indicates whether the number is positive or negative. This bit can be used instead as an ordinary number bit. The 16-bit unsigned number that results can represent the full range of 16-bit values from 0 to 65535. 32-bit unsigned numbers range from 0 to 4294967295.

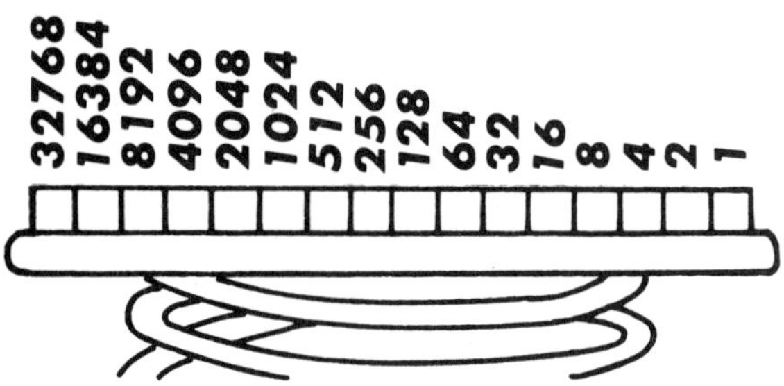

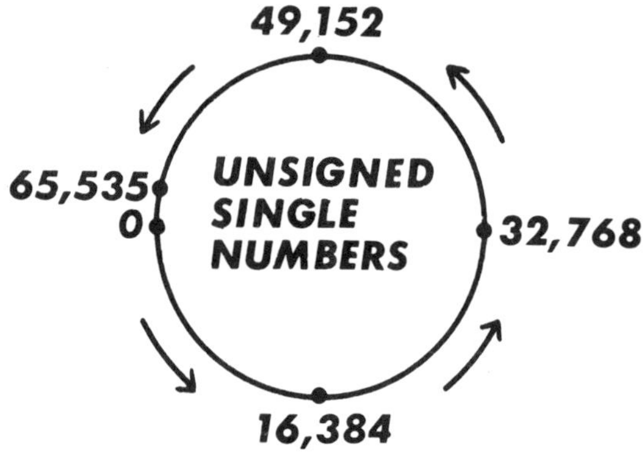

Whether or not a number is signed 16-bit or unsigned 16-bit is merely a question of how you look at it. To print a number as if it were unsigned, use `U.` ("U-dot") instead of `.`.*

```
20000 20000 + . -25536
20000 20000 + U. 40000

-1 U. 65535
```

To create an unsigned number, just type it in.

```
40000 U. 40000
```

Memory addresses are considered to be unsigned numbers. That's why the *memory space* of most small computers is 65535 bytes or *64K* (one *K* is 1024 bytes—the tenth power of 2). Fortunately, the operators `+` and `-` work for both signed and unsigned numbers, so you can correctly add an offset to an

* **MacForth** does not support unsigned number operators.

address with **+** . Many other single-number operators work correctly with unsigned numbers, such as **=** and **0=**. Unfortunately, you can't compare two addresses with **<**.

```
30000 40000 < . 0
```

That's because **<** interprets 40000 as the signed integer -25536. Use **U<** ("U-less-than") instead.

```
30000 40000 U< . -1
```

The unsigned operators required by the FORTH-83 Standard are:

Word	Stack	Action
U.	u	Prints an unsigned number.
U<	u u2 - f	Returns true if u1 is less than u2.
DU<	ud ud2 - f	Returns true if ud is less then ud2. This is the double-number equivalent to **U<**.
UM*	u u2 - ud	Multiplies u by u2 to give the unsigned double-number product ud. All values are unsigned.
UM/MOD	ud u - u2 u3	Divides the double-number ud by u to give the quotient u3 and the remainder u2. All values are unsigned.

The mixed-number operators **UM*** ("U-M-star") and **UM/MOD** ("U-M-slash-mod") are the FORTH primitives for multiplication and division. They are usually faster than the equivalent signed operations when all values are known to be unsigned.

```
: TENTH ( n - n2 n3)
\ divides n by 10. Leaves rem and quotient.
   0  ( makes n an unsigned double number)
   10 ( 10 is unsigned, too)
   UM/MOD ;

123 TENTH . . 12 3
```

Changing Bases

Decimal numbers are also called *base 10* numbers because they are based on the number 10. Computers usually translate decimal numbers to sequences of zeroes and ones, which are called *binary* or base 2 numbers. Sometimes you need to know exactly which pattern of bits a computer is using to represent a certain quantity. Rather than deal with long and often confusing binary numbers, you can group the bits four at a time into a single digit of the *hexadecimal* or base 16 system (*hex* for short). Here are the 16 possible combinations of four bits:

Binary	Decimal	Hex	Binary	Decimal	Hex
0000	0	0	1000	8	8
0001	1	1	1001	9	9
0010	2	2	1010	10	A
0011	3	3	1011	11	B
0100	4	4	1100	12	C
0101	5	5	1101	13	D
0110	6	6	1110	14	E
0111	7	7	1111	15	F

Any 16-bit memory address can be represented by four hex digits. How many of these hex values do you recognize?

Hex	Decimal	Interpretation
0000	0	The number *zero.*
00FF	255	The highest possible 8-bit value.
7FFF	32767	The largest positive signed 16-bit number.
8000	-32768	The largest negative signed 16-bit number.
FFFF	-1	The number *minus one.*
FFFF	65535	The largest unsigned 16-bit number; also the highest possible 16-bit memory address.

FORTH uses a special variable called **BASE** to decide which numeric base to use for interpreting and displaying numbers. Normally, numbers are treated as decimal numbers. You can make sure this is true by using the word **DECIMAL**. Here is a probable definition for **DECIMAL** (assuming you are somehow working in decimal in the first place):

```
: DECIMAL   10 BASE ! ;
```

Some of these alternate base commands are probably also included in your dictionary:

```
: BINARY   2 BASE ! ;
: OCTAL    8 BASE ! ;
: HEX     16 BASE ! ;
```

Numeric conversion is easy in FORTH.

```
DECIMAL 35  CR DUP BINARY . HEX .
100011 23
```

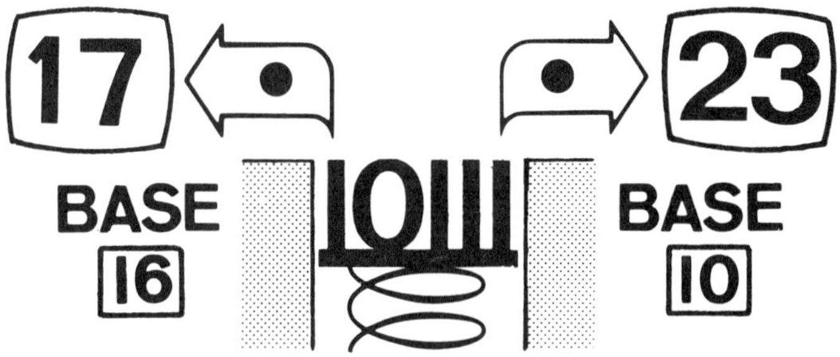

If you enter a number in hex, you should precede it with an extra 0 digit so that it doesn't accidentally look like something it shouldn't—better **0DEAD** than **DEAD**.

Here are two useful words which use **BASE**. Both words fetch and restore **BASE** so that they can display numbers in a given numeric base without disturbing the current **BASE**. The first word prints the current numeric base in decimal:

```
: BASE?   BASE @  DUP DECIMAL .  BASE ! ;

HEX      BASE?  16
DECIMAL BASE?  10
```

The second word displays a range of bytes starting at a given memory address.

```
: DUMP ( a n )
   BASE @ >R HEX              ( save BASE )
    CR ." ADDR: " OVER U.     ( starting address )
    CR OVER + SWAP            ( print each byte )
    DO I C@ U. LOOP
    R> BASE ! ;               ( restore BASE )
```

If you were to **DUMP** the beginning of the **POSTAGE-TABLE** we created in an earlier chapter, you would see something like this:

```
POSTAGE-TABLE 8 DUMP*

Addr: 2B40
0 28 28 28 3C 50 64 78
```

Word	Stack	Action
***/MOD**	n n2 n3 - n4 n5	Multiplies n by n2, then divides by n3 leaving remainder n4 and quotient n5. Uses a double-number intermediate.
***/**	n n2 n3 - n4	Like ***/MOD**, but leaves the quotient only.
BASE	- a	Variable containing the value of the current numeric base for all input and output conversion.
DECIMAL		Changes the current numeric base to decimal.

Exercises

1. Write the word **GROWTH?** which determines how long it takes a number (use 1000) to double for a given percent of growth. **GROWTH?** will act like this:

* **MacForth DUMP** expects starting and ending address as arguments.
To see **POSTAGE-TABLE**, use **POSTAGE-TABLE DUP 8 + DUMP**.

```
15 GROWTH? 5
```

1000 grows as 1150, 1322, 1520, 1748, and 2010.

2. The volume of a cone is given by the formula

   ```
   V = (π * r² * h) / 3
   ```

   where **V** is the volume, **r** is the radius, and **h** is the height. The volume of a sphere is given by

   ```
   V = (4 * π * r³) / 3.
   ```

   Define the words

   ```
   CONE ( r h - V) and
   SPHERE ( r - V).
   ```

3. Define **D>S** which truncates a double number to a single number. The definition is surprisingly short.

4. Create the operator **D~** which compares two double numbers for approximate equality. The amount by which the two numbers can differ and still be considered equal is stored in the variable **FUDGE**.

   ```
   2 FUDGE !
   3 S>D 4 S>D  D~ . -1
   3 S>D 5 S>D  D~ . -1
   3 S>D 7 S>D  D~ . 0
   ```

5. Write a smart **.S** which examines the current **BASE** and prints signed numbers if the base is decimal; otherwise it prints unsigned numbers.

   ```
   DECIMAL
   1 2 -3 .S
   STACK: 1 2 -3

   HEX .S
   1 2 FFFD
   ```

6. Define four operators **C+ C- C*** and **C/** to add, subtract, multiply, and divide complex numbers. A complex number is represented as a pair of numbers, real and imaginary magnitudes, with the imaginary magnitude on top. Complex mathematics follows the formulas

$$(a + bi) + (c + di) = (a + c) + (b + d)i$$
$$(a + bi) - (c + di) = (a - c) + (b - d)i$$
$$(a + bi) * (c + di) = ((a * c) - (b * d)) + ((a * d) - (b * c))i$$
$$(a + bi) / (c + di) = \frac{(a * c) + (b * d)}{c^2 + d^2} + \frac{((b * c) - (a * d))i}{c^2 + d^2}$$

7. Temperature conversion between Centigrade and Fahrenheit follows these rules:

$$°C = \frac{°F - 32}{1.8} \qquad °F = (°C * 1.8) + 32$$

Write the words **C>F** and **F>C** to convert from Centigrade to Fahrenheit and back again. Your words should be as accurate as possible. *Hint*: scale intermediate numbers by 10.

8. You decide to carpet your house. Since carpeting is sold by the square foot, you measure each (rectangular) room to find its dimensions in feet and inches. Define a word which converts these measurements to square feet.

```
15 FEET BY 18 FEET 4 INCHES ROOM?
275 SQUARE FEET
```

There are 144 square inches in a square foot. *Hint:* Let **FEET** and **INCHES** accumulate a total of inches. **ROOM?** expects to find two such totals on the stack.

10 Strings

Messages

We have already seen how . interprets the top stack item to be a signed integer, while U. interprets the same pattern to be an unsigned integer. The word EMIT interprets the top stack item as a printable character and prints it on the display.

```
65 . 65
65 EMIT A
```

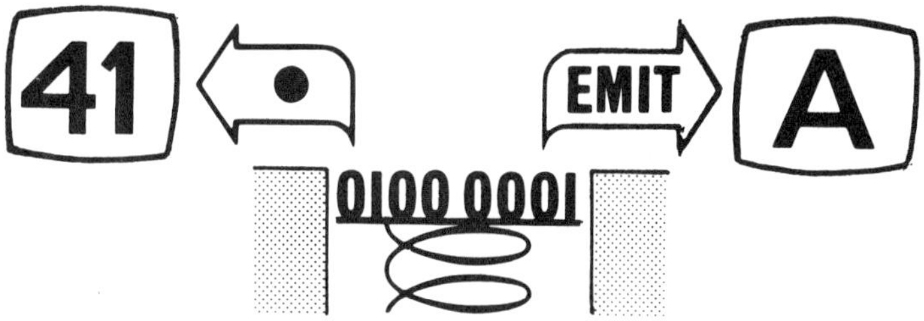

FORTH uses the 7-bit ASCII (*American Standard Code for Information Interchange*) patterns to represent printable characters. Any higher-order bits are usually 0, but may have a system-dependent meaning, like *blink this character*.

ASCII Character set (7-bit codes)

MSD / LSD	0	1	2	3	4	5	6	7
0	Null		SP	0	@	P	‘	p
1			!	1	A	Q	a	q
2			“	2	B	R	b	r
3			#	3	C	S	c	s
4			$	4	D	T	d	t
5			%	5	E	U	e	u
6			&	6	F	V	f	v
7	Bell		‘	7	G	W	g	w
8	Backspace		(	8	H	X	h	x
9	Tab		)	9	I	Y	i	y
A	Linefeed		*	:	J	Z	j	z
B		Escape	+	;	K	[	k	{
C	Formfeed		,	<	L	\	l	|
D	Return		-	=	M	]	m	}
E			.	>	N	^	n	~
F			/	?	O	_	o	Rubout

To use this chart, locate the character you want to display. The column gives you the most-significant hex digit (MSD), and the row gives you the least-significant digit (LSD) of the ASCII code. For example, the code for *small-z* is 7A (column 7, row A). The first printable character is the blank space (SP at hex 20).

The ASCII codes in the first two columns are for non-printing control-characters. They are named after the corresponding printable character found by adding hex 40 to the control character. For example, 07 is called control-G. The control characters also have special names, some of which appear in the chart above. Hex 0A (control-J) is called *Linefeed*, for example, because it is often used to reposition a cursor (or printer) to the left side of the current line.

You can display all the printable characters on your terminal with the word **CHARACTERS**.

```
: CHARACTERS   128 32 DO I EMIT LOOP ;
```

Many FORTHs support the command **ASCII,** which converts the character following it to an ASCII code and leaves it on the stack.

```
ASCII A . 65
```

ASCII also works within a definition.*

```
: DASHED-LINE   14 0 DO ASCII - EMIT LOOP ;
```

```
CR DASHED-LINE
--------------
```

Note that the last definition is equivalent to this one:

```
: DASHED-LINE2   ." -------" ;
```

The **."** word is *compile-only*, which means it can only be used within a definition. The equivalent word for use outside a definition is **.(** ("dot-paren"). MacForth uses **."** both inside and outside of definitions

```
CR .( ECHO ME!)
ECHO ME!
```

The word **.(** is useful for printing a message while **LOAD**ing a screen. Notice that it requires a matching **)** as the trailing delimiter.

Keyboard Input

One of the input primitives of FORTH is **KEY**, which waits for a key to be pressed, then leaves the ASCII code for that key on the stack. Type in the following line, then press <RETURN>:

```
KEY .
```

No Ok appears. **KEY** is waiting for you to press a key, so press "A".

```
65 Ok
```

---

* **polyFORTH** uses **[ASCII]** within a definition.

FORTH accepts the key immediately and prints Ok.

If the ASCII code returned by **KEY** is larger than 127 (hex 7F), then some high-order bits have been set by your system. You can screen out or *mask off* these bits with **127 AND**. The expression **KEY 127 AND** is guaranteed to leave a 7-bit ASCII code on the stack. We will talk more about masks and bit manipulation in a later chapter.

Try the simple word **ECHO**:

```
: ECHO
   BEGIN  KEY  DUP 127 AND EMIT  13 ( <Return>) =
   UNTIL ;
```

Control-M (13) is the <RETURN> key. Type **ECHO**; then type "ABC" and press <RETURN>.

```
ECHO ABC
```

Many FORTHs also provide a word that checks to see whether a key has been pressed without waiting for one. The word is called **KEY?** or something similar,* and leaves a flag which is *true* if a key has been pressed. You can use this word to allow yourself to interrupt a long loop by pressing a key.

```
: ENDLESS
   10000 0
   DO  I .  KEY? IF LEAVE THEN  LOOP
   KEY DROP ;
ENDLESS 0 1 2 3 4 5 ( key pressed here) Ok
```

The **KEY DROP** sequence is used to clear the unwanted key.

FORTH also provides the word **EXPECT** which reads an entire line from the keyboard. **EXPECT** reads each key in turn and moves it to a memory buffer of your choice until either a <RETURN> is pressed or the buffer is full. The number of characters read is stored in the variable **SPAN**. The <RETURN> itself is neither counted nor moved. **EXPECT** provides simple editing to allow the user to correct mistakes before hitting <RETURN>. This

* **UR/FORTH** and **MacForth** use **?TERMINAL** while **polyFORTH** uses **?KEY**.

includes recognizing and handling <Backspace> (control-H). Let's write a simple routine that uses **EXPECT**. We will need a buffer to hold the characters and a word to set up the arguments.

```
CREATE BUF  80 ALLOT  ( 80-byte buffer)
: READLINE
   CR BUF 80 ( a n) EXPECT
   CR SPAN ? ." Characters were read" ;
```

Execute **READLINE** <RETURN>, then type "A SIMPLE LINE", followed by a <RETURN>.

```
READLINE
A SIMPLE LINE
13 Characters were read
```

A word called **QUERY** which works very much like **READLINE** is used by FORTH to read the next line of text to be interpreted. The characters are stored in the array whose address is given by **TIB**, and the count is stored in the system variable **#TIB.** MacForth keeps the count in the variable **TIB. SIZE**.

String Representation

When **READLINE** reads a line from the keyboard to a buffer, a single 7-bit ASCII code is stored in each consecutive byte of the buffer, with the high-order bit cleared to 0.

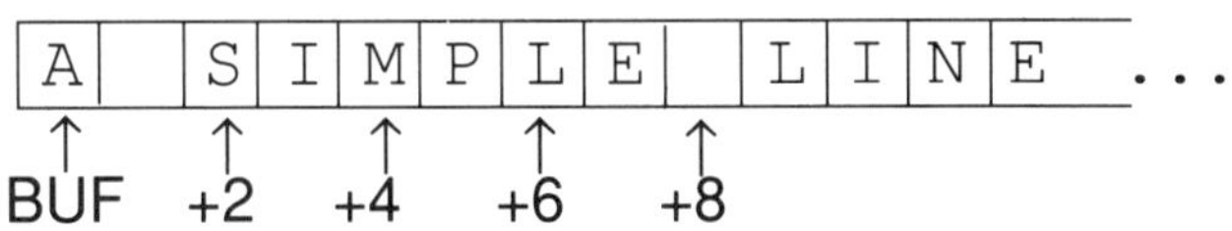

The expression **BUF SPAN @** gives the address of the first byte of the buffer and the number of bytes actually read into **BUF**. The phrase **SPAN @** is usually used in a definition, since it may be changed by the FORTH interpreter with every line you type. These two arguments, starting address and length, exactly represent a consecutive sequence (or *string*) of ASCII characters in memory. We will call this pair of arguments a *text string*. In stack notation, we will refer to a text string as **(a n)**.

You can display a text string with the command **TYPE**. **EXPECT** a string into **BUF** and then **TYPE** it out on your display.

```
: ECHO-BUF   CR BUF 80 EXPECT  CR BUF SPAN @ TYPE ;
```

```
ECHO-BUF
A SIMPLE LINE
A SIMPLE LINE
```

You could also have examined the string with **DUMP**, since **DUMP** expects the same arguments as **TYPE**, that is, starting address and length. MacForth users, don't forget that **DUMP** wants the starting and ending addresses, as in **BUF DUP SPAN @ + DUMP**. In fact, strings are often used to represent arrays of arbitrary bytes as well as sequences of ASCII characters.

Moving and Filling Strings

The word **CMOVE** is the primitive for moving sequences of bytes from one memory location to another, one byte at a time. **CMOVE** needs the *from* address, the *to* address, and the number of bytes to move. The byte at the lowest memory address (the *leftmost* byte) is moved first. If the *from* and *to* memory areas overlap, **CMOVE** may end up moving bytes which have already been moved.

You can exploit this effect to fill an arbitrary memory area with a repeating pattern of your choice. If you want to build a string of 10 stars in **BUF**, first put a star in the leftmost byte.

```
ASCII * BUF C!
```

Now **CMOVE** for 9 more bytes.

```
BUF BUF 1+ 9 CMOVE
```

Check your results.

```
BUF 10 TYPE **********
```

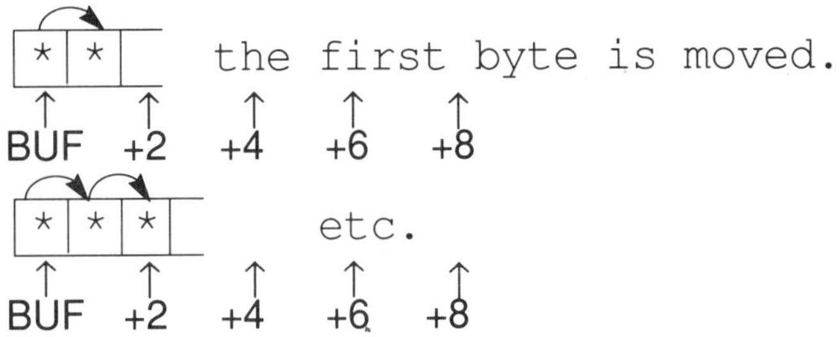

Here are some common FORTH words based on **CMOVE**:

```
: FILL ( a n c)
\ fill memory with n bytes of pattern c.
\ Only the low-order byte of the pattern is used.
   OVER 0= IF DROP 2DROP EXIT THEN
   SWAP >R  OVER C!  DUP 1+ R> 1- CMOVE ;

: ERASE ( a n)   0 FILL ;
\ fill memory from address a with n zeroes.

: BLANK ( a n) BL FILL ;*
\ fill memory from address a with n blanks.
```

Most FORTHs include the constant **BL** (32) for an ASCII blank.

To move a string safely when the *to* address is higher than the *from* address, use **CMOVE>** ("C-move-up").† **CMOVE>** is identical to **CMOVE**, except that the *rightmost* byte is moved first.

Packing Strings

Each string you read with **READLINE** replaces the previous string that was stored in **BUF** and resets **SPAN**. If you want to save a string, you must move the characters from **BUF** to another memory location. You must also save the character count or *length* of the string. The preferred format for saving strings in memory is to store the length in the first byte of an array, followed by the characters in the string. Storing "A SIMPLE LINE" would look like the example at the top of the following page.

* **polyFORTH** users should add **32 CONSTANT BL** to their prelude.

† **polyFORTH** uses **<CMOVE** instead.

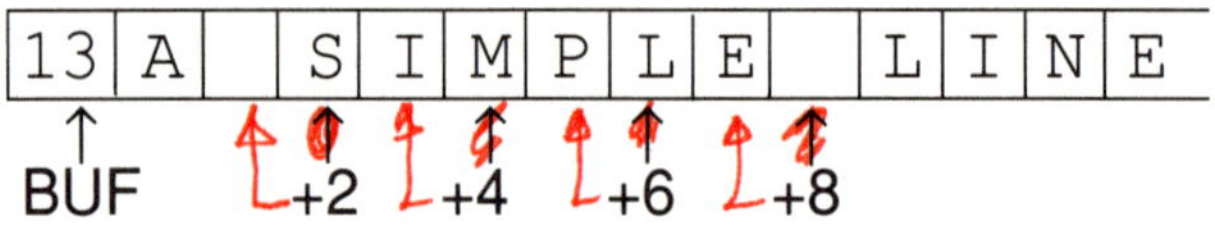

A string in this form is called a *counted string*. Since only one byte is used to hold the length, the maximum length of a counted string is 255 characters. Zero-length strings are allowed and are called *null* strings.

Let's create a second buffer and pack the string in **BUF** and **SPAN** into it.

```
CREATE BUF2 81  ALLOT          ( one more byte for count)

BUF BUF2 1+ SPAN @ CMOVE       ( move the chars)
SPAN @ BUF2 C!                 ( save the length)
```

This is even easier if you first define the word **PLACE**.

```
: PLACE ( a n a2)
\ pack string a n into counted string a2.
   2DUP >R >R  1+ SWAP CMOVE>  R> R> C! ;*

BUF SPAN @ BUF2 PLACE
```

Now you can refer to a string simply by pushing the address of the counted string on the stack. An address used to refer to information this way is called a *pointer*. We can say that the address left by **BUF2** *points* to a counted string. The word **COUNT** converts the counted string back into the more useful text string argument pair.

```
BUF2 COUNT TYPE A SIMPLE LINE
```

COUNT could be defined this way:

```
: COUNT ( a - a+1 n)   DUP 1+ SWAP C@ ;
```

You can convert a text string back into a counted string with the expression **DROP 1-**, but only if you're sure that the string was counted to begin with.

---

* A shorter definition is possible:

```
: PLACE   2DUP C!  1+ SWAP CMOVE ;
```

However, the longer definition allows a string to be packed into its own buffer

String Manipulation

When a string is represented as a text string argument pair, you can duplicate it with **2DUP** and drop it with **2DROP**. Bear in mind, however, that the string itself is not affected by the stack manipulation. **2DUP** does not produce a duplicate copy of the string, nor does **2DROP** destroy it. To make a true copy of a string, you must **CMOVE** or **PLACE** it in another memory location.

Splitting a string into smaller parts is easier with a text string. You can drop characters from the left side of the string by adding a constant to the starting address while decreasing the length by the same amount. Since "A SIMPLE LINE" is still in **BUF2**, let's drop the first two characters and print what remains.

```
BUF2 COUNT  SWAP 2+ SWAP 2- TYPE SIMPLE LINE
```

The original string has not changed.

```
BUF2 COUNT TYPE A SIMPLE LINE
```

Shortening a string this way is a common operation, and you might find the word **/STRING** handy.

```
: /STRING ( a n u - a2 n2)
\ drop the first u chars from a string.
   ROT OVER + ROT ROT - ;
```

/STRING works like this:

```
BUF2 COUNT  9 /STRING TYPE LINE
```

Dropping characters from the right of the string is even easier—just decrease the length.

```
BUF2 COUNT  5 - TYPE A SIMPLE
```

These simple string operations can be combined to select any part of a string.

```
BUF2 COUNT  2 /STRING 5 - TYPE SIMPLE
```

Once a part of a string, called a *substring*, is selected, it can be copied with **CMOVE** or **PLACE** to a separate memory area for further processing.

-Trailing

The length of a string can be kept on the stack or stored in memory. Alternately, it can be computed from the string itself. First, you must prepare a string buffer by filling it with blanks. FORTH provides a temporary but suitable memory area called **PAD**, which is guaranteed to be at least 84 bytes long. Then **EXPECT** or **CMOVE** the string into **PAD**. When you want the string in its text (two-argument) form, push the address and maximum length of the string in **PAD** on the stack and call **-TRAILING. -TRAILING** effectively shortens the string to remove trailing blanks by altering its length.

```
: ACCEPT ( - a n)
\ get a string from the user.
   PAD 80 BLANK
   PAD 80 EXPECT
   PAD 80 -TRAILING ( a n - a2 n2) ;

: NAME?
   CR ." Your name please: " ACCEPT
   CR ." Thank you, " TYPE ;

NAME?
Your name please: Martin
Thank you, Martin
```

String to Number Conversion

Single digits from 0 to 9 can be directly obtained from their ASCII codes (hex 30 to 39) by subtracting an ASCII "0". The following short program shows you how to prompt a user to select one of four items:

```
: SELECT? ( - n)
\ pick an item from 0 to 3.
   BEGIN  CR ." PLEASE SELECT AN ITEM:"
     KEY 127 AND DUP EMIT  ( echo)
     ASCII 0 -             ( convert)
   DUP 0< OVER 3 > OR      ( test range)*
   WHILE ." Oops!" DROP
   REPEAT ." Thank You" ;
```

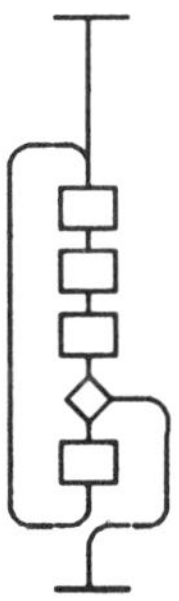

```
: SELECT? ( — n)
\ Pick an item from 0 to 3.
   BEGIN
      CR   ." PLEASE SELECT AN ITEM:"
      KEY ( c) 127 AND   DUP EMIT \ Echo.
      ASCII 0 - ( n)              \ Convert.
            DUP 0< OVER 3 > OR    \ Test range.
     WHILE   ." Oops!" DROP (  )
     REPEAT ( n) ." Thank You" ;
```

Converting a string of ASCII digits to a number is somewhat more difficult. FORTH provides the primitive **CONVERT**, which converts a string of ASCII digits to a double number. Digits are converted from left to right and in the current numeric base. Note that "A" is a valid digit in the hexadecimal base but not in the decimal base. The string to be converted must end with a blank. The length of the string is ignored, and conversion stops when the first non-digit character is encountered. By calling **CONVERT** repeatedly and examining each character that it stops at, you can build a sophisticated string-to-number conversion routine.

Let's construct a conversion routine that accepts a string of ASCII digits and converts it to a double number. The string can be optionally preceded by a

---

* **polyFORTH**, **L&P F83**, **MasterFORTH**, and **ZEN** would use **`WITHIN ( n n2 n3 - f)`** for this kind of range check. **`WITHIN`** is true if $n2 \le n < n3$.

`0 4 WITHIN NOT WHILE` or **`4 0 WITHIN WHILE`**

URFORTH users could define **`: WITHIN   OVER - >R - R> U< ;`**

minus sign, but can contain no other punctuation. Since you cannot assume that the string ends with a blank, you must arrange to add one. You must first copy the string to a buffer and then add the blank. The following sequence copies a string to **PAD** and prepares it for **CONVERT**:

```
PAD PLACE          ( copies the string to PAD)
BL PAD COUNT + C! ( adds a blank)
```

CONVERT requires a double-number accumulator on the stack, initialized to zero, and the starting address to be converted, minus one. It returns the double-number result and the address of the first non-digit character. Here is the word **VAL**, which sets up and calls **CONVERT**:

```
: VAL ( a n - d true | 0)
\ convert a string to a number.
\ Returns true if the number is valid.
\ If false, no number is returned.
   PAD PLACE  ( copies the string to PAD)
   BL PAD COUNT + C!  ( adds a blank)
   0 0                ( accumulator)
   PAD                ( starting address minus 1)
   CONVERT  ( d a - d2 a2)
   DUP C@ ASCII - =   ( leading minus sign?)
   IF   CONVERT       ( continue conversion)
        >R DNEGATE R> ( negative case)
   THEN  C@ BL =      ( successful conversion?)
   ?DUP 0= IF  2DROP 0  THEN ;*
```

The vertical bar | in the stack diagram means that *either* **d true** is returned *or* only a 0 is returned.

Use **ACCEPT** to read a string, and **VAL** to convert it to a number. Try some of the following examples:

---

* **polyFORTH** users: don't forget to substitute **[ASCII]** for **ASCII**.

MacForth doesn't support double numbers.
Substitute **0** for **0 0**, **NEGATE** for **DNEGATE**, and **DROP** for **2DROP**.

String	flag	(dn)	Comment
DECIMAL			Set base to decimal
“123”	-1	123	Successful conversion.
“12A”	0		“A” is not a digit.
HEX			Set base to hexadecimal.
“12A”	-1	12A	“A” is now a digit.
“54,321”	0		“,” is not allowed. “
-12ABC”	-1	-12ABC	Successful conversion.

Most FORTHs support imbedded punctuation. A number ending with a decimal point is usually interpreted to be a double number.

In general, a number containing any allowed punctuation is interpreted as a double number.

The following version of **VAL** supports imbedded punctuation. A decimal point can occur anywhere in the number. The number of digits to the right of the rightmost decimal point is returned in the variable **DPL**.

```
VARIABLE DPL

: VAL ( a n - d true | 0)
\ convert a string to a number.
\ Returns true if the number is valid.
\ If false, no number is returned.
   PAD OVER -  SWAP OVER >R CMOVE  BL PAD C!
   PAD DPL !  0 0 R> DUP C@ ASCII - = DUP >R - 1-
   BEGIN  CONVERT  DUP C@ ASCII . =
   WHILE  DUP DPL !  REPEAT
   R> SWAP >R  IF  DNEGATE  THEN
   PAD 1- DPL @ - DPL !  R> PAD = ( valid?)
   ?DUP 0= IF  2DROP 0  THEN ;

CR ACCEPT VAL . D.
123.45 -1 12345
DPL ? 2
```

Notice that this version of **VAL** puts its conversion buffer *below* **PAD**. This area is normally used for conversion and is at least 32 bytes long.

Most FORTHs provide **DPL** and some facility for converting strings to numbers. The name and nature of this facility, however, varies greatly.*

Number to String Conversion

You have already seen how to type numbers with the *dot* operators (**.**, **D.**, and **U.**). At times, you may want to add punctuation or otherwise control the way that a number prints. FORTH provides a flexible set of primitives to convert a double number to a string. Once you have a string, you can reformat it before printing it. And since single, signed, and unsigned numbers can be easily converted to double numbers, a number can be printed in any way you like.

The FORTH double number conversion primitives are

```
<#   "less-sharp"
#    "sharp"
#S   "sharp-S"
#>   "sharp-greater"
HOLD and SIGN
```

The symbols **<#** and **#>** are used as brackets to signal the beginning and end of conversion. As the conversion progresses, a string is constructed by the operators **#**, **#S**, **HOLD**, and **SIGN**. When the conversion is complete, **#>** pushes the address and length of this string on the stack. A possible definition for a word which prints an unsigned double number would be:

```
: DU. ( u )   <# #S #>  TYPE SPACE ;
\ print an unsigned double number.
```

---

* **MacForth** calls it **$>NUMBER**.

UR/FORTH uses **NUMBER? (a - d flag)** which converts the counted string at **a**.

```
:VAL DROP 1- NUMBER? ?DUP 0= IF 2DROP 0 THEN ;
```

polyFORTH uses **NUMBER (a - n | d)** which converts the counted string at **a**. Punctuation from the set ",-./:" is allowed. No punctuation returns a single number. Invalid numbers are errors.

```
: VAL DROP 1- NUMBER DPL @ 1+ 0>
    IF 'NUMBER CELL+ @ THEN TRUE ;
```

The sequence **<# #S #>** converts the number to a string, which is then printed by **TYPE**. The word **#S** converts all of the digits to characters in the string. No leading zeroes are printed unless the number is 0, in which case a single "0" is printed. The command **SPACE** prints an extra space. FORTH provides both **SPACE** and **SPACES**, which could be defined this way:

```
: SPACE   BL EMIT ;

: SPACES ( n )
  ?DUP IF  0 DO SPACE LOOP  THEN ;
```

The word **SIGN** adds a minus sign to the string if the number on top of the stack is negative. The definition of **D.**, which prints a signed double number, would be something like this:

```
: D. ( d )
\ print a double number.
   SWAP OVER DABS  ( save the sign)
   <# #S ROT SIGN #> TYPE SPACE ;*
```

The conversion words expect an unsigned double number to be on the stack. To convert signed numbers, you need a sequence like the one above to save and restore the sign for **SIGN.** Conversion proceeds from right to left, starting with the least significant digit, so **SIGN** is often the last word in the conversion sequence.

You can add punctuation as you convert with the word **HOLD. HOLD** takes an ASCII character and adds it to the string. Suppose you are programming a business application. Money in cents is represented by a signed double number. To print an amount of money, you will want, from right to left, two digits for the cents amount, a decimal point, the dollar amount, and a leading dollar sign. Here is a word that will do this for you:

---

* **MacForth** doesn't support double numbers, so use

```
: . ( n )  DUP ABS <# #S SWAP SIGN #> TYPE SPACE ;
```

polyFORTH takes the **SIGN** from the third number on the stack, so substitute **SIGN** for **ROT SIGN**.

```
: .MONEY ( d )
   SWAP OVER DABS
   <# # # ASCII . HOLD #S ASCII $ HOLD ROT SIGN #>
   TYPE SPACE ;*
```

Each **#** forces the conversion of one digit, even if the number is zero.

```
0 0    .MONEY $0.00
12345. .MONEY $123.45
-999.  .MONEY -$9.99
```

To print numbers in even columns, you can use the length of the string returned by **#>** to determine how many extra spaces should be printed on the left. The word **D.R**, defined below, right-justifies a number in a column of a given width. If the width is too small for the number, the width is ignored and the full number is printed.

```
: D.R ( d n)
\ print d right-justified in a field of width n.
   >R SWAP OVER DABS
   <# #S ROT SIGN #> R> OVER - SPACES TYPE ;†
```

Print a column of numbers with **D.R**.

```
CR 0. 5 D.R CR 123. 5 D.R CR -2. 5 D.R
    0
  123
   -2
```

* **MacForth**:

```
: .MONEY  DUP ABS
   <# # # ASCII . HOLD #S ASCII $ HOLD SWAP SIGN #>
   TYPE SPACE ;
```

polyFORTH:

```
: .MONEY  SWAP OVER DABS
   <# # # [ASCII] . HOLD #S [ASCII] $ HOLD  SIGN #>
   TYPE SPACE ;
```

† **MacForth** and **polyFORTH** users should rewrite these and subsequent definitions accordingly.

Most of the number printing words can be based on **D.R**.

```
: D.  ( d )   0 D.R SPACE ;
: U.  ( u )   0   D. ;
: .   ( n )   S>D D. ;
```

The conversion words build a string in a temporary area (usually just below **PAD**). Since there is only one temporary area, a converted string should be printed or moved to a string buffer before the next conversion is begun. This is why the definitions we have given **TYPE** the string immediately after conversion. With care, however, you can work directly with the string before printing it. Suppose you define **(D.)** to convert a signed double number to a string. You can base both **D.** and **D.R** on **(D.)** as follows:

```
: (D.) ( d - a n)
   SWAP OVER DABS  <# #S ROT SIGN #> ;

: D. ( d )   (D.)  TYPE SPACE ;

: D.R ( d n)   >R (D.) R>  OVER - SPACES TYPE ;
```

String Literals

In most FORTHs, a specific string, called a *string literal*, can be created by enclosing the string within double-quote marks. Like **."**, the string must be separated from the leading double quote by a blank. In some FORTHs, (MasterFORTH, ZEN, L&P F83) " returns a two-argument text string; in others (MacFORTH, UR/FORTH, polyFORTH), it returns a single-argument counted string which can be converted to a text string by **COUNT**.

```
: EG   " A String Literal" TYPE ;
```

or

```
: EG   " A String Literal" COUNT TYPE ;
EG A String Literal
```

TYPE is used to show that the string is on the stack in text string form. To hide the differences between FORTH implementations in subsequent examples, we will invent the word **(COUNT)**.

```
: (COUNT)   COUNT ;
```

or

```
: (COUNT)   ;
: EG   " A String Literal" (COUNT) TYPE ;
```

Some FORTHs allow one or more string literals to appear outside of a definition.* These strings are stored in a string stack, or **PAD**, or some other temporary location.

```
CR " Temporary String Literal" (COUNT) TYPE
Temporary String Literal
```

String Comparison

Many FORTHs include additional string commands for creating, storing, and comparing strings. We will present two typical string extensions which are based, in large part, on the commands you have learned so far.

Two strings can be compared with the word **COMPARE**. **COMPARE** returns -1 if the first string is *less than* the second, 0 if they are equal, and 1 if the first string is greater than the second.† *Less than* means that the string would appear first in a dictionary, that is, in *lexicographical* order. FORTHs vary in the number and order of the string arguments, but almost all return the *tri-state* flag. Here is a possible definition of **COMPARE**. Review the code carefully and make sure you understand it.

---

* **MasterFORTH** and **ZEN** allow one such string literal;
UR/FORTH and **MacForth** allow several such literals;
polyFORTH and **L&P F83** do not support interpreted string literals.

† **L&P F83** uses **COMPARE** **(a a2 n - - -1 | 0 | 1)**.
UR/FORTH uses **STRCMP** **(a n a2 n2 - - -1 | 0 | 1)**
MacForth and **polyFORTH** use **-TEXT** **(a n a2 - - -1 | 0 | 1)**. The **polyFORTH** **-TEXT** compares cell-by-cell and so length **n** must be even.

```
: -TEXT ( a n a2 - -1 | 0 | 1)
   OVER 0= IF  ROT 2DROP  EXIT  THEN
   SWAP 0 DO  OVER C@ OVER C@ - ( chars unequal?)
           IF  UNDO  C@ SWAP C@ > 2* 1+  EXIT  THEN
           1 1 D+
        LOOP  2DROP 0 ;

: COMPARE ( a n a2 n2 - -1 | 0 | 1)
   ROT  2DUP ( lengths) >R >R  MIN SWAP  -TEXT  DUP
   IF  R> R> 2DROP
   ELSE  DROP  R> R>  2DUP = ( lengths = ?)
     IF  2DROP 0  ELSE  > 2* 1+  THEN
   THEN ;
```

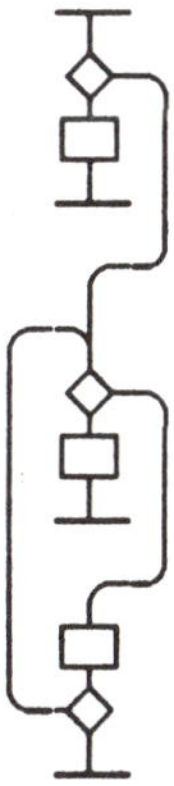

```
: -TEXT ( a n a2 — -1, or 0, or 1)
            OVER 0=
            IF   ROT 2DROP ( 0)
              EXIT
            THEN ( a n a2)
            SWAP 0 DO ( a a2)
               OVER C@ OVER C@ - ( Chars unequal? )
               IF   UNDO   C@   SWAP C@   > ( flag) 2*   1+
                  EXIT
               THEN ( a a2)
               1 1 D+
            LOOP   2DROP (  ) 0 ;
```

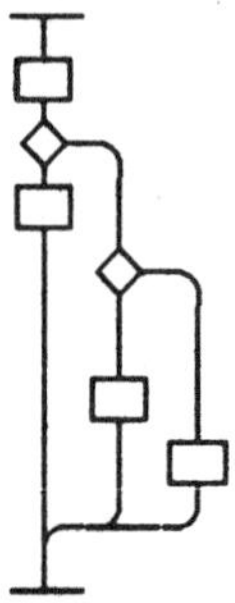

```
: COMPARE ( a n a2 n2 — -1,or  0, or 1)
   ROT ( a a2 n2 n) 2DUP >R >R
         MIN SWAP ( a min a2) -TEXT ( flag) DUP
         IF   R> R> 2DROP
         ELSE   DROP (  ) R> R> ( n2 n) 2DUP =
         ( Lengths = ? )
            IF   2DROP (  ) 0
            ELSE   > ( flag) 2*   1+
         THEN THEN ;
```

The phrase **2* 1+** converts *true* to -1 and *false* to 1. Notice how **-TEXT**, a useful primitive in itself, has been factored out of **COMPARE**. Here are some examples for you to try:

```
: "ANIMAL"    " ANIMAL" (COUNT) ;
: "AN"    " AN" (COUNT) ;
: "ANIMUS"    " ANIMUS" (COUNT) ;

"AN" "ANIMAL" COMPARE . -1
"ANIMAL" "ANIMAL" COMPARE . 0
"ANIMUS" "ANIMAL" COMPARE . 1
```

polyFORTH has a default name **WIDTH** of 3 characters, and would not be able to distinguish **"ANIMAL"** from **"ANIMUS"**. You can temporarily increase the **WIDTH** of a name to 31 characters by preceding it with a ~ ("tilde"). The ~ should precede the latter word.

```
~ : "ANIMUS"   " ANIMUS" ;
```

Another common string comparison word is **MATCH**, which finds one string within another.

```
MATCH ( a n a2 n2 - ??? 0 | n3 -1)
\ return the offset n3 of string a2 n2 in string a n.
\ Offset is zero if the match is found in the 1st position.
\ Returns invalid offset and 0 if no match is found.
   DUP 0= IF  2DROP 2DROP  0 TRUE  EXIT  THEN
   2SWAP  2 PICK OVER SWAP -
   DUP 0< IF  2DROP 2DROP  0 EXIT  THEN
   0  ( offset)  SWAP 1+ 0
   DO ( offset) >R
     2OVER 2OVER DROP  -TEXT 0=  ( equal?)
     IF  2DROP 2DROP  R> TRUE  UNDO EXIT  THEN
     1 /STRING  R> 1+
   LOOP  2DROP 2DROP  0 ;
```

UR/FORTH uses **STRNDX** **(a n a2 n2 – n3)** which returns the offset of the second string in the first. No match returns an offset of -1. polyForth uses **–MATCH** **(a n a2 n2 - a n -1 | a3 n3 0)** which finds the second string in the first. If a match is found, returns the substring following the match and 0; otherwise it returns a n and *true*. MacForth uses **MATCH** **(a n a2 n2 - a3 - -1 a4)** which finds the second string in the first. If a match is found, **MATCH** returns 0 and the address just past the match; otherwise it returns *true* and the address just past the string.

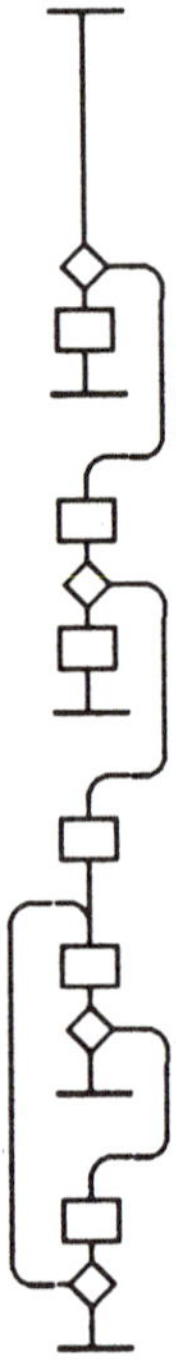

```
: MATCH ( a n a2 n2 - ??? 0 | n3 -1)
\ return the offset n3 of string a2 n2 in string a n.
\ Offset is zero if the match is found in the 1st position.
\ Returns invalid offset and 0 if no match is found.
         DUP 0=
         IF   2DROP 2DROP (  ) 0 TRUE ( 0 true)
            EXIT
         THEN ( a n a2 n2)
   2SWAP ( a2 n2 a n) 2 PICK ( a2 n2 a n n2)
         OVER SWAP - ( a2 n2 a n n-n2) DUP 0<
         IF   2DROP 2DROP ( a2) 0 ( a2 0)
            EXIT
         THEN ( a2 n2 a n n-n2)
         0 SWAP 1+ 0 ( a2 n2 a n offset n-n2+1 0)
         DO ( a2 n2 a n offset) >R ( a2 n2 a n)
            2OVER 2OVER DROP ( ... a2 n2 a) -TEXT 0=
            IF ( ... ) 2DROP 2DROP (  ) R> TRUE ( offset) UNDO
               EXIT
            THEN ( a2 n2 a n)
            1 /STRING   R> ( a2 n2 a n offset) 1+
         LOOP   2DROP 2DROP ( a2) 0 ;
```

```
: "MAL"    " MAL" (COUNT) ;

"ANIMAL" "AN"  MATCH . . -1 0
"ANIMAL" "MAL" MATCH . . -1 3
"ANIMAL" "ANIMUS" MATCH . DROP 0
```

Word	Stack	Action
.(ccc)		Displays the string <ccc>.
-TRAILING	a n - a2 n2	Removes trailing blanks from string a n, shortening it to string a2 n2.
BL	- c	ASCII space.
BLANK	a n	Fills memory at address a with n blanks.
CMOVE	a a2 n	Moves n bytes from address a to address a2, leftmost byte first.
CMOVE>	a a2 n	Moves n bytes from address a to address a2, rightmost byte first.
CONVERT	d a - d2 a2	Converts string at address a+1, accumulating number into d. Stops at first non-convertable character (at address a2).
COUNT	a - a+1 n	Unpacks string.
D.	d	Prints double number d.
D.R	d n	Prints double number d left-justified in a field n wide.
EMIT	c	Displays an ASCII key.
ERASE	a n	Fills memory at address a with n zeroes.
EXPECT	a n	Reads up to n chars or <Return> into the buffer at address a.
FILL	a n c	Fills n bytes at address a with the low-byte pattern of c.
KEY	- c	Reads an ASCII key.
KEY?	(- flag)	True if a key is pressed.
PAD	- a	Points to a temporary buffer.
SPACE		Prints a space.
SPACES	n	Prints n spaces.
SPAN	- a	Variable which contains the number of chars from the last **EXPECT**.
TIB	- a	Points to the FORTH terminal input buffer.
#TIB	- a	Variable which contains the number of chars in **TIB**.
TYPE	a n	Displays a string.
U.	u	Prints unsigned double number d.

Output conversion word set:

Word	Stack	Action
<#	d - d	Initializes for pictured numeric conversion.
#	d — d2	Converts one digit of d.
#S	d - 0 0	Converts all remaining digits.
HOLD	c	Adds char to conversion string.
SIGN	n	Adds "-" to conversion string if n is negative.
#>	d - a n	Ends conversion, leaving string.

String extensions:

Word	Stack	Action
/STRING	a n n2 - a2 n3	Drops n2 leftmost chars of string a n.
" ccc"	- a n	Creates the string literal <ccc>, delimited by double-quote marks.
ASCII	<c> - n	The ASCII code of the following character is left on the stack.
COMPARE	a n a2 n2	Compares string a n to string a 2 n 2. Returns true if string a n is less than string a2 n2 in lexicographical order, 0 if equal, and 1 if greater than.
MATCH	a n a2 n2 - ? 0 | n3 -1	Returns the offset n3 of string a2 n2 in string a n. Offset is zero if the match is found the the 1st position. Returns invalid offset and 0 if no match is found.
PLACE	a n a2	Moves and packs a string from address a to address a2 of length n.
VAL	a n - d true | 0	Converts a string to a - double number. True if conversion succeeds; otherwise the number is not returned.

Exercises

1. Write the word **<CMOVE>** which, unlike **CMOVE** or **CMOVE>**, safely moves an array of bytes either upwards or downwards in memory, even if the source and destination overlap.

2. Many FORTHs provide the word **UPPER** which converts a string to upper-case. **UPPER** only affects characters in the range of "a" to "z". Write **UPPER** and test it with some string literals which you have moved to **PAD**. If a string has a length 0, it should be properly ignored.

3. Define the word **LEX**, which splits a string into two at a given delimiter. The delimiter is removed and either string can be null (length 0). **LEX** is useful for breaking strings into meaningful substrings:

```
" VOLUME:NAME" ASCII : LEX
TYPE NAME        ( right string)
TYPE VOLUME      ( left string)
```

4. Write **S+ (a n)** which adds a string to the end of a counted string in **PAD**. The count byte at PAD should be adjusted accordingly.

5. Using the conversion words **<# # #S SIGN HOLD** and **#>,** Redefine **D.** to insert a comma between each three digits, starting from the right. Your new definition of **D.** will act like this:

```
1234567. D. 1,234,567
```

6. Write a word which parses a date, such as "02/07/88", in a text string and returns the month, day, and year on the stack, with the year on top. Check your results by writing another word to convert the arguments back into a text string at **PAD**.

7. UR/FORTH keeps temporary strings in a circular string buffer. When the buffer fills, it wraps to the beginning, overwriting the oldest string. Write the word **+BUF** which allocates bytes from a circular memory buffer and packs a given string there.

```
+BUF ( a n - a2)
\ allocates n+1 bytes in a circular buffer and moves
\ string a n there.
\ Returns the address of the now counted string a2.

: "TEST"  " This is a test." (COUNT) ;

"TEST" +BUF CR COUNT TYPE
This is a test.
```

11 Defining Words

Compile time

We have seen how the defining words **:** **CONSTANT**, **VARIABLE**, and **CREATE** can be used to add new words to your dictionary. **CREATE** is used to build variables, arrays and tables. In the way of review, let's use **CREATE** to build a two-dimensional array or *matrix*. A matrix can be *unraveled* into a normal one-dimensional array by allocating the first row in memory, followed by the second, and so forth. Suppose you want to build a *3 by 5* (3 rows of 5 columns) array of cells. To find the third cell of the second row, you would skip 5 cells (the first row) from the beginning of the matrix, and then skip two more (the first two columns of this row). This is expressed by the formula

```
'item = 'matrix + ([row# * #cols] + col#)
```

where		
	row#	means row number,
	col#	means column number,
	#rows	means number of rows,
	#cols	means number of columns, i.e., **bytes/row**,
	'matrix	means starting address of matrix, and
	'item	means address of item at the given row# and col#

A matrix of bytes is completely described by its two dimensions: **#rows** and **#cols**. The dimensions must be remembered somehow when the matrix is created. The defining word **MATRIX** does all of this.

```
: MATRIX ( #rows #cols )( - 'matrix)
\ define a #rows by #cols-byte matrix.
   CREATE 2DUP  , ,   ( remember the dimensions)
   * CELLS ALLOT ;    ( #rows * #cols elements)
```

We haven't actually created any matrices yet. But we have specified what will happen when we do. The first stack diagram reminds us that when **MATRIX** is executed, it expects to find the two dimensions of the matrix on the stack. **CREATE** creates the matrix and each **,** compiles a dimension into the dictionary for later use. The **ALLOT** then allocates one cell for each element of the matrix. So the *compile-time* action of **MATRIX** is to create the matrix by compiling the dimensions and allocating space for the elements.

The second stack diagram tells us that when any matrix is executed (*runs*), it will leave the address of the first cell of data compiled into the dictionary, in this case, **'matrix**, that is, the cell containing **#cols**. This is exactly the same address that **CREATE** alone would leave. In fact, pushing the address of the first byte of compiled data on the stack is the default *run-time* action for any word created by a defining word. This makes sense when you realize that there's no point in compiling data into the dictionary if you can't find it afterwards.

Use **MATRIX** to make a 3 by 5 matrix.

```
3 5 MATRIX BOXES
```

What's on the stack now? Nothing yet! The defining word **MATRIX** has been executed. Its compile-time action is to create the matrix **BOXES**.

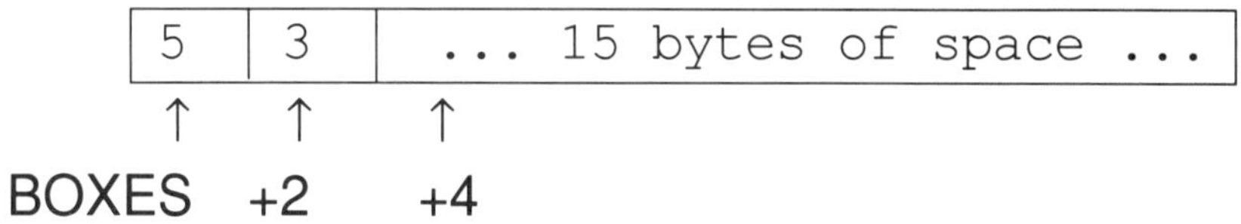

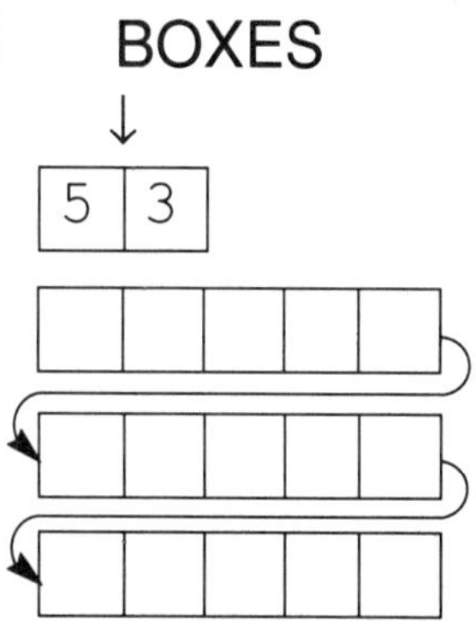

The dimensions 3 and 5 are compiled into the dictionary, and 15 cells of storage are allocated for the elements of the matrix. Only the word **MATRIX** has run, and not the matrix **BOXES**. Be sure you understand this before reading further.

The run-time action of **BOXES** is to leave the address of the first cell of the matrix on the stack, which contains the dimension **#cols**:

```
BOXES ? 5
```

If you're not sure where this number came from, try rereading the section on arrays.

You could say that **BOXES** is a member of the *class* matrix, created by the defining word **MATRIX**.

Separating the compile-time action of the defining word from the run-time action of the defined word is the key to understanding defining words.

With the address returned by **BOXES** you can define a word which will find the address of any element within **BOXES**, given its row and column number. Bear in mind that when you count items in FORTH, you usually start from zero.

```
: ELEMENT ( row# col# 'matrix - 'element)
\ finds the address of the element at row# and col#.
   DUP >R @   ( retrieve #cols = cells/row)
   ROT * +    ( apply formula for offset)
   2+ CELLS  R> ( addr of first element) + ;
```

See if it works.

```
100  0 2 BOXES ELEMENT !   ( 1st row, 3rd col)
150  1 1 BOXES ELEMENT !   ( 2nd row, 2nd col)
```

```
0 2 BOXES ELEMENT ? 100
1 1 BOXES ELEMENT ? 150
```

By using **CREATE**, we can create data structures of any complexity. This is because we can use the full power of FORTH (including other defining words) to compile the data in whatever form we wish.

Run Time

The default run-time action of any word made with **CREATE** is to leave the address of the internal data storage area (called the *body*) of the word on the stack. The size, format, and initial contents of this area are determined by the words which follow **CREATE** in the defining word. For example, here is a definition for the defining word **VARIABLE**:

```
: VARIABLE ( - )( - a)   CREATE  0 , ;
```

Using this definition, any variable of the class **VARIABLE** will have a one-cell body initialized to zero. When the variable is executed, it will leave the address of this body on the stack.

Once the address of the body of a word is known, the data stored within the body is available for further processing. The word **DOES>** lets you specify the run-time action to be done on this data. In other words, **DOES>** lets you extend the default run-time action of any defined word. Here is a definition of the word **VALUE** which is identical to the FORTH word **CONSTANT**:

```
: VALUE ( n )( - n)   CREATE ,   DOES> @ ;
```

Be sure you understand what is happening and when. The compile-time action of **VALUE** is to **CREATE** a word with a one-cell body initialized to the value n which is on the stack when the word is defined.

```
5 VALUE FIVE
```

At this point, the defining word **VALUE** has run, but the defined word **FIVE** has not. What's on the stack right now?

```
.S
<-Top
```

Normally, you would expect that **FIVE**, or any word made by **CREATE**, would leave the address of its body on the stack. In this case, when **FIVE** runs, you would expect to find the address of the body of **FIVE**, which contains the number 5, on the stack. However, the **DOES>** within **VALUE** extends this default action with a @, so that the value (5) in the body is returned rather than its address.

```
FIVE . 5
```

You can use **DOES>** to make the run-time action of **MATRIX** *smarter*. Simply incorporate the action of **ELEMENT** within the definition of **MATRIX**.

```
: SMART-MATRIX
\ defines a #rows by #cols byte matrix.
\ Finds the address of the element at row# and col#.
   CREATE ( #rows #cols )
     2DUP , ,         ( remember the dimensions)
     * CELLS ALLOT    ( #rows * #cols elements)
   DOES> ( row# col# - 'element)
     DUP >R @    ( retrieve #cols = bytes/row)
     ROT * +     ( apply formula for offset)
     2+ CELLS R>   ( addr of first element) + ;
```

The stack diagrams for compile-time and run-time action follow the **CREATE** and **DOES>** words, respectively. You will find this smarter matrix easier and more natural to use.

```
3 5 SMART-MATRIX COLLECTOR
100  0 2 COLLECTOR !
150  1 1 COLLECTOR !

0 2 COLLECTOR ? 100
1 1 COLLECTOR ? 150
```

You could have redefined **MATRIX** instead of renaming it to **SMART-MATRIX**. The old version of **MATRIX**, however, is *functionally different* from the new version. Functionally different means that the two words differ either in the arguments they expect or the results they produce. It is potentially confusing for two functionally different versions of a word to have the same name.

Whenever you change the function of a word, give the new version a new name.

You can use **DOES>** to add error or limit checking to a class of words. This version of **SMART-MATRIX** uses **MAX** and **MIN** to keep the row and column numbers within the bounds of the matrix.

```
: SMARTER-MATRIX
\ defines a #rows by #cols byte matrix.
\ Finds the addr of the element at row# and col#.
\ Limits the row# and col# to lie within the matrix.
   CREATE ( #rows #cols —)
     2DUP , ,   ( remember the dimensions)
     * CELLS ALLOT    ( #rows * #cols elements)
   DOES>  ( row# col# — ^element)
     DUP  >R        @ MIN 0 MAX  ( limit col#)
     SWAP R@ CELL+ @ MIN 0 MAX  ( limit row#)
     SWAP R@ @   ( retrieve #cols = bytes/row)
     ROT * +    ( apply formula for offset)
     2+ CELLS R>  ( addr of first element) + ;
```

FORTH allows you to add error checking to words, but does not require that you do so. Contrast this to other programming languages, which use extensive error checking even when it is not needed.

All objects which can be represented in computer memory fall into one of two classes: data and operations to be done on data. Most programming languages allow you to design and create data structures, sometimes called *records* or *types*. Similarly, they allow you to group data operations into *subroutines*, *modules*, *functions*, or *programs*. The FORTH construct **CREATE—DOES>** lets you define a class of *objects* by specifying both the data organization and the data operation for objects of that class. You can think of an object as either a smart data structure, or else as a program with built-in data storage. The structure and behavior of an object is conveniently presented by the **CREATE—DOES>** in the definition of the defining word for that object.

FORTH's ability to define a class of objects with **CREATE—DOES>** *is its single most powerful feature.*

Compilation Addresses

Sometimes you need to define a word before you know what its definition should be! You might be designing a word which calls several other words, not all of which have been written yet. You could define dummy words or *stubs* to indicate the undefined words, and then replace them with final definitions later. Or suppose you want to write a simple version of a word, to be replaced with a more sophisticated word when necessary. There is a way to apparently defer and otherwise manipulate the run-time action of a word in FORTH.

Normally, when compiling a definition, the address of each word which appears in the definition is compiled into the dictionary. This *compilation address* tells the FORTH interpreter where to begin executing a word. You can find the compilation address of a word with the command **'** ("tick"), followed by the name of the word. For example, executing **' DUP** leaves the compilation address of **DUP** on the stack. You can then execute the word at this address with the word **EXECUTE**.* So the sequence **' DUP EXECUTE** does the same thing as **DUP**.

```
1 2 3  ' DUP EXECUTE  .S
1 2 3 3 <-Top
```

MacForth: **'** returns the address of the definition. **EXECUTE**, however, executes a *token*, equivalent to a compilation address. In this and subsequent examples involving **EXECUTE**, substitute **TOKEN.FOR** for **'**.

```
1 2 3 TOKEN.FOR DUP EXECUTE .S
```

You can save the compilation address in a variable for future use, as in the following example.

```
: THING1  ." FIRST ACTION " ;
: THING2  ." SECOND ACTION " "†


VARIABLE ACTION
' THING1 ACTION !
ACTION @ EXECUTE FIRST ACTION
' THING2 ACTION !
ACTION @ EXECUTE SECOND ACTION
```

* **polyFORTH**: **'** returns the address of the body of the definition, which **EXECUTE** executes.

† **polyFORTH**: name them **1THING** and **2THING**, or else precede each with a ~ (tilde).

Notice that you have a consistant *action* (**@ EXECUTE**) on the *data* in the variable **ACTION**. This suggests that you can make a defining word to describe words like **ACTION**. Consider this definition of **DEFER:**

```
: DEFER
   CREATE  CELL ALLOT
   DOES>   @ EXECUTE ;
```

polyFORTH, MacFORTH, MasterFORTH and ZEN can use **@EXECUTE** for **@ EXECUTE**. L&P F83 and URFORTH should use **PERFORM** instead.

The compile-time action of **DEFER** is to create a deferred word, whose action will be specified later.

```
DEFER SURPRISE
```

SURPRISE, like all objects of the class **DEFER**, has internal storage for one compilation address. The run-time action of **SURPRISE** is to retrieve and execute this compilation address.

Parameter Addresses

Unfortunately, we can't initialize or change the action of **SURPRISE** because we no longer know the location of its body, where the compilation address is normally stored. This is because the address of the body (also called the *parameter address*) is used by the sequence **DOES> @ EXECUTE** in **DEFER** and is no longer available to us.

The solution to this problem is to use the command **>BODY** ("to-body") to change the compilation address of a word into its parameter address. polyFORTH doesn't need **>BODY** since **'** already returns the parameter field address. You could define **: >BODY ;** in your prelude, or just eliminate it from examples. Once you know the parameter address of a word, you can directly access the data stored in the word. Now you can set the action of **SURPRISE** like this:

```
' THING1   ' SURPRISE >BODY !*
SURPRISE FIRST ACTION

' THING2   ' SURPRISE >BODY !
SURPRISE SECOND ACTION
```

>BODY can be used to access the body of any word. You can use it to examine and change the value of the word **FIVE** defined earlier.

```
' FIVE >BODY ? 5
4 ' FIVE >BODY !
FIVE . 4
```

It is even possible to change the value of a constant this way, although a FORTH-83 Standard program is not allowed to do so.

If you are interested in a value which often changes, use a **VARIABLE.** *If it seldom changes, use a* **VALUE**, *and if it never changes, use a* **CONSTANT.**

You can use **'** within a definition, but this can lead to one of the most confusing constructs in FORTH:

```
: CONFUSION
\ planned obfuscation.
   ' THING1 DROP ;†

CONFUSION THING2 FIRST ACTION
```

What happened? The compilation addresses of **'**, **THING1**, and **DROP** were compiled into the definition of **CONFUSION** in the usual manner. When **CONFUSION** was executed, **'** ran, leaving the compilation address of the following word, which was then **THING2**, on the stack. Then **THING1** ran, printing "FIRST ACTION". Finally, **DROP** dropped the compilation address of **THING2**, which was never used.

---

* **MacFORTH**: in this example, **'** is used once with **EXECUTE** and once to find the body of **SURPRISE**:

```
TOKEN.FOR THING1   ' SURPRISE !
```

† **MacFORTH** users may skip the next paragraph, since both **'** and **TOKEN.FOR** work the same way inside and outside of a definition.

The word `[']` ("bracket-tick") is a variation of `'` for use within a definition.* Its usage is best illustrated with an example. Let's use it to improve **DEFER** to print a warning if an uninitialized definition is executed.

```
: WARNING   ." UNINITIALIZED "  ;

: DEFER
\ improved definition.warns of uninitialized values.
   CREATE  ['] WARNING ,
   DOES>   @ EXECUTE ;
```

The new **DEFER** works like this:

```
DEFER FORGOTTEN
FORGOTTEN UNINITIALIZED

' THING1 ' FORGOTTEN >BODY !
FORGOTTEN FIRST ACTION
```

The `[']` in **DEFER** compiles the compilation address of the following word **WARNING** as a *numeric literal*. This means that when **DEFER FORGOTTEN** is executed, `[']` will push the compilation address of **WARNING** on the stack. This is used by `,` to initialize the body of **FORGOTTEN** to the **WARNING**.

You could improve the readability of the sequence `' NAME >BODY !` with a word like **IS**:

```
: IS   ( n )
\ sets the body of the following word to the value n.
    ' >BODY ! ;
```

Read this definition carefully. This is exactly the case which we described above in the **CONFUSION** example. The word **IS** can be used to set the value of any body.

---

* **MacFORTH**: in the following discussion, substitute `'` for `[']` when it is used to find the body of a word and **TOKEN.FOR** for `[']` when it is used with **EXECUTE**.

```
: DEFER   CREATE  TOKEN.FOR WARNING ,  DOES> @EXECUTE ;
: IS   [COMPILE] '  ! ;
```

```
' THING2 IS FORGOTTEN
FORGOTTEN SECOND ACTION

10 IS FIVE FIVE . 10
```

This definition of **IS** cannot be used within a definition.

Positional Case

An array or table of compilation addresses lets you assign an action to an index into the array. The idea of relating a number to an action is sometimes called *vectored execution* and appears in programming languages as *positional case statements* or something similar. In the following example, television channel numbers are each given an action. The action could be to set an electronic tuner, but in this case, we will simply have it print out a channel identification. **MAX** and **MIN** are used to ensure that something reasonable is done even for meaningless channel numbers.

```
: KNXT   ." KNXT" ;
: KNBC   ." KNBC" ;
: KTLA   ." KTLA" ;
: KABC   ." KABC" ;
: KHJ    ." KHJ " ;
: KTTV   ." KTTV" ;
: KCOP   ." KCOP" ;
: N/A    ." NO STATION" ;

CREATE CHANNELS
' N/A  ,  ' N/A  ,  ' KNXT ,  ' N/A  ,
' KNBC ,  ' KTLA ,  ' N/A  ,  ' KABC ,
' N/A  ,  ' KHJ  ,  ' N/A  ,  ' KTTV ,
' N/A  ,  ' KCOP ,  ' N/A  ,
: CHANNEL ( channel# )
\ identify a TV channel using CHANNELS.
   0 MAX 14 ( decimal) MIN CELLS
   CHANNELS + @ EXECUTE  SPACE ;
```

```
-1 CHANNEL NO STATION
 0 CHANNEL NO STATION
 1 CHANNEL NO STATION
 2 CHANNEL KNXT
 3 CHANNEL NO STATION
 4 CHANNEL KNBC
99 CHANNEL NO STATION
```

Word	Stack	Action
DOES>		Used in the form **: <class> CREATE ... DOES> xxx ;** **<class> ccc** extends the run-time action of the new word **ccc** to include the code sequence **xxx**.
' ccc	- a	Leaves the compilation address of the word **ccc** on the stack.
['] ccc	- a	Like **'** , but for use within a definition only. When the definition runs, leaves the compilation address of the word **ccc** which followed it in the definition.
EXECUTE	a	Executes a word given its compilation address.
>BODY	a- a2	Converts a compilation address into a parameter (body) address.

Exercises

1. Write the defining word **STRING**. The compile-time action of **STRING (n)** is to create a string buffer for a string up to **n** bytes long. The run-time action of a string buffer **(- a)** is to leave the address of this buffer on the stack.

```
10 STRING REPOSE
: IMPOSE  " Stay a while " (COUNT) REPOSE PLACE ;
REPOSE COUNT TYPE Stay a while
```

2. Design the defining word **COUNTER**. When executed, an object of the class **COUNTER** increments an internal counter. You will need a word **RESET** to initialize the counter and a word **EXAMINE** to print its value.

```
COUNTER KILROY
RESET KILROY

KILROY KILROY KILROY
EXAMINE KILROY 3
```

   You can put counters like this in words to see how many times they've been executed.

3. Design a flip-flop generator that changes state each time it's called. Flip-flops leave their previous state, either a 0 or a -1, on the stack. The **RESET** function in the previous example should work on flip-flops too:

```
FLIP-FLOP DUPLEX
DUPLEX . 0
DUPLEX . -1
DUPLEX . 0
RESET DUPLEX DUPLEX . 0
```

4. Write **2VALUE** as the double-number equivalent of **VALUE**. Be sure **2VALUE** stores the high-order cell of the number in the low-order cell of the body.

5. Assume the variable **COLORED** represents a hardware register for setting the color of text on a graphic screen. Write a defining word which creates colors. The run-time action of a color is to store its value in **COLORED**.

```
4 COLOR YELLOW    5 COLOR VIOLET

YELLOW COLORED ? 4
VIOLET COLORED ? 5
```

6. Write the defining word **POINT** which stores the two-dimensional coordinates of a point. When a point runs, these coordinates are multiplied by the value **SCALE** before being pushed on the stack.

```
10 12 POINT 1OBJECT  8 13 POINT 2OBJECT

1 IS SCALE
1OBJECT . . 12 10

2 IS SCALE
1OBJECT . . 24 20
2OBJECT . . 26 16
```

7. The defining word **FOOD** makes a food category with a given initial price in pennies and an initial quantity of zero. The quantity may be inspected with **HOWMANY** and increased with **MORE**.

```
89 FOOD HAMBURGER
69 FOOD FRIES

HOWMANY HAMBURGER 0

12 MORE HAMBURGER
10 MORE FRIES
HOWMANY HAMBURGER 10
```

Each time a food is executed, its quantity is decremented by one. Furthermore, its cost is added to the variable **TOTAL**.

```
VARIABLE TOTAL 0 TOTAL !

HAMBURGER
TOTAL ? 89
HOWMANY HAMBURGER 11

FRIES FRIES FRIES
TOTAL ? 296
```

12 Compiling Words

Every word in the FORTH dictionary has a name, an action, and a body. The name and its associated linkage is called the *header*. The header can usually be subdivided into a *name field* and a *link field*, which points to another name or link field. In modern FORTHs, this is not always true. The action is specified by the *code field*. The body of the word, also called its *parameter field*, holds the data on which the code field acts. Together, these three fields completely describe the word.

Headers

The header is built by **CREATE** when a new word is first defined. All of the defining words use **CREATE** to create and name new words. **CREATE** reads the name which follows and packs it into the dictionary as a header for future reference. **CREATE** also creates a code field whose default action is to push the address of the parameter field on the stack. The parameter field is empty at this time.

When you type in a line and press <RETURN>, FORTH reads each word and looks in the dictionary for a matching header. The dictionary is searched in reverse chronological order, so if a word has been defined more than once, FORTH finds the most recent definition first. The header is followed by the corresponding code field or a pointer to it, which in turn is followed by the parameter field (or a pointer to it). Once the code field is found, it is either executed or else converted to a compilation address and compiled.

Colon Definitions

The parameter field of a colon definition contains the sequence of compilation addresses of the words which make up the definition. Consider this high-level definition of **WITHIN**:

```
: WITHIN   OVER - >R - R> U< ;
```

The body of **WITHIN** would contain the compilation address of **OVER** followed by the compilation address of **-** and so on. Let's assume that **OVER** is a machine-code primitive and not itself a colon definition. This means that it is the machine processor, and *not* FORTH, which executes the word **OVER**. FORTH simply maintains a register, usually called the *instruction pointer* or *I register*, telling the machine what to execute *next*. In this case, the **I** register points to the compilation address of **-** within the body of the definition **WITHIN**.

OVER, like all machine-code definitions called from FORTH, will eventually end with a special sequence of instructions called *the address interpreter* or simply NEXT. NEXT has two important jobs:

1. Execute the machine code associated with the compilation address pointed to by the **I** register.*

---

* The association between the compilation address and the machine code it executes varies greatly between FORTH implementations.

  For Indirect threaded-code (ITC) FORTHs, the compilation address points to the code field, which contains a pointer to the machine code.

  For Direct threaded-code (DTC) FORTHs, the compilation address points to the code field, which contains the machine code, usually a JMP or CALL elsewhere.

  For Token threaded-code (TTC) FORTHs, the compilation address is an index to an execution vector.

  For Subroutine threaded-code (STC) FORTHs, there is no address interpreter. FORTH compiles directly to machine code, and the **I** register is simply the machine instruction pointer.

2. Increment the **I** register to point to the next compilation address.

These two steps take place more or less simultaneously. By repeating them, NEXT will sequentially execute all the compilation addresses in a definition.

How does the **I** register get pointed into the colon definition in the first place? When the **I** register points to the compilation address of a colon definition, like **WITHIN**, NEXT executes the machine code associated with that colon definition. *The action of all colon definitions is the same.*

1. Save the current value of the **I** register by pushing it on the return stack.
2. Point the **I** register to the first compilation address in the colon definition (in this case, **OVER**) and execute NEXT.

Eventually, the **I** register will be incremented to point to the compilation address of the word **EXIT** (or its equivalent) compiled by ; at the end of the definition. **EXIT** has only one job—to restore the previous value of the **I** register by popping it from the return stack.

This would return the address interpreter to the word that contained **WITHIN**. Eventually, this word too will end with an **EXIT**, and control will be returned to the word which called it. As each word **EXIT**s in turn, control will be passed upward until it reaches the highest level of execution. This level is called the *outer interpreter* or *text interpreter*. The outer interpreter, like the address interpreter, has two important jobs:

1. Request a line of input. The input comes either from the user at the keyboard or from mass storage. We will take a closer look at this in the next chapter.
2. Find the code field associated with each word of input, either compiling or executing it as appropriate.

By repeating these two steps indefinitely, FORTH compiles and executes all programs according to the commands given in the input.

Compiling Versus Interpreting

When you enter a line from the keyboard or **LOAD** a screen, the text interpreter immediately finds and executes each word that it reads. This is called the *interpret state* of FORTH. On the other hand, once the interpreter starts a colon definition, it compiles the address of each word that it reads. This is the *compile state* of the language.

FORTH keeps track of which state it is in with the variable **STATE**. **STATE** is zero while interpreting and non-zero while compiling. Let's define a word to see what state we're in.

```
: STATE?
   STATE @ IF ." COMPILING" ELSE ." INTERPRETING" THEN ;
```

Try it out from the keyboard.

```
STATE? INTERPRETING
```

Now try it in a definition.

```
: TEST   STATE? ;
TEST INTERPRETING
```

The **STATE?** in **TEST** is compiled and doesn't run until **TEST** itself is executed in the interpret state. What we need is some way of executing a word in the middle of a definition. FORTH provides the pair of words **[** ("left-bracket") and **]** ("right-bracket") to let us change states at will. The **[** puts us in interpret state; the **]** returns us to compile state. They are normally used in pairs to bracket the sequence to be executed.

```
FORGET TEST
: TEST   [ STATE? ] ; INTERPRETING
TEST
```

This time, the bracketed **STATE?** runs as expected. But the brackets cause us to change states, so the message "INTERPRETING" is printed. And because **STATE?** is interpreted, it is never compiled. When **TEST** runs, it has nothing to do.

To see the message "COMPILING," we need a **STATE?** that will execute while FORTH is in the compile state. We can use the command **IMMEDIATE** to modify a word so that it runs while compiling. **IMMEDIATE** must appear immediately after the definition of the word you wish to modify:

```
FORGET STATE?

: STATE?
   STATE @ IF ." COMPILING" ELSE ." INTERPRETING" THEN ;
  IMMEDIATE

: TEST   STATE? ; COMPILING

TEST
```

The immediate word **STATE?** now runs while compiling, leaving **TEST** with nothing to do.

Making a word **IMMEDIATE** is a permanent change. If you ever need to compile an immediate word, however, you can force its compilation with the command **[COMPILE]** ("bracket-compile").

```
: TEST-AGAIN   [COMPILE] STATE? ;

TEST-AGAIN INTERPRETING
```

Words which run while compiling are called *compiler words* and are, by definition, **IMMEDIATE**. You have already used compiler words like **IF** and **THEN** in flow-of-control structures. You may even have noticed that the semicolon which ends a definition must be a compiler word, since it must *run* in order to restore FORTH to the interpret state. Furthermore, you have seen that the semicolon causes the word **EXIT** (or its equivalent) to be compiled at the end of the definition.

Literals

Compiling words let you mix data and code within the same definition. Suppose, for example, you put a number inside of a definition.

```
: FOUR+   4 + ;
```

If FORTH were simply to compile the number 4 into the definition where it occurs, the inner interpreter would try to execute a word at compilation address 4, which is not what you mean. And yet, the logical place to save a number is inside the definition where it occurs. What we need is some way to include the number within the definition while shielding it from execution.

When the text interpreter reads the definition, it compiles the following sequence into the body of **FOUR+**:

Address	Contents
BODY	compilation address of `lit`
CELL+	the number four
CELL+	compilation address of `+`
CELL+	compilation address of `EXIT`

The compilation address of the *run-time component of a numeric literal*, which we will call `lit`, is compiled in front of the 4. When `lit` runs, it must do two things:

1. First, it must push the number which follows it onto the stack.
2. Then it must move the `I` register past this number to the next compilation address.

Here is a possible high-level definition of `lit`:

```
: lit ( - n)
\ run-time code for a numeric literal
   R@ @         ( retrieves number)
   R> CELL+ >R ( adjusts I register) ;
```

How does it work? When **lit** runs, the **I** register is pointing to the next compilation address to be executed in **FOUR+**, in this case, the number 4. Because **lit** is a colon definition, it has the same action as all colon definitions, that is, to save the **I** register on the return stack. **R@** copies this address to the data stack and **@** replaces it with the 4. The next sequence, **R> CELL+ >R**, adds one cell to the return address, moving it past the 4. When **lit** returns (via its **EXIT**) to **FOUR+**, the address interpreter continues execution at the **+** instruction.

The final result is that the number 4 is saved and restored *literally* as the number 4. The literal 4 is saved *in-line*, that is, mixed in with the compilation addresses. Other kinds of literals can be saved in-line with the same technique. Consider, for example, the string literals from the chapter on strings. They could be compiled this way:

```
: FELIX ( - a n)   " CAT" ;
```

Address	Contents
BODY	compilation address of (")
CELL+	the byte count 3
1+	the ASCII bytes for "C" "A" and "T"
3 +	compilation address of EXIT

```
: (") ( - a n)
\ run-time string literal.
   R> COUNT       ( retrieves string)
   2DUP + >R ;    ( adjust I register)*
```

In this case we are taking advantage of the fact that if you have a two-argument text string, the phrase **2DUP +** returns the address just past the end of the string.

---

* **MacFORTH** and other 68000-based FORTHs compile compilation addresses on *even* byte boundaries. The phrase **1 AND +** forces an odd address to the next even address.

```
: (")   R> COUNT  2DUP + 1 AND + >R ;
```

You can make your own numeric literals with the compiling word **LITERAL**. **LITERAL** takes a number from the data stack and builds it into a literal. This number is often calculated between the commands **[** and **]** just before the **LITERAL**. For example, we could have defined **FOUR+** this way:

```
: FOUR+   [ 4 ] LITERAL  + ;
```

This definition produces exactly the same code as the previous definition.

LITERAL is used to best advantage whenever a calculation results in a constant value. Rather than compile each step of the calculation into a definition, you can perform the calculation between **[** and **]** and save the results as a literal. The calculation is made at compile time rather than at run time. This saves both time and memory.

Suppose, for example, that you have a four-cell status array called **STATUS** and that you are especially interested in the second cell. The phrase

```
[ STATUS 2 CELLS + ] LITERAL
```

is likely to be much faster and smaller than the phrase

```
STATUS 2 CELLS +
```

LITERAL can also be used to create *headerless* variables, arrays, and tables. Suppose, for example, you need a table with several powers of 10 for use in the definition **POWERS**.

```
HERE ( * )  1 , 10 , 100 , 1000 , 10000 ,

: POWERS ( n - n2)
\ returns nth power of 10 for small n.
   CELLS ( * ) LITERAL + @ ;
```

HERE pushes the address in the dictionary where the table is constructed on the stack. **LITERAL** takes this address off the stack and compiles it into **POWERS**. The (*) is simply a comment, similar to a footnote, to remind you what the **LITERAL** refers to.

Some FORTHs object to a change in the **DEPTH** of the stack between the colon and the semicolon. If your FORTH complains, use the following technique instead:

```
HERE  1 , 10 , 100 , 1000 , 10000 ,

: POWERS ( n - n2)
\ returns nth power of 10 for small n.
   CELLS [ DUP ] LITERAL + @ ;  DROP
```

The definition of **[']** itself can be based on **LITERAL**.

```
: ['] ( - a)
\ compile an address literal.
    ' [COMPILE] LITERAL ;  IMMEDIATE*
```

Constructing Compiler Words

When **LITERAL** runs, it must compile the address of **lit** into the word currently being defined. It must also pop a number from the stack and compile it into the dictionary following **lit**.

```
: LITERAL ( n ) ( - n)
\ compiles a numeric literal.
   ['] lit , ( add lit)  , ( add n.) ;   IMMEDIATE
```

You can see from the two stack diagrams, which specify separate compile-time and run-time actions, that compiling words are closely related to defining words.

You can think of compiler words as local versions of defining words. They specify both the in-line storage of data *during compilation of a definition, and the run-time* action *to be performed on this data when the definition is later executed.*

---

* **MacForth** would use:

```
: [']   [COMPILE] ' ; IMMEDIATE
```

Since the action of adding a compilation address to the dictionary is a part of every compiling word, it has been factored out into the command **COMPILE**. Here is a more readable definition of **LITERAL**, using **COMPILE**:

```
: LITERAL ( n ) ( - n)
\ compiles a numeric literal.
   COMPILE lit  ( add lit)  , ( add n.) ;  IMMEDIATE
```

Word	Stack	Action
STATE	- a	Variable holding the interpret state. A non-zero value means compile state.
[		Sets the interpret state.
]		Sets the compile state.
IMMEDIATE		Alters the latest definition so that it executes during compilation.
[COMPILE]	**<name>**	Adds the compilation address of **<name>** to the definition in progress, even if **<name>** is **IMMEDIATE**.
LITERAL	n - n	Compiles n into the current definition. When the definition is later executed, n is pushed on the stack.
COMPILE	**<name>**	Adds the compilation address of **<name>** to the definition in progress.

State-dumb and State-smart

All words in the FORTH-83 Standard have the same action regardless of the state of the system and are therefore said to be *state-dumb*. You have already seen how you must use `'` outside of a definition and `[']` inside of a definition to achieve the same results. And while you can use a `."` to print a message from within a definition, you must use `.(` to print a message outside of a definition.

You probably also have some words in your FORTH which apparently act the same way inside and outside a definition—perhaps **ASCII** or string literals. If so, these words are *state-smart*, that is, they examine **STATE** and take interpretive or compile-time actions accordingly. If compiling, they compile data and a run-time word which mimics their own interpretive action.

Flow-of-control Compiling Words

The flow-of-control operators like **IF**, **BEGIN**, and **LOOP** are all compiling words. They construct in-line conditional and unconditional branch instructions, using a small set of flow-of-control primitives. A *System Extension* to the FORTH-83 Standard suggests the following names for these primitives:

Word	Stack	Action
BRANCH		Unconditionally transfers control to the in-line address which follows.
?BRANCH		If the flag is false, transfers control to the address which follows; otherwise, skips this address and continues normal execution. Pronounced "question-branch."
<MARK	- a	Marks the destination of a backward branch by pushing its address on the stack. Pronounced "backward-mark."
<RESOLVE	a-	Uses the destination address left by **<MARK** to cause a transfer of control from the end of the dictionary to this address. The address must immediately follow a **BRANCH** or **?BRANCH**. Pronounced "backward-resolve."
>MARK	- a	Marks the destination of a forward branch by pushing its *fix-up* address on the stack. Pronounced "forward-mark."
>RESOLVE	a -	Calculates and compiles a destination address into the fix-up address left by **>MARK** to cause a transfer of control to the end of the dictionary. This address must immediately follow a **BRANCH** or **?BRANCH**. Pronounced "forward-resolve."

For example, the **IF—THEN** operators could be defined this way:

```
: IF    COMPILE ?BRANCH  >MARK ;   IMMEDIATE
: THEN    >RESOLVE ;   IMMEDIATE
```

Here is a definition of **MAX** along with the *object code* it produces:

```
: MAX    2DUP < IF   SWAP   THEN   DROP ;
```

Address	Contents
BODY	compilation address of **2DUP**
CELL+	compilation address of **<**
etc.	**?BRANCH ...**
	... forward to Label A
	compilation address of **SWAP**
Label A	compilation address of **DROP**
	compilation address of **EXIT**

Aliases

It is possible to use compiling words to substitute one code sequence for another. For example, if your FORTH doesn't have **2DUP**, you could define it this way:

```
: 2DUP    OVER OVER ;
```

If you use this **2DUP** within a definition, you will compile instructions to do several things.

1. Execute **2DUP** from the definition, which means pushing the **I** register on the return stack and resetting it to point to the first **OVER**.
2. Execute **OVER** and **OVER** again.
3. Execute **EXIT** (compiled by **;**), popping the **I** register from the return stack.

Actions 1 and 3 are the overhead of calling one high-level colon definition from another. It would be significantly faster to simply substitute the phrase **OVER OVER** for **2DUP** whenever it occurs in a definition.

```
: 2DUP   COMPILE OVER COMPILE OVER ;   IMMEDIATE
```

The technique of substituting one sequence for another is called *macro expansion*. In deference to FORTH's macro-assembler, however, we will call it *aliasing*. In this case, **2DUP** is an *alias* for **OVER OVER**.

The power of compiling words lies in their ability to substitute low-level command sequences for high-level constructions.

It is possible to create new flow-of-control operators as aliases of existing operators. For example, the popular variation of **DO** called **?DO** does not execute the following loop at all if the index is equal to the limit.* You could define **?DO** this way:

```
: ?DO   COMPILE 2DUP  COMPILE =
   [COMPILE] IF  COMPILE 2DROP
   [COMPILE] ELSE [COMPILE] DO ;  IMMEDIATE
: DO   COMPILE TRUE  [COMPILE] IF [COMPILE] DO ;  IMMEDIATE
:  LOOP   [COMPILE]  LOOP [COMPILE] THEN ;  IMMEDIATE
: +LOOP   [COMPILE] +LOOP [COMPILE] THEN ;  IMMEDIATE
```

This converts a **?DO—LOOP** construct into

```
2DUP = IF 2DROP ELSE DO ... LOOP THEN
```

DO LOOP and **+LOOP** also become aliases. **DO—LOOP** constructs are converted into

```
TRUE IF DO ... LOOP THEN
```

To create an alias, precede each **IMMEDIATE** *word in the sequence to be substituted with* **[COMPILE]** *; otherwise, precede it with* **COMPILE**.

* **MacFORTH** DO already includes this test.

Notice that all macros must be **IMMEDIATE**. This means that if you want to use one macro within another, you must precede it with **[COMPILE]**.

Exercises

1. Define the word **DLITERAL**, which acts like **LITERAL** but which saves and restores double numbers.
2. The construction **IF LEAVE THEN** is commonly found in **DO—LOOP**s. Write the alias **?LEAVE** to replace it.
3. Many FORTHs support the **BEGIN—AGAIN** construct which repeats the sequence between **BEGIN** and **AGAIN** indefinitely. Define **AGAIN**. Hint: base it on **UNTIL**.
4. Redefine : and ; to print the number of bytes occupied by each new word in the dictionary.

```
: NEW   1234 DUP 2DROP ;  Occupies 30 bytes.
```

5. Add the **FOR—NEXT** construct to your FORTH. This form of **DO—LOOP** takes a single argument **n** and executes the loop sequence **n+1** times.

```
: TEST  10 FOR I . NEXT ;
TEST 10 9 8 7 6 5 4 3 2 1 0
```

13 The Input Stream and Mass Storage

The text interpreter reads and operates on each word of input until the *input stream* is exhausted and then asks for more. Input normally comes from the lines you type in at the keyboard, unless you choose to **LOAD** a screen or a range of screens. We will use input stream to mean the input to the text interpreter, no matter where it is coming from.

The Input Stream

The text interpreter determines the source of the input stream by examining the system variable **BLK** ("b-l-k"). If the value of **BLK** is zero, it takes its input from the terminal input buffer (**TIB**). Otherwise, it uses the value of **BLK** as a block number and takes its input from that block. This is why you can never **LOAD** block number zero.

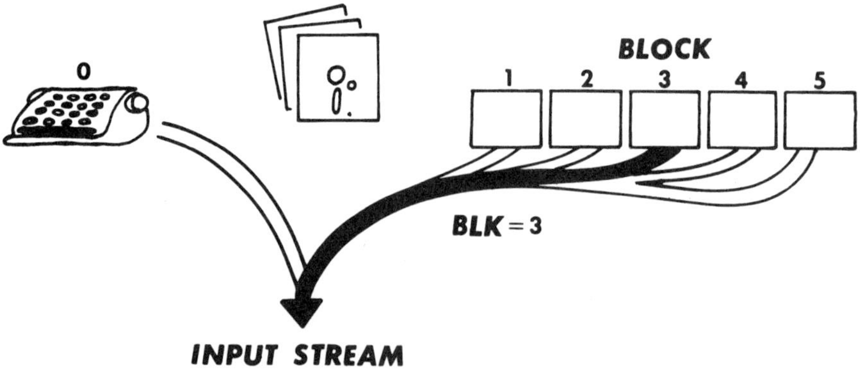

Since the input stream comes from either **TIB** or from a block, it will always be read from memory. You can think of the input stream as an array or string of characters whose starting address and length can be determined by the following word.

```
: SOURCE ( - a n)
\ determines the starting address and length in bytes
\ of the input stream.
   BLK @ ?DUP  ( from BLOCK ?)
   IF  BLOCK 1024  ELSE  TIB #TIB @  THEN ;*
```

The text interpreter uses the system variable **>IN** ("to-in") to keep track of where it is in the input stream. As it reads each word, it advances the index **>IN** to point to the next position to be read. This address and the number of characters remaining to be read is given by the expression

```
SOURCE >IN @ /STRING†
```

When the index in **>IN** is equal to the length of the input stream, there are no more characters to be read. The input stream is said to be "exhausted," and the text interpreter will request further input. The word **STOPS** takes advantage of this to immediately terminate a **LOAD** whenever it is executed from within a block. **STOPS** fools the text interpreter into thinking that the block has already been read.

```
: STOPS   1024 >IN ! ;
\ stops a LOAD immediately.
```

The word **MANY** works from the keyboard in a similar way; it causes the commands in the line just typed to be repeated until a key is pressed.

```
: MANY
\ re-execute the commands in the line just typed.
    KEY? NOT  IF 0 >IN !  THEN  ;
CR .( AGAIN!) MANY AGAIN! AGAIN! AGAIN! ( key pressed here)
```

* **MacFORTH** doesn't use **LOAD**, and interprets either from the keyboard or from text files.

```
: SOURCE   TIB @ TIB.SIZE @ ;
```

† At this point you may wish to review **/STRING** in the Strings chapter.

Be sure you understand why **MANY** must appear on the same line as the commands you want to repeat.

The Command WORD

You can use the command **WORD** to read the input stream. **WORD** uses the character on the top of the stack as a delimiter and reads the input stream up to the delimiter into a temporary packed string, returning the address of the string. Here is a simple word which simply reads and types the next word in the input stream:

```
: WHAT?
\ reads and types the next word in the input stream.
   BL ( delimiter) WORD  COUNT TYPE  ;

1 2 3 CR WHAT? OVER .S
OVER
1 2 3 <-Top
```

The **OVER** is read by **WHAT?** instead of by the text interpreter and so is never executed.

If the input stream is exhausted while it is being read, **WORD** returns with a string of whatever characters were available. If **WORD** is called when the input stream is already exhausted, this string has a length of zero.

```
CR . . . WHAT?
3 2 1 <-Top
```

The text interpreter itself uses **WORD** (or something similar) to read each word in the input stream. It then uses **FIND** (or something similar) to find the word in the dictionary from the packed name returned by **WORD**. The FORTH-83 **FIND** has a curious syntax which largely reflects the needs of a typical text interpreter.

Word	Stack	Action
WORD	c - a	Returns the address of a counted string read from the input stream up to the delimiter **c** or until the input is exhausted. Skips leading delimiters. The counted string is followed by a blank not included in the count. If more than 255 characters are read, the count is meaningless.
FIND	a - a 0 | a2 1 | a2 -1	Finds the name in the dictionary given by the counted string **a.** If the name is not found, returns **a** and 0. If the name is found, returns the compilation address **a2**and a *true* flag with one of two values: 1 meaning the word is **IMMEDI-ATE;** -1 meaning the word is not **IMMEDIATE**.

The text interpreter uses a sequence like **BL WORD FIND** to find a word in the dictionary. The state-smart word **ASCII** can also be based on **WORD**.

```
: ASCII ( - n)
\ used in the form: ASCII c
\ where c follows in the input stream.
\ Returns the 7-bit ASCII code of c.
   BL WORD 1+ C@   ( read the next char)
   STATE @   ( ASCII is state-smart!)
   IF  [COMPILE] LITERAL  THEN ;  IMMEDIATE
```

WORD skips leading delimiters.

```
ASCII             A . 65
```

This can lead to some unfortunate situations. Consider, for example, this definition of **.(**:

```
: .(
\ reads and TYPEs text up to the next ")".
   ASCII ) ( delimiter) WORD COUNT TYPE ;*
```

* Assume we are using a state-smart **ASCII**. Otherwise, use **LITERAL** like this:

```
: (   [ ASCII ) ] LITERAL WORD COUNT TYPE ;
```

The following message prints correctly:

```
.( PRINT ME) PRINT ME
```

But when the message is empty, strange things may happen.

```
.( )( IGNORE ME) ( IGNORE ME
```

What happens? When the text interpreter reads the **.(**, it leaves the index in **>IN** pointing just past the blank delimiter to the next right parenthesis. When **.(** is executed, **WORD** treats this right parenthesis as a leading delimiter and ignores it. **WORD** then reads the input up to the next right parenthesis into a packed string—which .(then prints.

This problem often occurs in words which use **WORD** to read the input stream with a non-blank delimiter. Such words should be based on **PARSE** rather than on **WORD**.

```
: PARSE ( c - a)
\ works like WORD, but doesn't ignore
\ leading delimiters.
   SOURCE >IN @ /STRING
   >R C@ OVER =   ( peek at next char in input)
   R> 0> AND      ( does it equal delimiter?)
   IF  DROP 0 PAD !   ( build empty string)
     1 >IN +!  PAD EXIT THEN  WORD ;
```

Both **.(** and **(** can now be safely defined with **PARSE**.

```
:  (   \ reads and ignores text up to the next ")".
   ASCII ) ( delimiter) PARSE  DROP ;

: .(   \ reads and TYPEs text up to the next ")".
   ASCII ) ( delimiter) PARSE  COUNT TYPE ;
```

Conditional Compilation

Some applications may need to run in several different environments. For example, words which control a printer may need to change with each new printer. While it is possible to write one word which controls several printers, it is more efficient to write one word for each printer. Once a printer is selected, only the word controlling that printer should be compiled.

One approach you might take to implement selective or *conditional compilation* is to put definitions onto separate screens in a file. You can then write a word which tests a condition and compiles the appropriate screen. The word might contain a code sequence like this:

```
DUP 1 = IF  8 LOAD  ELSE
DUP 2 = IF  9 10 THRU  ELSE
( otherwise:) DROP  11 LOAD
THEN THEN
```

It would be nice if this sequence could appear in interpret mode. Unfortunately, the **IF—ELSE—THEN** construct is compile-only and must appear within the body of a definition. Therefore, you must invent a name and compile the code sequence into its definition. Furthermore, since the new definition will be **LOAD**ing the screens, it will precede any definitions on these screens in the dictionary and so cannot be *forgotten* after the **LOAD**.

Alternately, you can design a class of *smart comments* for conditional code. These comments normally act like ordinary comments—any code they contain is ignored. But under certain conditions, smart comments *disappear* and the code they contain is read and processed by the text interpreter.

```
VARIABLE CHOOSE  ( smart comment selector)

: (1
\ the lefthand side of smart comment class 1.
\ If CHOOSE isn't 1, the code in the comment is
\ ignored.
   CHOOSE @ 1 - IF  ASCII ) PARSE DROP  THEN  ;
  IMMEDIATE

: (2
\ the lefthand side of smart comment class 2.
   CHOOSE @ 2 - IF  ASCII ) PARSE DROP  THEN ;
  IMMEDIATE

: )   ;  IMMEDIATE
\ the righthand side of a smart comment.
```

The dummy definition of `)` is necessary because when a smart comment is selected, all words included in the comment will be processed by the text interpreter, including the trailing `)`. For this same reason, the `)` must be preceded and followed by at least one blank.

```
2 CHOOSE !

(1 : HI ." HELLO" ; ) (2 : HI ." BONJOUR" ; )
CR HI  BONJOUR
```

String Arrays

We can combine string and input stream operators to generate arrays of strings. String arrays can be constructed with **STRING**, which is based on **WORD**.

```
: STRING ( c )
\ read a string up to delimiter c
\ Compile it into the dictionary.
   WORD COUNT  SWAP OVER  HERE PLACE  1+ ALLOT ;*

CREATE ASTRING
ASCII " STRING This is a test."

ASTRING COUNT TYPE This is a test.
```

Now suppose we need a string array to name various colors.

```
: STRINGS ( n )
   0 DO  [ ASCII / ] LITERAL STRING  LOOP ;

CREATE COLORS
5 STRINGS WHITE/RED/GREEN/YELLOW/KIND OF BLUE/

: .COLOR ( n )
   COLORS SWAP  ?DUP
   IF  0 DO  COUNT +  LOOP  THEN
   COUNT TYPE SPACE ;

1 .COLOR RED
4 .COLOR KIND OF BLUE
```

* FORTHs that require *even* address alignment might add the phrase **HERE 1 AND ALLOT** to the end of this definition.

Traversing a string array is simplified by using `0 C,` to compile a null string at the beginning of each array. MacFORTH and other *aligned* FORTHs would use `0,` instead.

```
: STRINGS ( n )    0 C, ( null string)
   0 DO  [ ASCII / ] LITERAL STRING  LOOP ;

CREATE COLORS
5 STRINGS WHITE/RED/GREEN/YELLOW/KIND OF BLUE/

: .COLOR ( n )
   COLORS SWAP
   1+ 0 DO  COUNT +  LOOP
   COUNT TYPE SPACE ;

1 .COLOR RED
4 .COLOR KIND OF BLUE
```

Mass Storage

The word **BLOCK** reads a block into a memory buffer and returns the starting address of that buffer. **BLOCK**, in essence, is a 1024-byte window into a file. MacFORTH users: **BLOCK** is only present if the optional BlockSupport is loaded. **BLOCK**s can be used for data storage, but not for source code, so **LIST** and **LOAD** are not provided. Words like **LIST**, **LOAD**, and even the editor itself are based on **BLOCK** (or a word very much like it). You might expect the following sequence to copy screen 2 to screen 4:

```
2 BLOCK 4 BLOCK 1024 CMOVE
```

The **2 BLOCK** reads block 2 into a buffer in memory and returns its address. The **4 BLOCK** returns the buffer address of block 4. You now have the three arguments required by **CMOVE**.

Unfortunately, you have no control over which buffer is selected by **BLOCK**. It could happen that block 4 is read into the same buffer as block 2, in which case you copy block 4 to block 4, which is not what you meant. You can solve this problem by using a third intermediate buffer in memory.

```
2 BLOCK PAD 1024 CMOVE
PAD 4 BLOCK 1024 CMOVE
```

Here, **PAD** is used as the intermediate buffer. **PAD** is only guaranteed to be 84 characters long, but on most FORTHs, it is much larger. If **PAD** is smaller than 1024 bytes on your system, substitute a suitable memory array.

```
CREATE TEMP-BUF 1024 ALLOT
```

Once screen 2 has been copied, you must tell FORTH that block 4 has been changed and needs to be (eventually) rewritten to mass storage. You can do this with the word **UPDATE**. **UPDATE** marks the most recently read **BLOCK** as updated or changed. (If you were in the editor, it would automatically **UPDATE** a screen when you changed its contents.) The complete sequence for copying screen 2 to screen 4 is

```
2 BLOCK PAD 1024 CMOVE
PAD 4 BLOCK 1024 CMOVE UPDATE
```

Now that you know how to copy one screen to another, you could write a utility to copy a range of screens the same way.

The FORTH-83 Standard also provides the word **BUFFER** which, like **BLOCK**, selects an available buffer and returns its memory address. Unlike **BLOCK**, however, the block number is *assigned to* the buffer and is not necessarily read into it from mass storage. **BUFFER** is designed for operating systems that require you to write a block before reading it for the first time. You can initialize a block this way:

```
10 BUFFER  1024 BL FILL  UPDATE
```

Block 10 is created and is initialized to blanks.

Reading Blocks

You now have all the words you need to write the **INDEX** function. **INDEX** reads a range of screens and types out any line that begins in the leftmost column (column 0).

```
: INDEX ( n n2)
\ prints any line in blocks n through n2
\ that begins in column 0.
   1+ SWAP                ( read each block)
   DO I BLOCK  1024 0   ( read each line)
     DO  DUP I + C@ BL -   ( column 0 not blank?)
       IF  CR  DUP I + 64 TYPE  THEN
       64 ( next line is 64 bytes away)
    +LOOP  DROP
   LOOP ;
```

Virtual Arrays

In writing **INDEX**, we took advantage of the fact that screens are exact multiples of lines, that is, there are exactly 16 lines per screen. This means that no line starts on one block and *crosses over* into the next block. So if a screen is brought into memory with **BLOCK**, all the lines on that screen are in memory too.

The lines on a screen spend most of their time in mass storage, and are brought into memory on demand. You could say that they exist in a *virtual* memory. As such, they don't take up valuable main memory space. In FORTH, virtual memory arrays are easy to implement, provided that the array fits entirely within a block. Here is a defining word which creates virtual arrays 1024 bytes (512 cells) long:

```
: VIRTUAL-ARRAY
   CREATE  ( block# ) ,
   DOES>   ( - a)   @ BLOCK ;
```

Notice that no **ALLOT** is necessary. Before you create a virtual array, you must decide which block to use.

```
4 VIRTUAL-ARRAY HOLD-IT
```

Block 4 of the active file is assigned to **HOLD-IT**. Save a string in **HOLD-IT** this way:

```
SAMPLE
" TRUST ME" HOLD-IT PLACE  UPDATE
```

The **UPDATE** is necessary to ensure that **HOLD-IT** will be rewritten to mass storage when the file is closed.

```
FLUSH SAMPLE

CR HOLD-IT COUNT TYPE
TRUST ME
```

No **UPDATE** is necessary here, since you are only reading **HOLD-IT**. **UPDATE** can be included in the defining word **VIRTUAL-ARRAY** itself, right after **BLOCK**.

If you are just as likely to write to a virtual array as you are to read from it, include UPDATE in the defining word for the virtual array.

A Simple Data Base Manager

In a simple data base manager, information is saved to and retrieved from mass storage in units called *records*. A record is typically subdivided into *fields* of numbers and text. For example, in a mailing list program, the records are the addresses themselves and the fields are the name, street number, city, state, zip code, and so on.

If the record size is fixed (unvarying) and evenly divides a block (1024 bytes), then the block location of a record in a file can be found by multiplying the record number by the record size (in bytes) and then dividing the product by 1024. The remainder of this division is the byte offset of the record within the block. If the records begin on a block other than block 0, you will need to add a constant offset to the block location.

Once the block location and byte offset of a record are known, the record and all fields in it can be treated as virtual memory arrays. Here's how to find the starting address of a record:

```
  4 CONSTANT FIRST-BLOCK   ( records start here)
128 CONSTANT RECORD-SIZE   ( 8 records per block)
```

```
: RECORD ( n - a)
\ determine the starting address of a virtual
\ record.
   RECORD-SIZE *
   1024 /MOD  FIRST-BLOCK +   ( offset block#)
   BLOCK +  UPDATE ;
```

Given the starting address, you can find all other fields just by adding an appropriate offset. You can even create the defining word **FIELD** to do this for you.

```
VARIABLE RECORD#   ( number of current record)

: FIELD
\ return the address of a field in the current
\ record.  A field is defined by its offset in
\ the record.
   CREATE   ( record-offset ) ,
   DOES>    ( - a) @   RECORD# @ RECORD + ;

 0 FIELD NAME      ( 20-byte name field)
20 FIELD STREET    ( 30-byte street field)
50 FIELD ZIP       (  9-byte zip code field)
```

Using the string operators from the chapter on strings, you can write a word which prompts the user for name, address, and zip code and uses this information to initialize a record.

```
CREATE BUF  4 ALLOT  ( temporary buffer)

: SELECT-IT
\ select a record and makes it current.
   CR ." USE WHICH RECORD? "  BUF 4 BL FILL
   BUF 4 EXPECT    ( assume a valid number:)
   BUF SPAN @ VAL ( dn flag)
    2DROP ( includes D>S) RECORD# ! ;

: READ-IT ( a n )
\ read and pack a field.
   OVER 1+ SWAP 1- EXPECT
   DUP  1+ SPAN @ ROT PLACE ;
```

```
: FILE-IT
\ request and file name, address, and zip.
   SELECT-IT   ( choose a record)
   CR ."    NAME: "     NAME 20 READ-IT
   CR ." STREET: "   STREET 30 READ-IT
   CR ."     ZIP: "      ZIP  9 READ-IT ;
```

Finally, **PRINT-IT** let's you see what's in a record.

```
: PRINT-IT
\ print requested record.
   SELECT-IT   ( choose a record)
   CR ."    NAME: "     NAME COUNT TYPE
   CR ." STREET: "   STREET COUNT TYPE
   CR ."     ZIP: "      ZIP COUNT TYPE ;
```

Word	Stack	Action
BLK	- a	Variable which selects a block number for input. If **BLK** is zero, input is taken from the terminal input buffer.
>IN	- a	Variable which contains the current offset of the input stream.
BLOCK	n - a	Reads block n from the active file into a memory buffer and returns the address of that buffer.
BUFFER	n - a	Assigns block n to a memory buffer and returns the address of that buffer. Block n may not be read from the active file into that buffer.
UPDATE		Marks the most recently read block for eventual rewriting to mass storage.

Exercises

1. Define a state-smart word **CONTROL** which, like **ASCII**, reads the character that follows it in the input stream, converting it to the appropriate control character.

   ```
   HEX CONTROL X . 18
   ```

2. Define the word **SLICES<** which reads the input stream to the delimiter ">" and prints each word on its own line.

```
SLICES< This is a test.>
This
is
a
test.
```

3. Write a version of **RECORD** which reads records into a memory buffer that you provide. The records can be any size less than 1024 bytes, but all records must be the same size. This means that a record can start on one block and end on another. By reading the record into a memory buffer, you are then able to access the fields with **CMOVE**. The syntax of the new **RECORD** is as follows:

```
RECORD ( record# buffer-address )
```

4. Modify the simple mailing list program to include city and state fields. Change **ZIP** from a 9-byte text field to a 4-byte double-number field. You will also need to modify **PRINT-IT** to print the new information.

5. Write a word to define an execution vector. Anything between **X[** and **]X** is compiled as a token or address for a later **EXECUTE**. Hint: define **]X** then use **X[** to compile tokens or addresses until you see a reference to **]X**.

```
: 1Thing   ." Thing 1 " ;
: 2Thing   ." Thing 2 " ;
: 3Thing   ." Thing 3 " ;

CREATE THINGS   3 X[ 1Thing 2Thing 3Thing ]X

: ACTION ( n )   1- CELLS THINGS + @ EXECUTE ;

1 ACTION Thing 1
3 ACTION Thing 3
```

14 Fixed and Floating Point Math

Bit Manipulation

The logical operators **AND** and **OR** presented in the chapter on flow of control are *bitwise* operators. This means they examine each pair of bits in the two operands independently. For example, suppose you **OR** two binary numbers together.

	0001001000110100	(hex `1234`)
OR	1010101111001101	(hex `ABCD`)
	1011101111111101	(hex `BBFD`)

Each bit in the answer is set to one if *either* of the two bits above it is set.

What if you **AND** the numbers 2 and 4?

	0000000000000010	(2)
AND	0000000000000100	(4)
	0000000000000000	(0)

Each bit in the answer is set to one if *both* of the two bits above it is set. In this case, all bits in the result are zero. If you were using 2 and 4 as boolean flags, you would get the surprising result that *true* **AND** *true* is *false*. To prevent situations like this, be sure that at least one of the flags is boolean, since boolean flags are either all zeroes (0) or all ones (–1).

You can use logical operators to manipulate bits within a number. They can be used to

- set a bit (to one);
- reset a bit (to zero);
- detect whether a bit is set or not;
- reverse a bit.

To set a bit, you can **OR** it with a one in the appropriate position. You can clear a bit by **AND**ing it with zero. We will number bits from right to left, starting with zero. If you want to set bit 3 of a number, you could **OR** it with binary 0000000000001000 (8).

	0001001000110100	(hex 1234)
OR	0000000000001000	(hex 0008)
	0001001000111100	(hex 123C)

You could clear it again with (hex) FFF7 **AND**.

	0001001000111100	(hex 123C)
AND	1111111111110111	(hex 7FFF)
	0001001000110100	(hex 1234)

To see whether bit 3 is set, **AND** it with 0000000000001000 (8).

	????????????????	
AND	0000000000001000	(8)
	000000000000?000	

If bit 3 is one, the result will be *true* (8); otherwise it will be *false* (0). The other bits are ignored or *masked out*.

Bits can be selectively reversed with the **XOR** ("x-or") *exclusive-OR* logical function. An exclusive-OR of two bits is one if either of the two bits (but not both) is one. In other words, if one of the two bits is set, the other will be reversed.

	1010101010101010	(hex AAAA)
XOR	1111111111111111	(hex FFFF or -1)
	0101010101010101	(hex 5555)

In some FORTHS (MasterFORTH, UR/FORTH, L&P F83, and other FORTH-83 Standard FORTHS), **NOT** is a bitwise operator, equivalent to **-1 XOR**; in others (PolyFORTH and MacFORTH), it is a logical operator, equivalent to **0=**.

Fixed-point Fractions

Numbers like 10.125 and .003 are called *fixed-point* numbers if the number of digits to the right of the decimal (or binary) point in their internal representation is fixed. Numbers like 6.0225×10^{23} (or its alternate representation 6.0225E23) are called *floating-point* numbers if their internal representation is in two parts: a fixed point number multiplied by a separate *exponent*. The exponent is usually a power 2 but is converted to a power of 10 for input and display. In floating-point representation, the number of accurate digits is fixed, but the decimal or binary point appears to *float* and can appear anywhere in the number.

FORTH programmers generally prefer fixed-point to floating-point math. For any given number size, fixed-point math is faster and more accurate than floating point but lacks its convenience and larger dynamic range. Real-time applications that read transducers and write to D/A converters or stepper motor controllers usually have well-understood algorithms of limited dynamic range. PID controllers, digital filters, and computer graphics are especially amenable to fixed-point solutions.

A common FORTH approach to implementing fixed-point numbers is to combine signed 16-bit integer math with signed 14-bit fractional fixed-point math. A 14-bit fraction is a signed 16-bit number with the binary point two positions from the left:

```
s#.## #### #### ####
```

where **s** is the sign bit and each **#** is a binary digit.

Binary	Hex	Decimal
01.00 0000 0000 0000	4000	1.0000
11.00 0000 0000 0000	C000	-1.0000
00.10 0000 0000 0000	2000	0.5000
00.01 0101 0101 0101	1555	0.3333

Fourteen-bit fractions have several charming properties:

- They can be added to each other with no adjustment.
- They can be multiplied by an integer with no adjustment.
- They can be multiplied together and adjusted with two left shifts.
- They can exactly represent +1 and -1, which is especially useful when working with sines and cosines.

To experiment with 14-bit fractional math, we need some way to enter fractions and some way to print them. Printing them is easy—just multiply them by 10000 to convert them to integers and print them with exactly four digits to the right of the decimal point. When you multiply a 14-bit fraction by an integer, you must shift the result left twice.

```
: FN* ( fn fn2 - fn3)†    *  2* 2* ;     \ Wrong!
```

This definition of **FN*** multiplies the two fractions with *****. Unfortunately, ***** discards the *leftmost* half of the double-number product, where all the precision is. Extra precision is preserved by using ***/** instead.

```
HEX      4000 CONSTANT ONE
         1555 CONSTANT 1/3   DECIMAL
: FN* ( fn fn2 - fn3)   ONE */ ;    \ Better.
```

Instead of multiplying the product by four, we are effectively dividing it by one quarter.

† Here we are using **fn** to mean *14-bit fraction*.

Many FORTHs support mixed-precision multiplication, called **M***, which multiplies two signed single-precision numbers to give a signed double-precision result. If **M*** and **D2*** are available, an alternate definition for **FN*** which uses multiplication only is

```
: FN* ( fn fn2 - fn3)   M*  D2* D2*  SWAP DROP ;
```

Now we are ready to print fractions.

```
: FN. ( fn )   \ print a 14-bit fraction.
      10000 FN*  DUP ABS 0
      <# # # # # [ ASCII . ] LITERAL HOLD # ROT SIGN #>
      TYPE SPACE ;
```

```
ONE FN. 1.0000
1/3 FN. 0.3333
```

To enter a fraction, follow the decimal point with exactly four digits.

```
1.2345
```

In most FORTHs, this will leave a double-precision 12345 on the stack. Assuming this is so, convert the number by *dividing* it by 10000 and then shift it twice to the right.

```
: FN/ ( fn fn2 - fn3)   ONE SWAP */ ;
: D>FN ( d - fn)   DROP  10000 FN/ ;
1.2345 D>FN FN. 1.2344
```

Some precision is unavoidably lost in the conversion, but the result is still accurate to about four decimal digits.

Fractions can be manipulated with **DUP** and **DROP**, and added and subtracted with **+** and **-** as usual.

```
1/3 1/3  2DUP + FN.  FN* FN. 0.6666 0.1110
```

Higher functions can be implemented with polynomial approximations, such as those found in *Computer Approximations*, by Hart et al (Fla: Krieger Publ,

1978). According to Hart, the cosine of an angle in radians between 0 an $\pi x/4$ is given to 7 digits by a third degree polynomial (#3820) of **x²**.

```
-.0003x⁶ + .0158x⁴ - .3084x² + 1
```

This can be implemented most quickly using Horner's method.

```
: FNCOS ( fn - fn2)    \ Hart 3820  COS of πfn/4
      DUP FN* ( x^2)
      [ -.0003 D>FN ] LITERAL    OVER FN*
      [  .0158 D>FN ] LITERAL +  OVER FN*
      [ -.3084 D>FN ] LITERAL +       FN* ONE + ;

ONE FNCOS FN. 0.7070
```

The correct answer is 0.7071. **FNCOS** is actually restricted to **x** between 0 and $\sqrt{2}$ (approximately 1.4142); otherwise the term **x²** overflows. Angles outside the permitted range can be easily transformed or *folded* to lie within the range. We will shortly explore one such technique. Polynomials are readily available for other trigonometric functions, logarithms, exponentials, power functions, and square and cube roots.

Mixed-precision Arithmetic

Unfortunately, neither single integers nor 14-bit fractions can represent handy numbers such as 3.1415... For both efficiency and convenience, you can use a *mixed-point* format which consists of a single number fraction and signed single integer, *with the integer on top of the stack*. Assume for the moment that single numbers are 16-bits wide.

```
s### #### #### #### . #### #### #### ####
```

Binary	Hex	Decimal
0000 0000 0000 0001 . 0000 0000 0000 0000	1.0000	1.00000
0000 0000 0000 0001 . 1000 0000 0000 0000	1.8000	1.50000
0000 0000 0000 0011 . 0010 0100 0011 1111	3.243F	3.14159

When we multiply and divide numbers in this format, we will need mixed-precision operators such as the **M*** we mentioned above. Many of these operators are probably already available in your FORTH. The easiest way to find out is to ' ("tick") them. If ' can't find a word, use the appropriate high-level definition provided below.

```
: D2* ( d - 2d)   2DUP D+ ;

: DU< ( ud1 ud2 - f )
   ROT SWAP 2DUP U<
   IF  2DROP 2DROP TRUE
   ELSE - IF  2DROP 0  ELSE U< THEN  THEN ;

: M+ ( d n - d2)   DUP 0< D+ ;
\ sign-extend n and add it to d.

: D+- ( ufn n - fn)   0< IF  DNEGATE  THEN ;
\ apply sign of n to ud.

: M* ( n n2 - d)
\ multiply n by n2 giving signed product d.
   2DUP XOR >R  ABS SWAP ABS  UM*  R> D+- ;

: M/ ( d n - n2)
\ divide d by n giving single quotient n2.
\ All are signed.
   2DUP XOR >R  ABS >R DABS R> UM/MOD  SWAP DROP
   R> 0< IF  NEGATE  THEN ;

: D* ( d d2 - d3 )
\ multiply two signed double numbers to give
\ a double product.
   ROT  2DUP XOR >R  ROT ROT  DABS 2SWAP DABS
   ROT  SWAP  >R >R  2DUP UM*
   2SWAP  R> UM* DROP  SWAP  R> UM* DROP  + +   R> D+- ;

2VARIABLE DENOM  \ holds denominator— simplifies stack.

: Q2* ( qn - qn2)
\ shift quad-precision q left once.
   2SWAP DUP >R  D2*  2SWAP  D2*  R> 0< NEGATE M+ ;
```

```
: D/MOD ( dn dn2 - dn-rem dn-quot )
\ divide two double numbers.
\ All numbers are signed doubles.
   2 PICK OVER XOR >R  DABS 2SWAP DABS 2SWAP
   DENOM 2!  0 0  32 0
   DO  DUP >R ( save hi bit)  ( Q2* >= DENOM?)
     Q2*  2DUP DENOM 2@ DU< NOT  R> 0< OR
     IF  DENOM 2@ D-  2SWAP  1 M+  2SWAP  THEN
   LOOP  2SWAP  R> D+- ;
```

The next set of words employ both double and triple-precision numbers. They are used to construct **M*/**.

```
: UT/D ( utn ud2 - ud-quot)
\ used by >F for input conversion.
   DENOM 2!  0  32 0
   DO  DUP >R ( save hi bit)  ( Q2* >= DENOM?)
     Q2*  2DUP DENOM 2@ DU< NOT  R> 0< OR
     IF  DENOM 2@ D-  2SWAP  1 M+  2SWAP  THEN
   LOOP  2DROP ;

: U2/ ( u - u/2)   2/ 32767 AND ;

: UT* ( ud u - ut)
   >R  SWAP R@ UM*  ROT R> UM*  ROT M+ ;

: UT/MOD ( ut u - urem udquot)
   DUP >R  UM/MOD  ROT ROT  R> UM/MOD  ROT ;
```

The **M*/** operator is the double-precision equivalent of ***/**. It is used to scale a double number by a ratio of two single numbers.

```
: M*/  ( d n n2 - d*n/n2 )
\ the infamous M*/
   ABS >R  DUP ABS >R  OVER XOR ( sign )
   ROT ROT  DABS R> UT*  R> UT/MOD
   ROT ( rem ) DROP  ROT D+- ;

123456. 1 3 M*/ D. 41152
```

Mixed-precision Aliases

Mixed-precision fractions, with the binary point between the signed single-precision integer and the single-precision fraction, can be manipulated with **2DUP** and **2DROP** and added and subtracted with **D+** and **D-**. However, it is to our advantage to hide the precision of these operators by calling them **FDUP, FDROP, F+**, and **F-**, respectively. This lets us increase the fixed-point precision or even change to floating-point numbers without changing the source code.

The easiest way to substitute **FDUP** for **2DUP** is to define it this way:

```
: FDUP   2DUP ;
```

If **FDUP** is implemented this way, however, it will be much slower than **2DUP**. To increase the performance of **FDUP**, we can *alias* it to be **2DUP**.

```
: FDUP   COMPILE 2DUP ;  IMMEDIATE
```

If you don't understand what's happening here, you may wish to review the chapter on compiling words. This definition of **FDUP** will work only inside a definition. A better *state-smart* version will work either inside or outside a definition.

```
: FDUP   STATE @ IF  COMPILE 2DUP  ELSE  2DUP  THEN ;
  IMMEDIATE
```

Since we have several aliases to make, let's create a defining word called **ALIAS**.

```
: ALIAS
\ alias two definitions.
\ The second will act like the first.
   CREATE  ' ,  IMMEDIATE
   DOES> STATE @ IF  @ ,  ELSE  @ EXECUTE  THEN ;

ALIAS F+   D+       ALIAS F-   D-       ALIAS F2*  D2*
ALIAS FU<  DU<      ALIAS F<   D<       ALIAS F2/  D2/

ALIAS FABS DABS     ALIAS FMAX DMAX     ALIAS FMIN DMIN
ALIAS F=   D=       ALIAS F0=  D0=
```

```
ALIAS FNEGATE DNEGATE

ALIAS FDUP  2DUP     ALIAS FSWAP 2SWAP
ALIAS FDROP 2DROP    ALIAS FOVER 2OVER   ALIAS FROT  2ROT

ALIAS F@ 2@          ALIAS F! 2!

: F0<  SWAP DROP 0< ;

: FVARIABLE   2VARIABLE ;

: FCONSTANT   2CONSTANT ;

: FLITERAL   [COMPILE] DLITERAL ;   IMMEDIATE
```

We will also need a constant to tell us how many bytes of memory a mixed-point number occupies. Assume for now that single-precision numbers occupy 2 bytes.

```
4 CONSTANT F#BYTES    \ bytes/mixed-fraction.
```

Mixed-precision Fractions

Mixed-point multiply and divide are not simple aliases of existing operators. Possible definitions for them are given below. Here we are using **r** to mean *real* or *floating-point number*. A properly aliased set of mixed-point operators is indistinguishable from floating operators.

```
: F* ( r r2 - r3)    \ mixed-point multiply
   ROT  2DUP XOR >R  ROT ROT FABS FSWAP FABS
   ROT  2DUP UM*  DROP >R  2OVER UM*  >R >R
   ROT UM*  2SWAP UM* D+  R> ROT ROT  R> R> D+
   ROT 0< NEGATE M+ ( rounds )  R> D+- ;

: F/ ( f f2 - fn-quot )   \ mixed-point divide
   2 PICK OVER XOR >R  FABS DENOM F!
   FABS 0  ROT ROT 0  33 0
   DO  DUP >R ( save hi bit)  ( Q2* >= DENOM?)
     Q2*  FDUP DENOM F@ FU< NOT  R> 0< OR
     IF  DENOM F@ F-  2SWAP  1 M+  2SWAP  THEN
   LOOP  FDROP  1 M+ DUP 0< M+ D2/ ( rounds )
   R> D+- ;
```

Now that we can add, subtract, multiply, and divide mixed-point fractions, we can implement routines to enter and display them.

```
: [NIP] ( n n2 - n2)    \ more practice with aliasing.
   COMPILE SWAP COMPILE DROP ;  IMMEDIATE

: F. ( r )    \ print a mixed-point fraction.
   DUP >R  FABS  SWAP 10000 UM* [NIP]  0
   <# # # # #  ASCII . HOLD  [NIP]  #S  R> SIGN  #>
   TYPE SPACE ;

: F? ( a )   F@ F. ;

CREATE TENS
1. , , 10. , , 100. , , 1000. , , 10000. , , 100000. , ,

: >F ( d - r)
\ converts most recent double number to mixed fraction.
\ Used like  3.14159 >F
   DPL @  0< ABORT" Needs decimal point"
   DPL @ 5 > ABORT" Use 0->5 digits after decimal"
   DUP >R  DABS  0 ROT ROT
   DPL @ 2* CELLS TENS + 2@  UT/D R> D+- ;
```

Here are some examples of their use:

```
3.14159 >F FCONSTANT PI

PI F. 3.1415

2.0 >F F. 2.0000
0 2 F. 2.0000

: CIRCUM ( r - r2)    [ PI 0 2 F* ] FLITERAL  F* ;
\ calculates circumference of a circle given radius r.

100. >F CIRCUM F. 628.3172

\ Useful constants

3.14159 >F FCONSTANT PI
1.57079 >F FCONSTANT PI/2
0.78540 >F FCONSTANT PI/4
0.31831 >F FCONSTANT 1/PI

0.69315 >F FCONSTANT LN(2)
0.30103 >F FCONSTANT LOG(2)
1.44270 >F FCONSTANT 1/LN(2)
3.32193 >F FCONSTANT 1/LOG(2)
```

```
2.71828 >F FCONSTANT E#
```

Finally, lets look at mixed-point functions for calculating sines and cosines. First, we will use another polynomial approximation from Hart, this time for the sine of π**x**/4.

```
: FNSIN ( fn - fn2)    \ Hart 3040  SINE of πfn/4
   DUP  DUP FN* ( x^2)
   [   .0025 D>FN ] LITERAL    OVER FN*
   [ -.0807 D>FN ] LITERAL +        FN*
   [   .7854 D>FN ] LITERAL +        FN* ;
```

```
ONE FNSIN FN. 0.7070
```

FNSIN operates on 14-bit signed fractions in the range of 0 to π/4. What we need now is a way to take a mixed-fraction, map it into this range, find the sine or cosine, and translate the result back to a mixed fraction. Bear in mind that **FNCOS** and **FNSIN**, our two primitives, operate on π**x**/4 and not on **x** itself. For this reason, a good first step would be to multiply the angle, which we assume to be in radians, by 4/π.

```
1.27324 >F FCONSTANT 4/PI
```

```
PI/4 4/PI F* F. 0.9999
```

Of course, if the result is one, then the angle is π/4. More important, if the angle is less than π/4, then the result will lie in the proper range for **FNSIN** or **FNCOS**. If the angle is equal to or greater than π/4, then we need to place the angle in one of eight possible divisions or *octants* of a circle and express it as an octant number and a remainder.

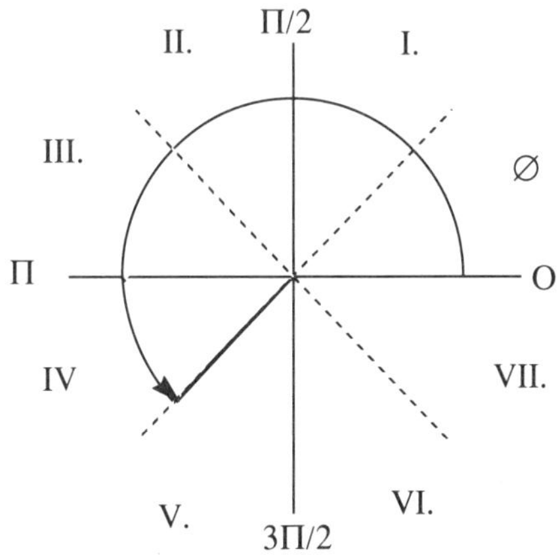

The remainder will lie within the range of 0 to π/4, which is what we want. If the angle lies outside of octant number 0, we will use trigonometric identities to bring it back into this range.

```
: /OCTANT ( r - fn octant)
\ transform angle r into smaller angle fn and
\ integer octant number.
   DUP ( sign) >R  FABS  8 MOD ( octant) >R
   0 D2/ 1 M+ ( rounds) D2/ DROP  R>
   R> 0< IF  >R  1 SWAP -  7 R> -  THEN ;

0.39270 >F FCONSTANT PI/8

PI PI/8 F+ FCONSTANT 9PI/8

9PI/8 4/PI F* /OCTANT . FN. 4 0.5000
```

After multiplying by 4/π, the phrase **8 MOD** determines the octant. The next **0** restores the integer part of the mixed fraction and **D2/ 1 M+ D2/ DROP** converts it to a positive 14-bit fraction. The remainder of the definition maps negative angles into positive angles. As you can see, an angle of one and one eighth π is in octant 4, plus one half an octant more.

```
CREATE SINES
' FNSIN , ' FNCOS , ' FNCOS , ' FNSIN ,
' FNSIN , ' FNCOS , ' FNCOS , ' FNSIN ,

: SINE ( fn octant - r)
   DUP >R  1 AND IF  1 SWAP -  THEN
   R@ CELLS SINES + @ EXECUTE
   DUP 0< D2* D2* ( fn - r)
   R> 4 AND IF  FNEGATE  THEN ;

: FSIN ( r - r2)
   4/PI F* /OCTANT SINE ;

: FCOS ( r - r2)
   4/PI F* /OCTANT  2+ 7 AND SINE ;

PI/8 FSIN F. 0.3826
PI/8 FCOS F. 0.9238
```

In **SINE**, we use the trigonometric identity

```
sin(x) = cos(π/4 - x)
```

where **1 SWAP -** is equivalent to π/4 - **x**. In **FCOS**, we use the identity

```
cos(x) = sin(π/2 + x)
```

where adding 2 to the octant is equivalent to adding π/2 to the angle.

Floating-point Numbers

Conservative FORTH programmers disdain floating-point for higher-performance fixed-point arithmetic. "If you need to use floating-point arithmetic," they say, "then you don't understand the problem." Nevertheless, virtually all major FORTH vendors offer a floating-point package. Most of these extensions closely follow the hardware or firmware floating-point support on the host system, such as the 8087 co-processor or the Macintosh SANE interface. Software-only floating-point implementations usually follow the guidelines in *The FVG Standard Floating-Point Extension* by Duncan and Tracy (*Dr. Dobbs Journal* Sep. 1984).

Virtually all floating-point (FP) extensions provide the four functions **F+ F- F*** and **F/**. Most packages keep FP numbers on a separate FP stack. Hardware implementations use the separate FP stack provided by the hardware. Software FP packages achieve better performance if FP numbers are kept on the normal data stack. It is possible to make the separate FP stack a compilable option. Imagine a definition of **F+** in a software FP system.

```
: F+   [FPOP]  ( ...add numbers here...)  [FPUSH] ;
```

If FP numbers are kept on a separate stack, **[FPOP]** would pop an FP number from that stack and push it on the data stack. **[FPUSH]** would have the reverse action. For greater speed, you could redefine **[FPOP]** and **[FPUSH]** to do nothing before compiling the FP extension.

```
: [FPOP]   ;  IMMEDIATE
: [FPUSH]   ;  IMMEDIATE
```

The existence of a separate FP stack implies the existence of FP stack operators such as **FDUP FDROP FSWAP FOVER** and **FROT**. In most packages, **F@** and

F! move FP numbers to and from **FVARIABLE**s, and **FCONSTANT**s such as **PI** aid readability. FP numbers can be compared with **F<** and **F>**. **F=** may be provided, but comparing floating-point numbers for equality is a questionable practice and should be avoided. It is meaningful, however, to compare an FP number to zero with **F0=** or **F0<**. **FABS FNEGATE FMAX** and **FMIN** are usually also provided.

The method of inputting a real number varies from FORTH to FORTH. Most FORTHS install some kind of automatic conversion when the FP extension is compiled. The usual conversion rule is that real numbers must contain an uppercase E, particularly in MasterFORTH, UR/FORTH, MacFORTH, and all derivatives of the FVG Standard.

2E or **2.E** or **2.0E** or **2E0** etc.*

You must be in **DECIMAL** or strange things happen.

To print a real number, use **F.** , but first set the number of places to the right of the decimal with **PLACES**.†

```
4 PLACES
3.14159E F. 3.1416
```

Now let's see what's involved in writing a floating-point package, in case you would like to experiment with one. First, we need a proper floating-point representation. The most efficient representation for FORTH seems to be a normalized double-precision signed mantissa and a single-precision signed exponent, with the exponent on top.

* **PolyFORTH** numbers containing a period and followed by at least one non-blank character are converted to floating point when the floating-point extension is compiled. For example,

`2.0` Would be a *real* 2 while

`2.` Would be a *double-precision* 2.

† **PolyFORTH**'s **F.** is an exception to this rule, and takes the number of places from the stack. If you would like compatibility with the FVG standard, redefine **F.** this way:

```
VARIABLE Places
: PLACES ( n )   Places ! ;
: F. ( r )   Places @ F. ;
```

s.1### #### #### #### #### #### #### ####	normalized mantissa
s### #### #### ####	exponent as a power of 2.

where s is the sign bit and each # is a binary digit. The high-order bit of the mantissa is the sign bit. The remaining bits form an unsigned normalized mantissa, with the second highest bit set to one. The binary point is to the left of this bit. This gives the mantissa 31 bits, or about nine digits of precision, and an exponent with an unheard of dynamic range.

Hex Mantissa	Exponent	Decimal Real	
40000000.	1	1.E	
C0000000.	2	-2.E	
40000000.	0	.5E	
70000000.	-1	.875E	or 1.75E-1
0.	0	0	

To multiply and divide double-precision mantissas, we are going to need a few more math operators.

```
: DU2/ ( d - d2)
   D2/  [ HEX ] 7FFF [ DECIMAL ] AND ;

: T+ ( tA tB - tC)
\ add two triple numbers.
   >R  ROT >R  ROT SWAP >R >R
   0 SWAP 0 D+  0 R> 0 D+  R> 0 D+  R> R> + + ;

: TU2/ ( t - ut)
\ shift triple number right unsigned.
   0 SWAP DU2/  >R >R  DU2/  R> + R> ;

2VARIABLE MULTIPLIER

: DUM* ( ud1 ud2 - uqproduct)
```

```
\ multiply unsigned double numbers to unsigned quad result.
   MULTIPLIER 2!  0 0 ( accumulator) 2SWAP   32 0
   DO  DUP ( pseudo-carry) >R Q2* R>  0< ( carry set?)
     IF  >R  MULTIPLIER 2@ 0 T+  R>  THEN
   LOOP ;

: QUM/ ( uq ud - udquotient)
\ divide unsigned quad uq by unsigned dividend ud.
   DENOM 2!  32 0
   DO  DUP >R ( save hi bit)  ( Q2* >= DENOM?)
     Q2*  2DUP DENOM 2@ DU< NOT  R> 0< OR
     IF  DENOM 2@ D-  2SWAP  1 0 D+  2SWAP  THEN
   LOOP  2DROP ;

: DUM*/ ( ud ud2 ud3 - ud4)   >R >R DUM*  R> R> QUM/ ;
\ (ud * ud2)/ud3  with quad-precision intermediate.
```

Writing the various stack manipulation and memory access words is also straightforward.

```
: FDUP     DUP 2OVER ROT ;

: FDROP    2DROP DROP ;

: FSWAP    >R ROT >R  2SWAP  R> R> SWAP 2SWAP ROT ;

: FOVER    >R >R >R  FDUP   R> R> R>  FSWAP ;

: FROT     >R >R >R  FSWAP  R> R> R>  FSWAP ;

: F@    DUP 2+ 2@  ROT @ ;

: F!    SWAP OVER !  2+ 2! ;

: F,   , , ,   ;

: FCONSTANT  CREATE  F,  DOES>  DUP 2+ 2@  ROT @ ;

: FVARIABLE  CREATE  0 0 0  F, ;

: FLITERAL   ROT ROT [COMPILE] DLITERAL [COMPILE] LITERAL ;
  IMMEDIATE
```

Rather than support a fancy system of infinities and other *not-a-numbers*, the only special case we will handle is zero. A zero number will have a zero mantissa, which can be easily tested with the expression **OVER 0=**.

```
: f0= ( r - r f)   OVER 0= ;
```

```
: F0= ( r - f)   ROT 2DROP 0= ;
```

Changing the sign of the mantissa is easy, but we must not change the sign of zero.

```
HEX 8000 DECIMAL CONSTANT -MAX#*

: FNEGATE ( r - r2)
\ 2's complement of r
   OVER IF  >R -MAX# XOR R>  THEN ;

: FABS ( r - r2)
\ absolute value of r.
   >R  -MAX# 1- AND  R> ;
```

Packing and unpacking the sign bit from the mantissa is also easy.

```
: UNPACK ( d - ud sign)   DUP FABS ;

: PACK ( ud sign - d)   -MAX# AND OR ;
```

Probably the simplest function to implement is `F*` since exponents add and mantissas multiply. We do, however, need some way to normalize and round the quad-precision result.

```
: QNORM ( q - t exp)
\ normalize q to bit 30; leave adjustment as exp.
   2DUP OR 2OVER OR OR ( any non-zero bit?)
   IF  1 ( count) >R
      BEGIN  DUP 0< NOT
      WHILE  Q2*  R> 1- >R  REPEAT
      >R >R  SWAP DROP  R> R>  TU2/  R>
   THEN ;

: ROUND ( t - ud exp )
\ assumes hi bit is zero.
   -MAX# 0 0 T+  ROT DROP
   DUP 0< DUP IF  >R  DU2/ R>  THEN ;

: F* ( r r2 - r3)
```

* For 32-bit FORTHS, change 8000 to 80000000.

```
   f0= IF  FSWAP  THEN
   FOVER F0= IF  FDROP EXIT  THEN
   ( exp2 ) >R  ROT ( exp ) >R
   UNPACK >R  2SWAP UNPACK >R  DUM*
   QNORM ( t exp ) >R
   ROUND ( d exp ) R> + ROT ROT
   R> R> XOR PACK  ROT R> R> + +  1+ ;
```

The other arithmetic primitives **F+ F-** and **F/** follow a similar pattern.

```
: DNORM ( d - t exp)
\ normalize d to bit 30, leaving adjustment as exp.
   2DUP D0= IF  0 0 EXIT  THEN
   1 ( exp) >R
   BEGIN  DUP 0< NOT WHILE  D2*  R> 1- >R  REPEAT
   0 ROT ROT  TU2/  R> ;

: -NORM ( ud n - ut)
\ denormalize ud by n bits.
   32 MIN >R  0 ROT ROT
   R> ?DUP IF  0 DO  TU2/  LOOP  THEN ;

: F+ ( r r2 - r3)
   FOVER F0= IF  FSWAP  THEN
   f0= IF  FDROP EXIT  THEN ( exp2 ) >R
   ROT R@ - ( del = exp - exp2)  DUP 0< ( r2 > r?)
   IF  NEGATE ( del) >R  UNPACK >R  2SWAP UNPACK
     R> R> ROT OVER  ( signs) XOR SWAP >R >R
   ELSE  DUP R> + >R >R  UNPACK >R  2SWAP UNPACK >R
     2SWAP R> R> R> SWAP ROT DUP >R ( signs)
     XOR >R  ( R: exp sign xor) THEN
   -NORM ( t )  ROUND ( d exp )
   R> SWAP >R  0< IF  D-  ELSE  D+  THEN
   DNORM ( t exp ) >R  ROUND ( d exp ) R> R> + +
   R> SWAP >R  PACK  R> R> + ;

: F- ( r r2 - r3)  FNEGATE F+ ;

: F/ ( r r2 - r3)
   f0= ABORT" Zero divide"
   FOVER F0= IF  FDROP EXIT  THEN
   ( exp2) >R  ROT ( exp) >R
   0 0 2ROT UNPACK >R  2ROT UNPACK >R  D2*  QUM/
   DNORM ( t exp) >R  ROUND ( d exp)
   R> + ROT ROT  R> R> XOR PACK  ROT R> R> SWAP - + ;
```

For a simple four-function package, we lack only the primitives for input and output.

```
: D>SHIFT ( d u - d2)
\ double shift d u bits to the right arithmetically.
   0 MAX  ?DUP IF  0 DO  D2/  LOOP THEN ;

: F. ( r )
   OVER >R  FABS  DUP 0>
   IF  0 0 ROT  0
     DO  Q2*  LOOP  Q2*  999999999. DMIN
         2SWAP  DU2/
   ELSE  NEGATE D>SHIFT  0 0 2SWAP  THEN
   500000000. 1073741824. DUM*/
   <# # # # # # # # # #
   [ ASCII . ] LITERAL HOLD  2DROP
   #S R> 0< SIGN #> TYPE SPACE ;

: FLOAT ( d - r)
   2DUP D0= IF  0 EXIT  THEN
   SWAP OVER  DABS  1 ( count) >R
   BEGIN  DUP 0< NOT WHILE  D2*  R> 1- >R  REPEAT
   DU2/  ROT PACK  R> 31 + ;

: >F ( d - r)
\ convert most recent double number to real.
\ Used like  3.14159 >F
   DPL @  0< ABORT" Needs decimal point"     FLOAT
   DPL @ ?DUP
   IF  1 0 ROT  0 DO  10 0 DUM* 2DROP  LOOP  FLOAT F/  THEN
;

3.14159 >F F. 3.141589999

3.14159 >F FCONSTANT PI

PI PI F* F. 9.869587719
```

>F converts a double to a real number, and **F.** prints it. This simple version of **F.** clips the real number to only a part of its dynamic range, limiting it to 999999999. Numbers less than .000000001 are printed as zero. A more sophisticated version would use logarithms to change the number from a power of 2 to a power of ten before printing.

Exercises

1. The exclusive-OR function **XOR** can be built from **AND** and **OR** according to the following formula:

   ```
   A XOR B = (((A AND (NOT B)) OR ((B AND (NOT A)))
   ```

   where **A** and **B** are the arguments and **NOT** is the bitwise operator. Define **NOT** using **XOR**, then define **XOR** using **AND OR** and **NOT**. Test your function.

2. According to HART (#2521), the logarithm of a number to the base two can be approximated to four digits of accuracy with the ratio of two polynomials

   $$\frac{.5020x^2 + .9514x - 1.4533}{x + .3521}$$

   where $.5 \le x < 1$. Add the function **FNLOG2 (fn - fn2)** to the 14-bit fraction operators. Test your result with .5, .75, and **ONE**.

3. Numbers which are smaller than .5 or larger than 1 can be normalized to a 14-bit fraction and an integer exponent power of 2. The fraction should lie within the range $.5 \le \text{fn} < 1$, that is, bit 14 should be clear and bit 13 set. Write the word **FNORM (r - fn exp)** to reduce a mixed-point number to this range. Ignore negative numbers for now.

4. Using **FNORM**, write the word **FLOG2 (r - r2)** which finds the logarithm of base two of its mixed-point argument. The logarithm of a normalized fraction and exponent is calculated by taking the logarithm of the fraction and adding it to the exponent. The logarithm of zero should return exactly one. The logarithm of a negative number is meaningless—return an answer of zero.

5. The 8087 floating-point coprocessor *long real* is a 64-bit format.

sign |	exponent |		mantissa ... |	
63	62	52	51	0

The exponent is biased by 1023, that is, an exponent of one would appear in the number as 1024. The bias is used as the the sign of the exponent. The sign of the long real is actually the sign of the mantissa. Assume that in an 8087 floating-point package running on a 16-bit FORTH, the long real would appear on the data stack as four items in decreasing significance, with the *least* significant on top. Write the word **`XFORM ( n n2 n3 n4 - r)`** to unpack an 8087 long real and repack it as a software floating-point real number. Use the following test cases:

HEX .S	XFORM	DECIMAL F.
3FF0 0 0 0		1.000000000
BFF0 0 0 0		-1.000000000
3FD5 5555 5555 5556		.333333333
4009 21FB 5444 2D18		3.141592653

15 Assemblers and Metacompilers

Assemblers

All FORTHs have a built-in assembler for writing selected words directly in machine code. FORTH code is inherently more portable than machine code in that it can run unchanged on different computers. Nevertheless, there are times you may wish to consider the extra speed of machine code. The format of the FORTH assembler differs greatly from machine to machine and differs between FORTHS as well. You should consult your system documentation for details.

Most programs spend roughly 80 percent of their time in 20 percent of their code. If you rewrite this 20 percent of a FORTH program in machine code, you will see a dramatic increase in the speed of execution. A good compromise between speed and portability is to first write your entire program in FORTH and then to replace selected words with machine code. This way, the original FORTH source code is available if you ever need to move your program to a different computer. You can even keep the FORTH source code on screens near the machine-code source.

Colon definitions take the form:

```
: <name>    ( sequence of FORTH words)    ;
```

Machine-code definitions take instead the form:

```
CODE <name>    ( machine instructions)    NEXT   END-CODE
```

The defining word **CODE** creates a dictionary entry with the given name and prepares FORTH to assemble machine-code instructions. When the definition is later invoked by its name, control will pass to the first machine instruction. The macro **NEXT*** returns control back to the FORTH address interpreter at the point just past where the **CODE** definition was invoked. The word **END-CODE**, sometimes called C; ("C-semi"), ends the definition.

Let's look at a typical **CODE** definition:

```
CODE + ( n n2 - n3)
   AX POP  BX POP             ( pop the arguments)
   BX AX ADD                  ( add them)
   AX PUSH                    ( push the result)
   NEXT                       ( return to FORTH)
END-CODE
```

Here we are using the instruction set of the Intel 8088 CPU. Notice that the register arguments precede the opcodes, that is, **AX POP** instead of **POP AX**. The register and opcode names vary from FORTH to FORTH, even if the CPU is the same. Nevertheless, in most FORTHs, the arguments precede the opcode. The register **AX** would typically be a constant used as the argument to the opcode generator **POP**. This implies that both **AX** and **POP** *run* while the **CODE** definition is assembled.

***CODE** definitions are interpreted and not compiled.* This means that you can *calculate* operands to be used as arguments to opcodes. Assume, for example, that the **#** ("sharp") operator, appearing within a **CODE** definition, means *immediate data.*

```
CODE 2+ ( n - n2)
   AX POP                     ( pop the argument)
   2 # AX ADD                 ( add 2)
   AX PUSH                    ( push the result)
   NEXT                       ( return to FORTH)
END-CODE
```

Suppose you are interested in the third entry in a cell array called **STATUS**.

```
CODE WHATSIT ... STATUS 3 CELLS + # BX MOV ... END-CODE
```

* Sometimes you will see **NEXT JMP**. If so, you might consider redefining **NEXT** as a macro in the assembler like this:

```
: NEXT   NEXT JMP ;
```

The address of **STATUS 3 CELLS +** will be moved into the **BX** register, perhaps to be used as a pointer.

The word **;CODE** ("semi-code") is the machine-code equivalent of **DOES>.** Used inside of a defining word, **;CODE** sets the run-time action of any word subsequently defined by that word to be the machine-code sequence which follows it.

```
: CONSTANT
   CREATE ( n ) ,
   ;CODE ... ( machine code for constant ) ...  NEXT
END-CODE
```

The address of the data field containing **n** is pushed on the stack (as with **DOES>**) or else is found in a selected register.

Labels

FORTH-style assemblers seem to fall into two classes—those that use numeric labels (MasterFORTH and UR/FORTH), for flow of control and those that use structured conditionals (PolyFORTH, MacFORTH, and L&P F83). Numeric labels are numbered labels which are re-initialized for each **CODE** definition.

```
CODE 0<> ( n - f)
   BX POP  BX BX OR          ( set flag if n is not zero)
   TRUE # BX MOV             ( assume zero flag)
   1 L# JNZ                  ( jump to label 1 on zero flag)
     BX INC                  ( increment BX to 0)
   1 L: NEXT                 ( continue with NEXT at label 1)
END-CODE
```

Using structured conditionals, **0=** might look instead like this:

```
CODE 0<> ( n - f)
   BX POP  BX BX OR          ( set flag if n is not zero)
   TRUE # BX MOV             ( assume zero flag)
   0= IF                     ( skip to THEN on zero flag)
     BX INC                  ( increment BX to 0)
   THEN  NEXT                ( continue with NEXT)
END-CODE
```

Typically, conditionals are provided for branching on every possible CPU flag state.

Vocabularies

In an example above, we used the **#** operator as an opcode selector for immediate data. This differs from the normal meaning of **#**, which is to convert one digit of a number. How can **#** mean one thing outside of a **CODE** definition and another thing inside of it? Because words inside a colon definition are selected from the **ASSEMBLER** vocabulary.

Vocabularies are miniature dictionaries of words related to each other by function. A FORTH system typically has at least three vocabularies:

FORTH	This is the main vocabulary and contains the required words of the FORTH language like **DUP** and **SWAP**.
EDITOR	This vocabulary holds the words used by the screen editor.
ASSEMBLER	This vocabulary holds the words which generate machine code.

When the FORTH interpreter searches the dictionary for a word, it looks first in the most recently activated vocabulary, called the context vocabulary. It then searches any other active vocabularies in their order of activation, typically ending with the FORTH vocabulary. The order in which the vocabularies are searched is called the *search order*.

There are two important advantages to grouping words into vocabularies:

1. *Compilation speed.* Words in an inactive vocabulary are not part of the search order and will not be searched by the text interpreter. For example, if you are not editing a screen, there is no need to search for words in the **EDITOR** vocabulary.
2. *Reusing names.* You can use the same name to mean different things in different vocabularies. For example, the word **FILL** in the vocabulary FORTH is used to fill a memory area with a character. In a graphics application, you might also use it to fill a shape with a given pattern or color.

When you first run the FORTH language, the search order is simply the **FORTH** vocabulary. To make any other vocabulary the context vocabulary, simply execute it.

Assembler

The context vocabulary is set to **ASSEMBLER**, and the search order is changed to search first in the **ASSEMBLER** vocabulary and last in the **FORTH** vocabulary. The word **CODE** contains the command **ASSEMBLER**, so within a **CODE** definition, the **ASSEMBLER** vocabulary is searched first. To restore the search order to search only **FORTH**, execute **FORTH**.

How do you put new definitions into a vocabulary in the first place? By using the command **DEFINITIONS**, which sets the *current* vocabulary equal to the context vocabulary. All new definitions go into the current vocabulary. For example, to add the macro **PUSH10** to the assembler, you might use

```
ASSEMBLER DEFINITIONS
: PUSH10    10 # AX MOV    AX PUSH ;
FORTH DEFINITIONS
```

PUSH10 is now available while assembling machine code, that is, between the words **CODE** or **;CODE** and **END-CODE** or **C;**. When executed, it will assemble instructions to push a 10 on the stack.

Suppose you want to redefine **VARIABLE** to take an initial value, as in the FORTH Interest Group (FIG) FORTH dialect, but you don't want to lose the current definition of **VARIABLE**. In other words, you want two different kinds of **VARIABLE**, depending on the context. First, lets define the vocabulary **FIG**.

```
VOCABULARY FIG
```

PolyFORTH vocabularies select the entire word order. For example,

```
HEX 0137 DECIMAL VOCABULARY FIG
```

defines vocabulary 7 and specifies that this vocabulary will be searched first, followed by vocabulary 3 (**ASSEMBLER**), followed by vocabulary 1 (**FORTH**).

Then lets make **FIG** both the context and the current vocabulary while defining the new **VARIABLE**.

```
FIG DEFINITIONS
: VARIABLE   CREATE ( n) , ;
FORTH DEFINITIONS
```

Whenever you want an initialized variable, just say so.

```
10 FIG VARIABLE EXAMPLE  FORTH
EXAMPLE ? 10
```

For historic reasons, the **:** defining word sets the context vocabulary equal to the current vocabulary—the opposite action of **DEFINITIONS**.

Be aware that any colon definition can change the context vocabulary.

Word	Action
VOCABULARY <name>	Defines a new vocabulary. When the vocabulary is executed, it will become the context vocabulary, that is, the first vocabulary in the search order.
DEFINITIONS	Sets the current vocabulary equal to the context vocabulary. Subsequent definitions will be created in the current vocabulary.

The FORTH-83 Standard includes a vocabulary stack as an experimental extension. This special stack is often available as an optional extension to FORTH, so lets take a brief look at it.

The vocabulary stack determines the search order. The order in which vocabularies are pushed on the stack is the order in which they are searched, with the top vocabulary searched first. Before we push any vocabularies onto this stack, let's empty it.

```
ONLY
```

ONLY is a smart vocabulary which has the side effect of clearing the vocabulary stack, effectively removing all vocabularies, including FORTH, from the search order. **ONLY** then makes itself the context vocabulary.

```
1 2 3 DUP DUP ?
```

ONLY itself contains only about a dozen definitions. (Fortunately, one of them is **FORTH.**)

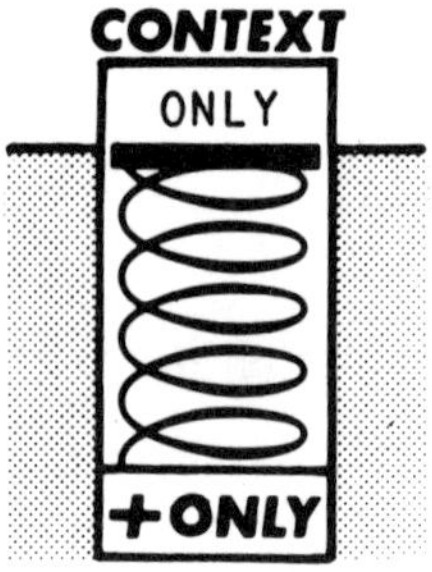

In diagram form, the vocabulary stack looks like this:

While **ONLY** seems to be present twice, it actually isn't on the vocabulary stack at all! The **ONLY** is *transient.* Like all context vocabularies, it is replaced when the next vocabulary runs.

```
FORTH DEFINITIONS
```

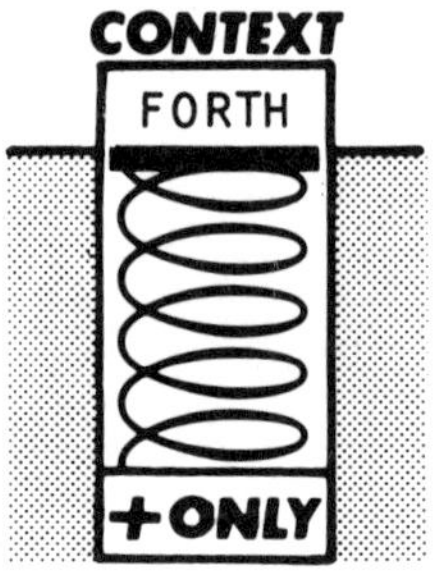

Now **FORTH** is the context vocabulary. FORTHs which use vocabulary stacks are usually optimized so that if the same vocabulary appears twice in the search order, it is only searched once. To make a vocabulary a permanent part of the search order, use **ALSO**, which pushes the context vocabulary onto the vocabulary stack.

```
ALSO
```

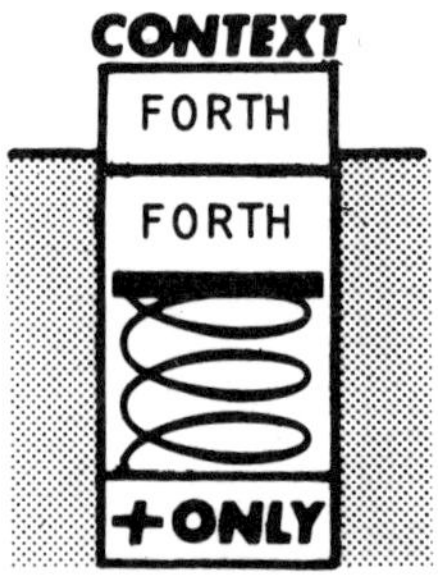

There is no way to pop an item from the vocabulary stack, but.you can always clear it with **ONLY** and start over. The normal search order is

`ONLY FORTH DEFINITIONS ALSO`

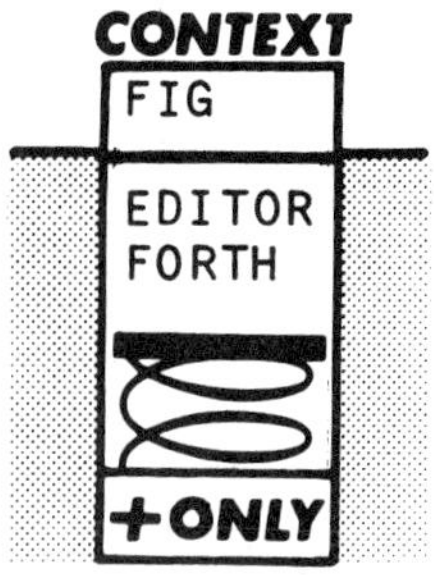

You can extend the search order as needed with **ALSO**.

`EDITOR ALSO`

The search order is **EDITOR** then **FORTH** then **ONLY**. The **ONLY** vocabulary sits *below* the stack and is not part of it.

The ONLY vocabulary is always searched and is usually searched last.

Building an Assembler

An assembler *assembles* opcodes and operands into bytes of machine-code instructions. A FORTH-style assembler adds these instructions to the end of the dictionary with `,` and `C,`. Let's examine a typical Intel 8088 CPU FORTH-style assembler.

Every CPU has a class of opcodes whose operands are *implicit*. In other words, once you know the opcode, you know which byte(s) to generate. Here are some of the 8088 opcodes with implied operands:

Opcode	Instruction (in hex)
CLC	F8
STC	F9
CMC	F5
IRET	CF

The action of each of these opcodes is the same; it is only the data, that is, the machine instruction, which changes. Whenever you see a group of words with the same action but different data, you should immediately think of **CREATE** and **DOES>**.

```
ASSEMBLER DEFINITIONS

: IMPLIED
\ generate implied operand instructions.
   CREATE ( n) C,   DOES> C@ C, ;

HEX      F8 IMPLIED CLC
         F9 IMPLIED STC
         F5 IMPLIED CMC
         CF IMPLIED IRET  DECIMAL
```

When **CLC** is executed in a **CODE** definition, F8 will be added to the end of the dictionary.

A second class of 8088 opcodes increment or decrement a 16-bit register. The register to be altered is packed into the low order three bits of the instruction according to the following table:

Register	Bit pattern (in binary)
AX	000
CX	001
DX	010
BX	011
SP	100
BP	101
SI	110
DI	111

A register leaves its bit pattern on the stack for the following operand.

```
0 CONSTANT AX      1 CONSTANT CX
2 CONSTANT DX      3 CONSTANT BX
4 CONSTANT SP      5 CONSTANT BP
6 CONSTANT SI      7 CONSTANT DI
```

```
: REGISTER
\ generate simple 16-bit register instructions.
   CREATE ( n) C,
   DOES> C@ OR C, ;

HEX       40 REGISTER INC
          48 REGISTER DEC  DECIMAL
```

Executing **BX INC** adds the instruction 43 (hex) to the end of the dictionary.

A third class of 8088 opcodes branch forward or backward a short distance. These relative branch opcodes need an address to branch to, from which they compute the relative distance. This relative distance, a one-byte number between -128 and 127, follows the opcode byte.

```
: BRANCH
\ generate a branch to the given address - HERE - 1.
   CREATE ( a) C,
   DOES> C@ C,  HERE - 1- C, ;

HEX       70 BRANCH JO  ( jump on overflow)
          7E BRANCH JLE ( jump if less than)
          75 BRANCH JNZ  DECIMAL  ( jump if not zero)
```

In its simplest form, an indefinite loop might look like this:

```
HERE  ( code sequence)  JNE
```

As long as the code sequence leaves the zero flag *false*, it will be repeated. Indeed, with structured conditional operators, the example might look like this:

```
BEGIN  ( code sequence)  0= UNTIL
```

With local labels, it would look instead like this:

```
1 L: ( code sequence)  1 L# JNE
```

What if the branch address is too far, that is, the relative distance does not fit in one byte? We can improve the definition of **BRANCH** to check for this.

```
: FAR? ( o)
\ objects if the displacement o is too big.
   128 + 256 U< IF  ABORT  THEN ;

: BRANCH
\ generate a branch to the given address - HERE - 1.
   CREATE ( a) C,
   DOES> C@ C,  HERE - 1-  DUP FAR?  C, ;
```

A correct opcode cannot be generated, and the error is *fatal*.

Exceptional Conditions

When an error occurs for which FORTH has no reasonable course of action, it *aborts* and returns to you with an error message.

```
HERE  1000 ALLOT  JNZ
JNZ ?
```

Aborting a program means that FORTH immediately stops whatever it is doing and returns to the normal keyboard text interpreter. You can force a program to abort anytime with the words **ABORT** or **QUIT**.

Word	Action
QUIT	Clears the return stack, changes to text interpret mode, and returns you to the keyboard.
ABORT	Clears the data stack and executes **QUIT**.

QUIT is normally used to end a program immediately. In the **CRAPS** program presented in the chapter on loops, for example, when you determine that the game is won or lost, you can **QUIT** the program without having to return through several layers of execution.

ABORT is more commonly used when you detect an error but are unable to take a corrective action. If you wish to specify the error message, use **ABORT"** ("abort-quote") instead.

```
: FAR? ( o)
\ objects if the displacement o is too big.
   128 + 256 U< NOT ABORT" Too Far" ;
```

If the displacement is too big, the message "Too Far" will be printed and the program will **ABORT**. Otherwise, no action is taken.

Word	Stack	Action
ABORT"	flag	Compiled in the form **ABORT" ccc"** If the flag is true, prints the message ccc and takes a system-dependent error action which includes **ABORT**.

The system-dependent error action can include automatically **FORGET**ing a defective definition or even tracing the execution path leading to the error. In addition, many FORTHs let you change the error action to something more suitable for the program at hand.

Metacompilation

Metacompilation is the process by which one FORTH creates another. The program which creates the new FORTH is called the metacompiler. The newly created *target* FORTH need bear little or no resemblance to its *parent*. For example, you might use a Motorola 68000 FORTH to create an Intel 8088 FORTH. Let's create a separate address space within our own so we can watch this process.

```
CREATE TARGET   32 ALLOT
TARGET 32 ERASE
```

Our target address space is a small one, only 32 bytes long. We have initialized it to zeroes. We'll also need some way to examine it.

```
: .## ( c)   0 <# # # #> TYPE SPACE ;
```

```
: REVIEW   BASE @ >R  HEX  \ show target address space.
   2 0 DO  CR 16 0 DO  J 16 * I + TARGET + C@ .##  LOOP LOOP
   R> BASE ! ;
REVIEW
```

```
00 00 00 00 00 00 00 00 00 00 00 00 00 00 00 00
00 00 00 00 00 00 00 00 00 00 00 00 00 00 00 00
```

Since this address space is within our own, we can **@** and **!** directly into it. Nevertheless, we would like to refer to the beginning of this space as *target address 0*, so we should have special forms of **@** and **!** which use the target address.

```
: T@ ( a)   TARGET + @ ;
: T! ( n a)   TARGET + ! ;

: TC@ ( a)   TARGET + C@ ;
: TC! ( c a)   TARGET + C! ;
```

All references to the target space will be through these words. We can make a new FORTH in a block or file simply by rewriting these words to use a virtual array.

As we generate code, we will be adding bytes and cells to the current end of the target address space. This is analogous to using **C,** and **,** to add to the end of the dictionary at **HERE**. We need a special form of these words to work in the target space.

```
VARIABLE TP   ( target pointer)   1 TP !

: THERE ( - a)   TP @ ;

2 CONSTANT TCELL   ( 2 bytes per target cell)

: TC, ( n)   THERE TC!  1 TP +! ;
: T,  ( n)   THERE T!   TCELL TP +! ;

: RENEW   TARGET 32 ERASE  1 TP ! ;   RENEW
```

Notice that we initialize **THERE** to 1 instead of to 0.

FORTH follows the unwritten rule that address 0 is not an address at all, but is rather a flag. The flag usually means that the address is invalid or the requested item is missing.

Let's add some bytes to the target.

```
RENEW  1 TC, 2 TC, 3 TC,  REVIEW
00 01 02 03 00 00 00 00 00 00 00 00 00 00 00 00
00 00 00 00 00 00 00 00 00 00 00 00 00 00 00 00
THERE . 4
```

These bytes can just as easily be characters in a string.

```
: TECHO   BL WORD COUNT
   DUP TC,  0 DO  COUNT TC,  LOOP  DROP ;
RENEW  TECHO ABC  REVIEW
03 41 42 43 00 00 00 00 00 00 00 00 00 00 00 00
00 00 00 00 00 00 00 00 00 00 00 00 00 00 00 00
```

You may recognize that hex 41, 42, and 43, are the ASCII characters for A, B, and C.

```
HEX  41 EMIT 42 EMIT 43 EMIT  DECIMAL ABC
```

These bytes could also be machine-code instructions. In fact, the machine-code primitives in the target FORTH are built by changing the opcode generators to use **TC,** instead of **C,**.

```
0 CONSTANT AX     1 CONSTANT CX
2 CONSTANT DX     3 CONSTANT BX
: REGISTER
\ generate simple 16-bit register instructions.
   CREATE ( n) C,
   DOES> C@ OR TC, ;
HEX     40 REGISTER INC
        48 REGISTER DEC  DECIMAL
RENEW  AX INC  CX DEC  REVIEW
00 40 49 00 00 00 00 00 00 00 00 00 00 00 00 00
00 00 00 00 00 00 00 00 00 00 00 00 00 00 00 00
```

Since we can compile strings in the target space, we can compile headers; and because we can assemble machine instructions, we can generate **CODE** definitions as well.

What about colon definitions? A colon definition compiles to a sequence of compilation addresses. Suppose that we have assembled **CODE** definitions for **SWAP**, **DROP**, and **EXIT**, and that their compilation addresses *in the target* are hex 10, 20, and 30, respectively. In most language compilers, the table associating names with addresses is called the *symbol table*. In FORTH, however, each symbol is a word whose action is compile its address into the target. Symbols have the same action on different data, so we make them with **CREATE** and **DOES>**.

```
: SYMBOL
\ associate a name with a compilation address.
   CREATE ( a) ,
   DOES> @ T, ;

HEX       10 SYMBOL SWAP
          20 SYMBOL DROP
          30 SYMBOL EXIT  DECIMAL
```

Actually, a symbol is created when it is first defined. At that time, the header and the code field are constructed, and the symbol is given the value of the compilation address *in the target*. This value is usually closely related to **THERE**. A more correct skeletal definition of **SYMBOL** would look like this:

```
: SYMBOL
\ associate following name with compilation address.
       ( construct link field in target here)
       CREATE  THERE ( convert to compilation address) ,
         ( construct code field in target here)
       DOES> @ T, ;
```

This version of **SYMBOL** does not construct a header in the target. Applications which run in the target but which do not have their own text interpreter can be *headerless* to save on target memory. To create a new FORTH in the target, however, **SYMBOL** will have to generate target headers.

```
: SYMBOL
\ associate following name with compilation address.
       ( construct link field in target here)
       >IN @ >R ( remember input stream pointer)
       BL WORD COUNT ( construct name field in target)
       DUP TC,  0 DO  COUNT TC,  LOOP  DROP
       R> >IN ! ( prepare to reread name)
       CREATE  THERE ( convert to compilation address) ,
         ( construct code field in target here)
       DOES> @ T, ;
```

Notice how **>IN** is manipulated to read the following name twice: once to move it to the target and once to create a symbol. **SYMBOL** must run whenever a new word is added to the target. That implies that **SYMBOL** is included in the metacompiler's version of **CREATE** and in any word based on **CREATE**, such as **CODE** or **:** (colon).

```
: CODE   SYMBOL  ASSEMBLER   ( etc.) ;
```

To avoid a proliferation of names, metacompiler versions of defining words have the same name as their normal FORTH counterparts, but are kept in a separate vocabulary. This vocabulary is the context vocabulary when the metacompiler runs.

Let's metacompile the word **NIP** for the new target FORTH.

```
: NIP   SWAP DROP ;
```

This definition looks like an ordinary definition, but a great many things are happening under the surface. First of all, the context is set so that the metacompiler version of **:** (colon) runs. This creates a new symbol called **NIP** which resides in another special vocabulary which we will call **SYMBOLS.** At the same time, the header and code field of **NIP** are created in the target. The symbol **NIP** gets the value of the compilation address of the target **NIP.** **:** (colon) then effectively changes state and enters the *metacompiler loop.*

The metacompiler loop reads each word from the input stream and looks it up in the special vocabulary **SYMBOLS**. Unlike the normal FORTH compiler loop, *instead of compiling each symbol, it executes it.* Executing a symbol causes it to compile its target compilation address into the target. So the symbols for both **SWAP** and **DROP** add their associated compilation addresses to the target definition of **NIP**.

When the metacompiler loop encounters the word ; (semicolon), it recognizes it as a special word and executes it without searching **SYMBOLS**. The metacompiler version of ; executes, in turn, the symbol **EXIT** and then leaves the metacompiler loop, changing state again. Executing the symbol **EXIT** causes it to add its associated compilation address to the end of the target **NIP**, completing the target definition.

Confused? Don't worry. A metacompiler typically juggles multiple address spaces and several vocabularies, and that would confuse anyone. The best way to learn how to use a metacompiler is to get one and practice generating tiny FORTHs with it.

Exercises

1. Redefine / (slash) to protect against division by zero.

   ```
   10 0 /
   / ?  Zero Divide
   ```

   Keep your definition in a new vocabulary called **SAFETY**.

2. Define an associative stack for use with local labels. Each **L:** pushes on the stack two items: a value, which is normally **HERE**, and a key, which is the label number. Each **L#** finds the key-value pair associated with the label number, or zero if no matching key is found.

```
HERE . 1000 ( for example)
1 L:  20 ALLOT  3 L:  10 ALLOT  5 L: HERE . 1030
1 L# . 1000
5 L# . 1030
3 L# . 1020
2 L# . 0
```

This simple version of local labels does not handle multiple references to the same label.

```
1 L# . 0
```

3. Extend the 8088 assembler to handle the string instructions

```
HEX    AC LODS     A6 CMPS     A4 MOVS
       AA STOS     AE SCAS     DECIMAL
```

The low order bit of the opcode is 0 if 8 bits are to be transferred on each operation and 1 otherwise. Adjust the syntax of the assembler so that string opcodes preceded by **BYTE** or by nothing set this bit to zero; those preceded by **WORD** set it to one.

```
HERE  BYTE LODS  C@ . AC
HERE  WORD LODS  C@ . AD
HERE  LODS  C@ . AC
```

Hint: use a variable as a flag holder. Assume it is initialized to *false* by **CODE**.

4. Change the metacompiler so that it builds the target somewhere in a disk file. You need only change the words **T@ T! TC@** and **TC!**.

Solutions to Problems

Chapter 2

```
1. : BLIP   CR INSET STAR ;

   : T   ROW BLIP BLIP BLIP BLIP ;

   : I   ROW BLIP BLIP BLIP ROW ;
   : C   ROW CR STAR CR STAR CR STAR ROW ;
   : E   ROW CR STAR ROW     CR STAR ROW ;

2. : BOOP   CR ." *   *" ;

   : H   BOOP BOOP ROW BOOP BOOP ;
   : U   BOOP BOOP BOOP BOOP ROW ;

3. : HI-TECH   H I CR ROW CR T E C H ;
```

Chapter 3

```
1. : TRIANGLE   CR ." THE AREA IS "  * 2/ . ;

2. : LIMIT   0 MAX 100 MIN ;

3. : CHANGE   0 ;
   : QUARTERS   25 * + ;
   : DIMES      10 * + ;
   : NICKELS     5 * + ;
   : PENNIES       + ;
   : FRANCS     27 * + ;
   : KRONOR     13 * + ;
```

```
: MARKS      40 * + ;
: TOKENS     75 * + ;

: INTO
   25 /MOD CR . ." QUARTERS"
   10 /MOD CR . ." DIMES"
   5  /MOD CR . ." NICKELS"
           CR . ." PENNIES" ;
```

4. 15, 1, 625, 64.

Chapter 4

```
1. a. OVER                  b. OVER SWAP
   c. SWAP DROP             d. ROT DROP
   e. ROT ROT SWAP          f. ROT SWAP
   g. ROT DUP 2SWAP         h. OVER SWAP

2. : 3DUP   2 PICK 2 PICK 2 PICK ;
   : NIP    SWAP DROP ;
   : TUCK   SWAP OVER ;

3. a. DUP * +
   b. DUP * SWAP DUP * +
   c. 3 * *
   d. + DUP *
   e. ROT ROT + SWAP /
   f. ROT ROT OVER +  ROT ROT SWAP - /
   g. DUP * 2DUP *  2SWAP DUP * OVER *  ROT -  ROT ROT    * +

4. : RECTANGLE
      ROT - ROT ROT  SWAP - *
      CR ." THE AREA IS " . ;

5. : POLY   DUP 3 - OVER * 17 + OVER * 4 - * 5 + ;
```

Chapter 5

Problem 1

```
: STAR    ." *" ;
: INSET   ."    " ;
: ROW      CR ." *****" ;
```

```
: COLUMN  CR STAR CR STAR CR STAR CR STAR ;

: BLIP   CR INSET STAR ;
\ a block-letter stem primitive.

\ Some block-letters:
: T   ROW BLIP BLIP BLIP BLIP ;

: I   ROW BLIP BLIP BLIP ROW ;
: C   ROW CR STAR CR STAR CR STAR ROW ;
: E   ROW CR STAR ROW     CR STAR ROW ;
```

Problem 2

```
: BOOP   CR ." *   *" ;
\ another block-letter primitive.

\ Some block-letters:
: H   BOOP BOOP ROW BOOP BOOP ;
: U   BOOP BOOP BOOP BOOP ROW ;
```

Problem 3

```
: HI-TECH   H I CR ROW CR T E C H ;
\ prints a giant message.
```

Chapter 6

Problem 1

```
VARIABLE X   2 X !   VARIABLE Y   5 Y !
: EXCHANGE ( a a2)   OVER @ OVER @  SWAP  ROT ! SWAP ! ;
\ exchanges the values at the two given addresses.
```

Problem 2

```
: FIG-VARIABLE ( n)   CREATE , ;
\ create a FIG-style variable with initial value n.
```

Problem 3

```
CREATE STACK  ( extra stack)  16 CELLS ALLOT
VARIABLE STACK-INDEX  ( next stack index)  0 STACK-INDEX !
\ Push and Pop from extra stack:
: PUSH ( n)
```

```
   STACK STACK-INDEX @ + !
   STACK-INDEX @ CELL + 15 CELLS MIN STACK-INDEX ! ;
: POP ( - n)
   STACK-INDEX @ CELL - 0 MAX  DUP STACK-INDEX !
   STACK + @ ;
```

Problem 4

```
: >P ( n ; P: - n)   PUSH ;   ( same as PUSH)
: P> ( - n ; P: n)   POP ;    ( same as POP)

: PDUP  ( P: n - n n)      P>    DUP  >P >P ;
: PSWAP ( P: n n2 - n2 n)  P> P> SWAP >P >P ;
: PDROP ( P: n)   P> DROP ;
```

Chapter 7

Problem 1

```
: MAX ( n n2 - n3)   2DUP < IF  SWAP  THEN  DROP ;
: MIN ( n n2 - n3)   2DUP > IF  SWAP  THEN  DROP ;
```

Problem 2

```
: 0> ( n - f)   NEGATE 0< ;
```

Problem 3

```
: NAND ( n n2 - n3)   AND NOT ;
```

Problem 4

```
: NOT ( f - f')   TRUE NAND ;   : AND ( f f2 - f3)   NAND NOT ;
: OR  ( f f2 - f3)   NOT SWAP NOT NAND ;
: XOR ( f f2 - f3)
   2DUP NOT AND  ROT ROT SWAP NOT AND  OR ;
```

Problem 5

```
CREATE DAYS/MONTH  00 C, ( January is month #1)
 31 C, 28 C, 31 C, 30 C, 31 C, 30 C,
 31 C, 31 C, 30 C, 31 C, 30 C, 31 C,
```

```
VARIABLE MONTH
VARIABLE YEAR

: DAYS ( - n)    \ compute the # of days in MONTH for YEAR.
   DAYS/MONTH  MONTH @ + C@
   MONTH @ 2 = YEAR @ 4 MOD 0= AND ( leap year?)
   IF  1+  THEN ;
```

Problem 6

```
VARIABLE SECRET#     \ the secret number.
VARIABLE OLD-ERROR   \ the prior guess error.
VARIABLE #GUESSES    \ the number of incorrect guesses.
VARIABLE SEED   1234 SEED !
: RAND ( - n)   SEED @ 5421 * 1+  DUP SEED ! ;
: RANDOM ( n - n2)    \ random number from 0 to n-1.
   RAND ABS  SWAP MOD ;

: GAME   \ set up the secret number.
   100 RANDOM 1+  DUP SECRET# !
   0 #GUESSES !  101 OLD-ERROR ! ;

: YOU-WIN!
   CR ." YOU WON IN " #GUESSES @ .  ." GUESSES! " ;

: GUESS ( n )    \ play "guess the number."
   1 #GUESSES +!
   DUP SECRET# @ =          IF  DROP  YOU-WIN!  ELSE
   DUP SECRET# @ - ABS 3 < IF  DROP  ." HOT!"  ELSE
   ( compute error size:)
      SECRET# @ - ABS  OLD-ERROR @  OVER OLD-ERROR !
   ( new-error old-error) < IF  ." WARMER"  ELSE  ." COLDER"
   THEN THEN THEN ;
```

Chapter 8

Problem 1

```
CREATE BOXES   \ create and initialize box array:)
 3 , 2 , 0 , 4 , 0 , 1 , 4 , 2 , 2 , 3 ,

: BOX? ( n )
\ select a box, deleting it from BOXES.
   9 MIN ( sizes 0-9)  0 ( assume no boxes)
   10 ROT ( check same or larger sizes)
```

```
   DO  DROP      BOXES I CELLS + @  ?DUP ( any boxes?)
     IF  I .  1- BOXES I CELLS + !  TRUE LEAVE  THEN  0
   LOOP  0= IF  ." NO BOXES"  THEN ;
```

Problem 2

```
: STARS ( n )    \ print n stars.
   ?DUP IF  0 DO  ." *" ( Star)  LOOP  THEN ;
```

Problem 3

```
: BOUNDS ( a n - n2 n3)   OVER + SWAP ;
\ convert address and length into DO — LOOP form.
```

Problem 4

```
: HISTOGRAM ( a n )
\ display array of cells as histogram.
   CELLS BOUNDS DO  CR I @ STARS  CELL +LOOP ;
```

Chapter 9

Problem 1

```
: GROWTH? ( n )
\ find how long it takes 1000 to double at this percent.
   >R  0 ( COUNT)  1000
   BEGIN  1 0 D+ ( increment count)
     DUP R@ 100 */ +  DUP 1999 >
   UNTIL  R> 2DROP . ;
```

Problem 2

```
: CONE ( n n2 - n3)   OVER * *       355 339 (  PI/3) */ ;
: SPHERE ( n - n2)    DUP DUP * *  1420 339 ( 4PI/3) */ ;
```

Problem 3

```
: D>S ( d - n)   DROP ;
```

Problem 4

```
VARIABLE FUDGE
```

```
: D~ ( d d2 - f)    \ true if d = d2 within fudge factor.
   D- DABS D>S  FUDGE @ > NOT ;
```

Problem 5

```
: .S
   CR ." STACK: "   DEPTH ?DUP
   IF  0 DO  DEPTH I - 1- PICK  BASE @ 10 = IF . ELSE U. THEN
         LOOP
   ELSE  ." EMPTY"
   THEN ;
```

Problem 6

```
: C+ ( cx cx2 - cx3)   ROT +        >R  +  R> ;
: C- ( cx cx2 - cx3)   ROT - NEGATE >R  -  R> ;
: C* ( cx cx2 - cx3)   2OVER 2OVER
   >R *  R> ROT * - NEGATE  >R  ROT * >R  *  R> -  R> ;

: C/ ( cx cx2 - cx3)   2OVER 2OVER
   2DUP  DUP * SWAP DUP * + ( c**2 + d**2)  >R
   >R *  R> ROT * - >R   ROT * >R  *  R> +  R>
   R@ / SWAP  R> / SWAP ;
```

Problem 7

```
: C>F ( n - n2)   18 10 */ 32 + ;
: F>C ( n - n2)   32 - 10 18 */ ;
```

Problem 8

```
: FEET ( n - n2)   12 * ;
: INCHES ( n n2 - n3)   + ;
: BY ;
: ROOM? ( n n2)   144 */  CR  . ." SQUARE FEET " ;
```

Chapter 10

Problem 1

```
: <CMOVE> ( a a2 n)
\ safely move n overlapping bytes from a to a2.
   >R  2DUP U< NOT IF  R> CMOVE  ELSE  R> CMOVE>  THEN ;
```

Problem 2

```
: UPPER ( a n)    \ convert a string to upper case.
   DUP 0= IF  2DROP EXIT  THEN
   OVER + SWAP DO  I C@ DUP ASCII a <  SWAP ASCII z > OR NOT
                 IF  I C@ BL - I C!  THEN
               LOOP ;
```

Problem 3

```
: /STRING ( a l n - a+n l-n)   ROT OVER +  ROT ROT - ;
\ truncates leftmost n chars of string.  n may be negative.

: SCAN ( a l byte - a2 l2)
\ returns shorter string from first position equal to byte.
   >R  BEGIN  DUP
       WHILE  OVER C@ R@ =  IF  R> DROP  EXIT  THEN  1 /STRING
       REPEAT   R> DROP ;

: LEX ( a n c - a2 n2 a3 n3)   \ splits string at the delimiter.
\ Rightmost string is on top.  Either string can have 0 length.
   >R 2DUP R> SCAN ROT OVER -  ROT ROT  DUP 0> NEGATE /STRING ;
```

Problem 4

```
: S+  ( a n)   \ add string to counted string at PAD.
   ( n ) >R   PAD COUNT + R@ CMOVE   PAD C@ R> + PAD C! ;
```

Problem 5

```
: D. ( d )
  <#  BEGIN  #  2DUP D0= NOT
        IF   #  2DUP D0= NOT
        IF   #  THEN THEN
                2DUP D0= NOT
      WHILE  ASCII , HOLD
      REPEAT  #>  TYPE SPACE ;
```

Problem 6

```
: VAL ( a n - d true | 0)
\ convert a string to a number.
\ Return true if the number is valid.
\ If false, no number is returned.
   PAD OVER -  SWAP OVER >R CMOVE  BL PAD C!
```

```
   PAD DPL !  0 0 R>  DUP C@ ASCII - =  DUP >R - 1-
   BEGIN  CONVERT  DUP C@ ASCII . =
   WHILE  DUP DPL !  REPEAT
   R> SWAP >R  IF DNEGATE  THEN
   PAD 1- DPL @ - DPL !  R> PAD = ( valid?)
   ?DUP 0= IF  2DROP 0  THEN ;

: PLACE ( a n a2)   \ pack string into counted string a2.
   2DUP >R >R  1+ SWAP CMOVE>  R> R> C! ;
: >DATE ( a n - month date year)
\ parse a string in the form 02/07/88
   ASCII / LEX  ASCII / LEX  ( a n a2 n2 a3 n3)
   VAL 0= ABORT" ?"  DROP ( D>S) >R
   VAL 0= ABORT" ?"  DROP ( D>S) >R
   VAL 0= ABORT" ?"  DROP ( D>S)  R> R> ;

: DATE> ( month date year)
   <#  0 ( S>D) # #  ASCII / HOLD  2DROP
       0 ( S>D) # #  ASCII / HOLD  2DROP  0 ( S>D) # # #>
   PAD PLACE ;
```

Problem 7

```
CREATE BUF  1024 ALLOT           \ circular string buffer.
VARIABLE BUFPTR  BUF BUFPTR !    \ pointer to latest string.
: +BUF ( a n - a2)
\ allocate n+1 bytes in a circular buffer and moves
\ string a n there.
\ Return the address of the now counted string.
   BUFPTR @ PLACE  BUFPTR @
   DUP COUNT +  DUP BUF 1024 256 - + U< NOT  ( wrap?)
   IF  DROP BUF  THEN  BUFPTR ! ;
```

Chapter 11

Problem 1

```
: STRING  CREATE ( n ) 1+ ALLOT ;
\ create a string buffer for strings up to n bytes long.
```

Problem 2

```
: COUNTER   \ create a counter.
   CREATE  0 ,  DOES>  1 SWAP +! ;

: RESET   \ reset a counter.
   ' >BODY  0 SWAP ! ;
: EXAMINE   \ print counter value.
   ' >BODY  @ . ;
```

Problem 3

```
: FLIP-FLOP   \ object which changes state alternately.
   CREATE  0 ,  DOES>  DUP @  DUP 0= ROT ! ;
```

Problem 4

```
: 2VALUE   \ double-number value.
   CREATE ( d ) , ,   DOES> ( - d)  2@ ;
```

Problem 5

```
VARIABLE COLORED
: COLOR   \ object which sets its value into COLORED.
   CREATE ( n ) ,  DOES> @ COLORED ! ;
```

Problem 6

```
VARIABLE SCALE
: POINT   \ 2CONSTANT scaled by SCALE.
   CREATE  ( n n2)  , ,
   DOES> ( - n n2)  2@  SCALE @ * SWAP  SCALE @ * SWAP ;
```

Problem 7

```
VARIABLE TOTAL

: FOOD
   CREATE ( n ) ,  0 ( quantity) ,
   DOES>  DUP 2@  TOTAL +!  1- 0 MAX  SWAP CELL+ ! ;

: HOWMANY       ' >BODY CELL+ @ . ;
: MORE ( n )    ' >BODY CELL+  +! ;
```

Chapter 12

Problem 1

```
: DLITERAL  ( d ) ( - d)
   SWAP  [COMPILE] LITERAL  [COMPILE] LITERAL ;  IMMEDIATE
```

Problem 2

```
: ?LEAVE   [COMPILE] IF  [COMPILE] LEAVE  [COMPILE] THEN ;
  IMMEDIATE
```

Problem 3

```
: AGAIN   0 [COMPILE] LITERAL  [COMPILE] UNTIL ;  IMMEDIATE
```

Problem 4

```
: :    HERE  ( old) : ;
: ;    [COMPILE] ;  HERE SWAP -  ." Occupies " . ." bytes." ;
  IMMEDIATE
```

Problem 5

```
: FOR    0 [COMPILE] LITERAL  COMPILE SWAP  [COMPILE] DO ;
  IMMEDIATE
: NEXT  -1 [COMPILE] LITERAL  [COMPILE] +LOOP ;  IMMEDIATE
```

Chapter 13

Problem 1

```
: CONTROL ( - n)
\ used in the form:  CONTROL c
\ where c follows in the input stream.
\ Return the 7-bit ASCII code of c.
   BL WORD  1+ C@ ( read the next char)  ASCII @ -
   STATE @ IF  [COMPILE] LITERAL  THEN ;  IMMEDIATE
```

Problem 2

```
: SLICES<   ASCII > WORD COUNT
   BEGIN  BL LEX  DUP
   WHILE  2SWAP  CR TYPE  REPEAT  2DROP  CR TYPE ;
```

Problem 3

```
  4 CONSTANT FIRST-BLOCK
100 CONSTANT RECORD-SIZE

: RECORD ( n a)    \ read virtual record into buffer.
   SWAP RECORD-SIZE *
   1024 /MOD FIRST-BLOCK + SWAP
   1024 OVER - >R  RECORD-SIZE R@ -  0>
   IF   OVER 1+ BLOCK  3 PICK
        RECORD-SIZE R@ /STRING  CMOVE
   THEN SWAP BLOCK + SWAP
        RECORD-SIZE R> MIN      CMOVE ;
```

Problem 4

```
 0 FIELD NAME   ( 20-byte)   20 FIELD STREET   ( 30-byte)
50 FIELD CITY   ( 20-byte)   70 FIELD STATE    (  3-byte)
73 FIELD ZIP    (  4-byte)

CREATE BUF   9 ALLOT

: FILE-IT   SELECT-IT  ( choose a record)
   CR ."   NAME:"   NAME 19 READ-IT
   CR ." STREET:" STREET 29 READ-IT
   CR ."   CITY:"   CITY 19 READ-IT
   CR ."  STATE:"  STATE  2 READ-IT
   CR ."    ZIP:"  BUF 9 EXPECT
   BUF SPAN @ VAL  DROP ZIP 2! ;

: PRINT-IT   SELECT-IT  ( choose a record)
   CR ."   NAME:"   NAME COUNT TYPE
   CR ." STREET:" STREET COUNT TYPE
   CR ."   CITY:"   CITY COUNT TYPE
   CR ."  STATE:"  STATE COUNT TYPE
   CR ."    ZIP:"  ZIP 2@ D. ;
```

Problem 5

```
: 1THING   ." THING 1 " ;     : 2THING   ." THING 2 " ;
: 3THING   ." THING 3 " ;
: ]X ;    ( dummy)
: X[   BEGIN  '  DUP ['] ]X - WHILE  ,  REPEAT  DROP ;
```

Chapter 14

Problem 1

```
: XOR ( n n2 - n3)
   2DUP NOT AND >R  SWAP NOT AND  R> OR ;
```

Problem 2

```
: FNLOG2 ( fn - fn2)   \ HART #2521.
   [   .5020 D>FN ] LITERAL   OVER FN*
   [   .9514 D>FN ] LITERAL + OVER FN*
   [ -1.4533 D>FN ] LITERAL + SWAP
   [   .3521 D>FN ] LITERAL +  FN/ ;
```

Problem 3

```
: FNORM ( r - fn exp)   2DUP D0= IF  EXIT  THEN
   0 ( count) >R
   BEGIN  DUP    WHILE  D2/  R> 1+ >R  REPEAT
   BEGIN  DUP 0= WHILE  D2*  R> 1- >R  REPEAT
   D2/ D2/ D2/   DROP  R> 1+ ;
```

Problem 4

```
: FN>F ( fn - r)   \ convert fn to r.
   DUP 0< D2* D2* ;

: FLOG2 ( r - r2)   \ logarithm base 2.
   2DUP D0= IF  2DROP  0 1  ELSE
    DUP  0< IF  2DROP  0 0  ELSE
    FNORM >R  FNLOG2 FN>F  0 R> F+  THEN THEN ;
```

Problem 5

```
HEX
: T+ ( tA tB - tC)    \ add two triple numbers.
   >R  ROT >R  ROT 2>R
   0 SWAP 0 D+  0 R> 0 D+  R> 0 D+  2R> + + ;

7FFF CONSTANT MAX#    8000 CONSTANT -MAX#

: DU2/ ( d - d2)   D2/ MAX# AND ;
: TU2/ ( t - ut)   \ shift triple number right unsigned.
   0 SWAP DU2/  >R >R  DU2/  R> OR R> ;
DECIMAL

: PACK   ( ud sign - d)   -MAX# AND OR ;

: ROUND ( t - ud exp )    \ assumes hi bit is zero.
   -MAX# 0 0 T+  ROT DROP  DUP 0< DUP IF  >R  DU2/ R>  THEN ;

HEX
\ Xlate from 8087 format:
: XFORM ( mh mm mm ml - r)   DROP SWAP ROT  ( ml mm mh )
   DUP 7FF0 AND 10 / 3FF - ( exp ) >R  DUP ( sign ) >R
   0F AND 10 OR  5 0 DO  TU2/  LOOP  ROT ROT  TU2/
   ROUND  ROT ROT  R> PACK  ROT R> + 1+  .S ;
DECIMAL
```

Chapter 15

Problem 1

```
VOCABULARY SAFETY   SAFETY DEFINITIONS
: / ( n n2 - n3)   DUP 0= ABORT" Zero Divide" ;
FORTH DEFINITIONS
```

Problem 2

```
10 CONSTANT MXL#

VARIABLE FWDS
\ associate stacks can be "popped" from the middle, or wherever
\ the key is found.   Emptied by READY.
   CELL ALLOT  ( pointers)  MXL# 2* CELLS ALLOT  ( pairs)
```

```
: READY   FWDS 2 CELLS + FWDS ! ;
\ initializes associative stack.
: LPUSH ( n key)   \ pushes value and its key.
   FWDS 2@ = ABORT" Full"  FWDS  @ 2!  2 CELLS FWDS +! ;

: LPOP  ( key - value true | 0 0)   \ pops value given key.
   FWDS @  FWDS 2 CELLS +  2DUP - ( not empty?)
   IF  DO  DUP ( key) I @ =  ( found?)
         IF  DROP  I CELL+ @  ( move last pair into slot)
             2 CELLS NEGATE FWDS +!
             FWDS @ 2@  I 2!  TRUE  UNDO EXIT
         THEN  2 CELLS
      +LOOP  0 0
   THEN  2DROP DROP  0 0 ;

: L: ( n )  HERE SWAP  LPUSH ;   \ enter local label.
: L# ( n )  LPOP DROP ;          \ resolve local label.
```

Problem 3

```
ASSEMBLER DEFINITIONS
VARIABLE ?WORD   \ switch.  1 : WORD ref ;   0 : BYTE ref.

: WORD   1 ?WORD ! ;
: BYTE   0 ?WORD ! ;

: STRCODE   \ assemble string instructions.
   CREATE  ( n)  C,   DOES> C@  ?WORD @ OR  C,  0 ?WORD ! ;

FORTH DEFINITIONS
```

Problem 4

```
  5 CONSTANT FIRST-BLOCK

: >FILE ( a - a2)
\ convert target address into memory address.
   1024 /MOD FIRST-BLOCK + BLOCK + ;

: TC@ ( a - n)  >FILE C@ ;
: TC! ( n a)    >FILE C!  UPDATE ;

\ Assume 2 bytes per cell, low-order byte at lower address:
: T@ ( a - n)   DUP TC@  SWAP 1+ TC@    256 * + ;
: T! ( n a)     >R  DUP 255 AND R@ TC!  256 * R> 1+ TC! ;
```

Index

About the Authors

Martin Tracy has been a full-time FORTH programmer since 1978. He is the founder of Advanced Micromotion, Inc., and vice president of the FORTH Interest Group. Mr. Tracy serves as the secretary of the ANS X3J14 FORTH committee and is the FORTH columnist for Dr. Dobb's Journal. He is currently a project manager at FORTH, Inc.

Anita Anderson has worked as a freelance writer and editor since 1979 and has co-authored several books. She is currently a professional technical writer and editor of the office of Academic Computing at the University of California, Los Angeles, specializing in mainframe and micro computers.